Winning with Words

Winning with Words

Volume 1

How to Write Effectively

Published by

World Book Encyclopedia, Inc.
a Scott Fetzer company
Chicago

Acknowledgments

The publishers gratefully acknowledge the following for permission to use copyrighted material.

16,56 From *Writers at Work: The Paris Review Interviews,* 1st series, edited by Malcolm Cowley. Copyright © 1958 by The Paris Review, Inc. Reprinted by permission of Viking Penguin Inc.

34 Reprinted from *The Technique of Clear Writing,* by Robert Gunning. New York: McGraw-Hill Book Co. Used with permission of Gunning-Mueller Clear Writing Institute, Inc.

37 From *The Wild Flag* (Houghton Mifflin). © 1943, 1971 E. B. White. Originally in *The New Yorker.*

51 Specified selection from *Stuart Little* by E. B. White. Copyright 1945 by E. B. White. Text copyright renewed © 1973 by E.B. White. Reprinted by permission of Harper & Row, Publishers, Inc.

56 From *Writers at Work: The Paris Review Interviews,* 2nd series, edited by George Plimpton. Copyright © 1963 by The Paris Review, Inc. Reprinted by permission of Viking Penguin Inc.

63 "The Definitive Word," by Bruce Feinstein. *New York Times* Magazine, Sept. 25, 1983. Copyright © 1983 by the New York Times Company. Reprinted by permission.

79 © 1983 Gabriele Lusser Rico, *Writing the Natural Way.* Published by J. P. Tarcher, Inc. 9110 Sunset Boulevard, Los Angeles, California.

ISBN 0-7166-3171-7
Library of Congress Catalog Card No.84-51396
a/hd

Photo Acknowledgments

Credits should be read from top to bottom, left to right, on their respective pages.

Staff

Publisher
William H. Nault

Editorial

Editor in chief
Robert O. Zeleny

Senior editor
Scott Thomas

Permissions editor
Janet T. Peterson

Editorial assistant
Valerie Adams

Writers
James Clark
Rena Moran

Researcher
Kathy Florio

Art

Executive art director
William Hammond

Art director
Roberta Dimmer

Assistant art director
Joe Gound

Photography director
John S. Marshall

Photographs editor
Randi Sherman

Designers
Harry Voigt
Kristin Nelson

Illustrations
William Petersen

Production artist
Ann Tomasic

Product production

Executive director
Peter Mollman

Manufacturing
Joseph C. LaCount, **director**

Research and development
Henry Koval, **manager**

Pre-press services
Jerry Stack, **director**

Production control
George Luehring

Film separations
Alfred Mozdzen

Adviser
Geraldine La Rocque
Director of Teacher Education
University of Northern Iowa
Cedar Falls, Iowa

Contents

Introduction

The title of this first volume of WINNING WITH WORDS is *How to Write Effectively.* It is a straightforward kind of title and, as a good book title should, accurately describes the content. The "how to" part promises something to the reader—that he or she, upon finishing the book, will know *how to* write effectively. But what, exactly, is effective writing?

We all assume that we know what writing is—the marking, with a tool on a surface, of letters that add up to words. This definition, although accurate, leaves out something basic to the process. Letters are symbols; they represent the sounds of speech. Words are also symbols; they represent things, ideas, even nuances, which we perceive with our five senses. The word *apple* is, thus, only a symbol that represents a firm, rounded, often red-skinned edible fruit. All people who read the English language know that the letters *a, p, p, l,* and *e,* spelled together in that order, signify a particular kind of fruit. The word, therefore, is nothing but a code used to transfer the image of an apple from the mind of a writer into the mind of a reader. This transference of images, this communication of thought, from one human being's mind into another's is really what writing is all about.

The final word of our title is *effectively,* an adverb that modifies the verb *write.* In this context, *effectively* means "in a manner that causes some desired result." So the full title—*How to Write Effectively*—promises the reader that he or she will learn how to get desired results from his or her writing.

Anytime we pick up a pen and write something down on paper we have some specific result in mind: to be understood; to make others see as we see; to make others comprehend as we comprehend. The problem, of course, is transferring with some degree of exactness all of those thoughts we have rattling around in our heads. Although 5,000 years old, writing is still an inexact means of communication, still subject to a reader's interpretation and to a writer's limitations. Few of us are able to find the right words and place those words in the right sequence to achieve any measure of total understanding. This book is designed to help the writer find those words and place them in the best possible sequence to achieve that better understanding.

Becoming an effective writer involves learning a craft, a technique. The craft includes mastering the rules of writing; developing structure in one's writing; exposing oneself to good writing and learning from the example; and practicing what one has learned.

Mastering the rules of writing is fundamental. All functioning systems require rules. Writing, as we all know from years of school, has more than its share. The rules, however, serve a purpose beyond badgering students and stifling creativity. They are basic to effective writing, ensuring that your writing gets the results that you desire. Uniform codes of spelling, punctuation, grammar, and syntax assure communication. As long as a period, like a red light, always signals a stop, the writer knows that his or her reader will, in fact, stop. Many rules of writing are covered in Chapter 2, "Writing Clearly," and in Appendix A at the back of the book.

Developing structure in one's writing requires advance planning. This planning is accomplished with an outline. Like spelling and grammar rules, outlines are devices that we are exposed to early and often. Teachers hammer away at outlines, however, for good reason. Outlines are the blueprints, the designs, from which a writer builds his or her words and sentences into images and ideas that a reader can comprehend. Outlines provide the steel and concrete upon which effective writing, like a finished tower, rests.

All writing has structure. Even a single sentence, if it is to be understood, requires the structure supplied by a subject and predicate. Effective writing, however, demands appropriate and logical structure. An effective personal letter is written in an appropriate form. The same is true of any business letter that gets results. The same is true of book reports, term papers, office memos, formal reports, even short stories and novels.

The structure of various kinds of writing is examined throughout *How to Write Effectively*. Chapter 4, "Writing for School," reviews the forms of various writing assignments. Chapter 5, "Writing for Work," dissects resumés, memos, business letters, and reports. Appropriate structure for personal correspondence is the subject of Chapter 6; and Chapters 7 and 8 discuss how writing intended for publication is developed and formatted.

Another aspect of the craft of writing is exposing oneself to good writing; developing an eye and an ear for style; and learning to trust one's creative impulses. No single book can teach these lessons. They are picked up from reading other writers' works and recognizing how various problems are attacked and solved. However, read the section on style in Chapter 2, "Writing Clearly." Examine Chapter 3, "Writing Creatively," and play the various games suggested in the text. Your responses may be surprising.

The final, and perhaps the most important, technique of learning to write effectively is practice. Writing is a craft. Like other crafts—running hurdles, sewing, playing the piano, playing baseball—performance improves with practice. If you want to learn to write, then write. With each attempt, the quality of your work will improve.

Following the various discussions of forms of writing throughout the book, you will find a heading—*Give It a Try*—that announces an exercise in writing. These exercises are practice sessions. If you complete all of these practice sessions, you will find that you have absorbed a good deal of the technique of effective writing. The title of this book promises you, the reader, instruction on how to master the craft of writing. The practice sessions are an important part of that instruction. Give it a try.

Getting Ready to Write

Whether you are a student assigned to write a term paper, an employee making out an annual report, a club secretary writing up the minutes of a meeting, a guest responding to a formal invitation, or an aspiring novelist, you will need to do some groundwork before you can begin to write. This involves more than simply sitting down with pad and pencil. It requires self-discipline and an environment that is both quiet and conducive to concentration. Effective writing is not produced in noisy rooms or in the company of a blaring television. Writing is a solitary craft. It is pursued alone, and it is only accomplished with willpower and after a good deal of practice.

Writing, like any other craft, is learned through trial and error. Good, solid work is not produced on the first attempt, nor, perhaps, on the second or even the third. Writers, whether amateur or professional, revise their work, reread, and revise yet again. The good writer is relentless in his or her attention to detail and accuracy.

Effective writing demands time. It cannot be hurried or be done well overnight. Certain tools are necessary: paper, pens, a typewriter, and, of course, reference books—dictionaries, thesauruses.

Chapter 1 deals with these preliminaries to effective writing: time, place, and tools. It also covers audience—the person or persons for whom you will be writing.

Time

Professional writers—those who make their living from the craft—work as regularly as any wage earner, settling to their tasks at a certain hour and for a certain length of time each working day. Most likely, you go to school, or manage a household, or work full-time outside of the house. You may do all three. You may not have large blocks of time to devote to writing. So when do you find the time to write? The truth is, you do not find the time. You *make* the time.

Perhaps you have never looked at it this way, but our means of counting time gives each of us 8,760 hours each year: 24 hours per day times 365 days. Let's say you set aside 1,000 of those hours for writing, less than 12 percent of the total. What might you write in a thousand hours? Suppose you produce, on the average, one typewritten page of 250 words every 2 hours. The amount of copy that you would turn out in a year would fill a book of average length—125,000 words. But perhaps you weren't planning to write enough copy to fill a book, or you feel you can't devote that much time to writing. Even so, you can see that if you write for only about an hour each day, you can produce about 46,000 words each year, which is not bad for a part-time writer.

Procrastination does not produce manuscripts.

An environment conducive to effective writing is private, quiet, and well-lit. You need the space to spread out the tools of writing—pens, pencils, a typewriter, paper, and reference books.

What's the best time to write? It depends on the individual. Some people get up early to put in a few hours before leaving for work or school. Others prefer to write in the evening. Still others set aside part of the weekend for writing.

Once you have set aside time for writing, establish a routine and stick to it. If necessary, force yourself to begin writing at the appointed hour. Remember, following a routine is vital to learning to write, just as following a routine is important to learning any other craft.

Many of us procrastinate, or put things off. Some people think that professional writers procrastinate more than others. We have all heard about how writers fidget, file their nails, check the time, sharpen and resharpen pencils, and neatly arrange and rearrange their desks. They make a pot of coffee, examine the refrigerator's contents, and gaze out the window—anything to avoid getting down to work. Most of these stories, however, about professional writers' habits are exaggerations. Procrastination does not produce manuscripts, and no manuscripts means no money for the writer.

If you put off the writing task, you, of course, will not starve, but you also will not master the craft. Writing must, and will, be put aside from time to time. But, procrastination should not become a habit.

You have probably heard the expression *writer's block*. It's used to describe those frustrating times when a writer stares at a blank piece of paper and cannot think of anything to say. You will probably experience it yourself. But for most professional writers, writer's block is an unaffordable luxury. Thoughts of not eating help most writers recover from this malady fairly quickly.

Writer's block is often linked with the absence of inspiration. Common wisdom says that if you are not inspired, you cannot write. However, almost any idea can offer inspiration. As you get into the swing of writing, you will find there are many more ideas around than you could possibly handle in a lifetime. Actually, there is more hard work than inspiration involved in molding ideas into useful manuscripts. Because writing is such hard work, writers sometimes say that they really hate to write. Perhaps some do, but on the whole that is nonsense. If writers didn't like to write, there would not be so many of us.

Place

Now that you have found the time to write, you must decide *where* you will do so. As we said earlier, writing is a solitary task. If you are going to write, you must get away by yourself and draw deep within yourself. It's up to you to choose the place.

Some Professional Writer's Places

As James Thurber's eyesight faded towards blindness, he often wrote in his head, wherever he happened to be. When he spoke about his work in public, Thurber joked about his writing habits:

> I never quite know when I'm not writing. Sometimes my wife comes up to me at a party and says, "Thurber, stop writing." She usually catches me in the middle of a paragraph. Or my daughter will look up from the dinner table and ask, "Is he sick?" "No," my wife says, "he's writing something." I have to do it that way on account of my eyes . . . My usual method is to spend the mornings turning over the text in my mind. Then . . . I call in a secretary and dictate to her . . . It took me ten years to learn.[1]

According to literary legend, Thomas Wolfe occasionally made a refrigerator his desk, writing in longhand while

Privacy can be hard to come by.

standing at the appliance. Refrigerators were shorter then, and Wolfe with his 6 foot, 6-inch frame could write comfortably this way.

So ingrained was the writing habit in Thomas Mann that he always wrote regularly, even during an ocean voyage. Mann confessed that during rough weather it did unsettle his stomach to look out a window and see the horizon appear and disappear as the ship met the ocean waves.

Before word processors came to newspaper city rooms, reporters wrote amid the din of clacking typewriters. Although most of the noisy typewriters are gone now, reporters still must contend with ringing phones, shouts for copy, and loud conversations at the next desk. War correspondents have often produced stories amid the noise and danger of battle.

Your Writing Place

You may live in an apartment or in a house without an extra room to set aside for writing. If this is the case, you can do with a desk or a table tucked in a corner of your bedroom or the living room. You may decide to do your writing at the kitchen or dining room table.

You might also do some of your writing at your local library. Students in particular may need to use library resources to complete writing assignments. Also, libraries generally are quiet places and may be the answer for writers who cannot seem to get much done at home.

Ideally, of course, you should have a separate room for writing. You might think of this room as your office or study and spend a great deal of your time there. However, unless you are wealthy, do not rent office space outside of your house. Even if your income from writing could eventually pay the office rent, such an expenditure remains questionable.

Your writing desk or table should be about 29 or 30 inches high for greatest comfort. If you have a typing table, it should be lower, about 26 or 27 inches high. If you type on a higher table or stand, you may strain your neck and back muscles.

You will need adequate lighting; an architect's lamp works well for this purpose. Of course, you need not buy a new lamp if you already have one that properly illuminates your writing area.

Tools

You have set aside time for writing and have found a place in which to write. Now it's time to assemble the tools you will need.

We'll assume that you already have the most comon writing tools—pens, pencils, erasers, and sheets or pads of paper. If you do not have to produce typewritten copy, these may be the only writing tools you will need, other than reference books.

If you must produce typewritten or printed copy, you will, of course, need a typewriter or a word processor.

Typewriters

Choosing a typewriter is largely a matter of budget and personal preference. There are three kinds of typewriters: manual, electric, and electronic. Manual typewriters are the least expensive of the three, but are also the slowest. Electric typewriters cost more, but allow you to type faster and, in many cases, produce neater copy.

Electronic typewriters, which are the most expensive of the three, look like electric typewriters, but contain a tiny computer. This computer, called a *microprocessor*, allows the typewriter to perform certain functions automatically, such as underlining and setting margins. Most electronic typewriters also allow the typist to store information in a device called *memory*. When such information is needed at a later time, the typist simply presses a key, and the information is retyped automatically. See pages 286–289 for more information on electronic typewriters.

A word of caution: You do not need to spend extra money to buy a typewriter that allows you to use a variety of type faces. If you already own such a machine, do not use italic or script type as your major type face. It's best to use an ordinary type face like those shown below.

Pica

```
We the people of the United States,
in order to form a more perfect
```

Elite

```
We the people of the United States,
in order to form a more perfect
```

Sans-serif

```
We the people of the United States,
in order to form a more perfect
```

You will notice that you also have a choice of type sizes available: pica or elite. There are advantages to both. Pica is larger than elite and is, thus, easier to read. Elite will save you money on paper; it allows twenty percent more characters per page than pica.

You will also need a device to correct typing errors. You can apply a quick-drying liquid preparation that whites out type, allowing you to type over errors. Or you can use correction tape, a paper device that you place on the paper and then strike with the appropriate key, whiting out the error. Some electric and electronic typewriters include built-in correction ribbons that allow the typist to correct errors. Of course, if you wish, you may stick with the good old typewriter eraser.

Some writers do their first draft in longhand. Others compose on the typewriter. Still others dictate first drafts to a tape recorder. There is no best way. Do whatever suits you the best.

Your final draft should be typed on 8½- by 11-inch bond paper. Sixteen-pound bond is the lightest weight paper you should use; twenty-pound costs more, but is preferred. Do not use erasable paper. It does not absorb ink, and the type smears, creating a messy page.

Before you begin typing, make sure your typewriter keys are clean. The ribbon should be changed frequently as well.

Word Processing Equipment

A word processor can be an effective writing tool. When you use one, the material you type is stored on a magnetic

Word processors are the writer's newest tool. The machine allows a writer to add, delete, or move letters, words, lines, and even paragraphs without retyping.

disk, card, or tape. On most word processors, your words and sentences appear on a video display device resembling a television screen. Correction devices are not necessary because you can simply type over any errors. A word processor also allows you to add, delete, or move letters, words, lines, and paragraphs without retyping everything you have written. In fact, you can revise a document as many times as you wish without ever having to retype it.

When you finish typing, you can direct the word processor to print a copy of the document. Because the document is "saved" on a storage device, you can make further changes in the document and reprint it whenever you wish.

A word processor thus saves you considerable time as you write and especially as you revise what you have written. It eliminates the laborious task of retyping each new draft of a document. But before you decide to buy a word processor, give some careful thought to whether you do enough writing to justify the purchase. Keep in mind that you will spend from a few hundred to several thousand dollars on a word processor, depending on the quality and sophistication of the system.

Reference Books

Reference books are important tools of the writer's craft. Certain books are essential, such as a good dictionary and a style and grammar guide. Other books, for example, thesauruses and encyclopedias, are useful to almost any writer. The use of other reference books depends on the type of writing you do. You might, for example, need a historical or a geographical dictionary if you were writing about early pioneer settlements.

The following list of reference books is not meant to be comprehensive, nor are we suggesting that you acquire all or most of these books. It is offered simply as a guide.

Dictionaries

The American Heritage Dictionary of the English Language
> Edited by William Morris. Houghton Mifflin Co. Dell publishes an abridged edition in paper.

Bernstein's Reverse Dictionary
> Edited by Theodore M. Bernstein. Times Books.

The Random House Dictionary of the English Language—College Edition
     Edited by Laurence Urdang. Random House.

The Random House Dictionary of the English Language—Unabridged Edition
     Edited by Jess Stein. Random House.

The Random House Dictionary*
     Edited by Jess Stein. Ballantine Books.

Webster's New Collegiate Dictionary
     Merriam-Webster Inc.

Webster's Third New International Dictionary—Unabridged Edition
     Merriam-Webster Inc.

The World Book Dictionary
     Edited by Clarence L. Barnhart and Robert K. Barnhart. World Book, Inc.

Encyclopedias

Collier's Encyclopedia
     Macmillan Educational Corporation.

Encyclopedia Americana
     Grolier Incorporated.

The New Columbia Encyclopedia
     Edited by William H. Harris and Judith S. Levey. Columbia University Press.

The New Encyclopaedia Brittanica in 30 Volumes.
     Encyclopaedia Brittanica, Inc.

The World Book Encyclopedia
     World Book, Inc.

Thesauruses

Roget's International Thesaurus
     Thomas Y. Crowell, Co.

The New Roget's Thesaurus of the English Language in Dictionary Form
     Berkley Publishing Corp.

The Synonym Finder
     Edited by J. I. Rodale. Rodale Press Inc.

Webster's Collegiate Thesaurus
     Merriam-Webster Inc.

---

*Available in paper binding.

Reference books are as important to a writer as pen and paper. A dictionary, encyclopedia, and thesaurus kept close by help to ensure an error-free and factual text.

Webster's New Dictionary of Synonyms
Merriam-Webster Inc.

*Webster's New World Thesaurus**
Edited by Charlton Laird. New American Library.

Books of Quotations

Dictionary of Quotations
Edited by Bergen Evans. Delacorte Press.

Familiar Quotations (John Bartlett)
Little, Brown, and Company.

The Home Book of Quotations, Classical and Modern
Edited by Burton Stevenson. Dodd, Mead and Co.

Oxford Dictionary of Quotations
Oxford University Press, Inc.

*The Great Quotations**
Edited by George Seldes. Lyle Stuart, Inc.

The International Thesaurus of Quotations
Edited by Rhoda Thomas Tripp. Thomas Y. Crowell, Co.

The Quotable Woman, 1800–1981
Edited by Elaine Partnow. Facts on File, Inc.
Pinnacle Books publishes a paperback edition.

---

*Available in paper binding.

Almanacs and Statistical Sources

American Statistics Index: A Comprehensive Guide and Index to the Statistical Publication of the United States Government.
　　Congressional Information Service. Monthly.

Information Please Almanac*
　　A. & W. Pubs., Inc. Annual.

Statistical Abstract of the United States*
　　U.S. Bureau of the Census. Annual.

The People's Almanac*
　　Edited by David Wallechinsky and Irving Wallace. Doubleday & Co.

The People's Almanac 2*
　　Edited by David Wallechinsky and Irving Wallace. William Morrow & Co., Inc.

The People's Almanac 3*
　　Edited by David Wallechinsky and Irving Wallace. William Morrow & Co., Inc.

The World Almanac and Book of Facts*
　　Publisher varies. Annual.

Atlases

The National Atlas of the United States of America
　　U.S. Geological Survey.

The Times Atlas of the World
　　Times Books.

Rand McNally Cosmopolitan World Atlas
　　Rand McNally & Co.

The World Book Atlas
　　World Book Encyclopedia, Inc.

The World Book Atlas of the United States and Canada
　　World Book–Childcraft International, Inc.

General Biographical References

Webster's Biographical Dictionary
　　G. & C. Merriam Company.

Who's Who in America
　　Marquis Who's Who, Inc.

Who's Who in World
　　Marquis Who's Who, Inc.

---

*Available in paper binding.

Guides to Reference Books
Finding Facts: Interviewing, Observing, Using Reference Source
> By William L. Rivers. Prentice-Hall.

Guide to Reference Books
> By Eugene P. Sheehy. American Library Association.

How to Find Out
> By George Chandler. Pergamon Press, Inc.

Grammar, Style, and Usage Guides
A Dictionary of Modern English Usage
> By Henry W. Fowler. Oxford University Press, Inc.

A New Guide to Better Writing*
> By Rudolf Flesch and A. H. Lass. Warner Books.

Do's, Don'ts and Maybes of English Usage
> By Theodore M. Bernstein. Times Books.

Grammar and Style Guide
> World Books.

On Writing Well: An Informal Guide to Writing Nonfiction*
> By William Zinsser. Harper & Row.

The Careful Writer. A Modern Guide to English Usage
> Atheneum Pubs.

The Chicago Manual of Style
> University of Chicago Press.

The Elements of Style*
> By William Strunk, Jr. and E. B. White. Macmillan Publishing Co., Inc.

The Misspeller's Dictionary
> Simon & Schuster, Inc.

Words into Type
> By Marjorie E. Skillin and Robert M. Gay. Prentice-Hall.

Guides to Markets for Articles and Books
Literary Market Place
> R. R. Bowker, Co. Annual.

Writer's Market
> Writer's Digest Books. Annual.

---

*Available in paper binding.

Audience

The first three elements of getting ready to write—time, place, and tools—have been discussed. Before you actually begin writing, however, you must also give some thought to the person or persons for whom you will be writing, that is, your audience.

Almost all writing is directed at an audience. When you write a school paper, your audience is your teacher and possibly your classmates. Professional writers who work in the media, including advertising and public relations, sometimes write for the general public. At other times, they must tailor their writing to a specific segment of the general public, for example, women between the ages of 18 and 30.

When you write for work, your audience may be your supervisor, your co-workers, or people working under your supervision. You may write letters in response to customer complaints or as a means of getting new business for the company. Employers are your audience when you write a reśumé and cover letters.

Writing for the community involves a variety of possible audiences, including members of your club or community group, elected officials, community leaders, the editors of your local newspaper, and the community as a whole. When you are writing personal correspondence your audience may be friends, relatives, or acquaintances to whom you write letters or send invitations. You may write to companies to place an order, request information, or register a complaint. Perhaps you will express your opinions in letters to elected officials or newspaper editors. In addition, you may have to fill out applications for jobs or for credit. Even your journal or diary has an audience—you.

Finally, if you write for publication, you will need to worry about two audiences. Your first audience is always the editor or other person at the publishing company who decides whether to accept or reject your manuscript or proposal. Your other audience includes the people who most likely will read your article, poem, essay, short story, or book.

Why is it so important to consider your audience before you begin to write? First, your audience influences the content, emphasis, and tone of your writing. For example, suppose you are a student who decides to write about your recent trip to Europe. If you are writing for your history teacher, you will want to emphasize the places you visited, describing and explaining their historic importance. Most

Audience influences the content, emphasis, and tone of writing. The effective writer knows for whom he or she is writing.

likely, you will write in a formal tone appropriate for a school paper. On the other hand, if you are writing about your trip for your school newspaper, you might want to emphasize personal experiences. Your audience probably will be more interested in such anecdotes than in reading about famous buildings and battlefields. Your tone for such an article will be informal, even conversational.

Your audience also influences your choice of words. Novelists use different words when writing for children than when writing for adults. When scientists write for other scientists, they use different words than when they write for the general public.

You should also keep in mind how much, or how little, your audience knows about the topic. Don't insult your readers by telling them what they already know, but don't make the mistake of assuming they know more than they do.

You now have the basics of writing at your command: making time, finding space, using good tools, and concentrating on your audience. A fifth basic, writing clearly, is a challenge to master, one you will face each time you sit down to write. Our next chapter will show you how to develop a clear writing style.

References

1. **Malcolm Cowley, editor.** *Writers at Work,* vol. 1. New York: Viking, 1958, p. 96.

Writing Clearly

Learning to write clearly takes time and practice. One learns by writing, again and again. But mastering the craft is well worth the effort. The ability to write clearly will help you throughout life: at home, at school, on the job, and in the community. Writing, like speaking, is communicating, and communicating effectively is a powerful tool to have mastered. The ability to write *exactly* what one sees, feels, or understands about the world offers advantages, both personal and professional.

There are, of course, rules, and these are discussed throughout the chapter. Rules of grammar sound forbidding, but with practice, they become second nature, handy things to have around when one runs into problems.

Besides practice and mastering the rules, the ability to write clearly demands the ability to distinguish good writing from bad. Learning the difference is, in fact, the first step. Let's begin by looking at examples of writing that should be avoided.

Gobbledygook

During World War II, a man named Maury Maverick was appointed head of the Smaller War Plants Corporation (SWPC), a federal agency. Maverick had served in Congress and had also been mayor of San Antonio. He admired plain talk, written as well as spoken. The fogbound prose that government departments produced appalled him.

Judging from what they wrote, government employees never worked; they "performed tasks" or "maintained operations." They did not go by rules; they "followed established methods of procedure." They did not use buildings, offices, and equipment, but rather "utilized facilities to their maximum potential." An agency chief might never out-and-out fire someone, but could use "broad discretionary powers to initiate dismissal action."

Maverick called this mush *gobbledygook.* He isn't really sure where he got the word: "Perhaps I was thinking of the bearded turkey gobbler back in Texas who is always gobbledy-gobbling . . . At the end of his gobble there was a sort of gook."[1]

Maverick, in a memo to SWPC employees, declared war on gobbledygook. All people in his employ were to stop writing memos, letters, and reports in language designed

to avoid the issue and confuse the reader. He demanded messages that were direct and written in brief, simple sentences.

The war ended, the SWPC folded, and the enemy of gobbledygook returned to Texas. Maury Maverick added a new word to the language. He may even have had some influence on the Washington bureaucracy. But gobbledygook, unfortunately, lives on. We are still up to our ankles in oatmeal prose. As we shall see, it oozes not only from government, but from other sources as well.

Examples of gobbledygook.   Literary muddiness flows at various depths. In some cases, you may wade through gobbledygook, eventually find meaning and translate the stuff into English.

> If management continues to defer maintenance operations through failure to supply sufficient funds to make repairs as they naturally become necessary from time to time, the operating efficiency of the plant will be considerably lowered and, as a direct result, major construction tasks will then become imperative.
>
> **Translation:**
> If those in charge fail to provide a *little* money from time to time for repairs, the plant will become run down. At length it will cost a *lot* of money to put it in shape.[2]

The idea can be stated even more simply: spend a little now to avoid spending a lot later. The waters get even muddier in the following passage. See if you can translate.

> Reading is a processing skill of symbolic reasoning sustained by the interfacilitation of an intricate hierarchy of substrata factors that have been mobilized as a psychological working system and pressed into service in accordance with the purpose of the reader.
>
> **Translation:**
> Reading is decoding written or printed symbols called words.[3]

We reach muddy bottom with the following passage. A traveler on a British railroad wrote to complain that there was no dining car on the train. A company official replied:

> Whilst I can readily appreciate your frustration at the loss of breakfast, since in the circumstances you describe it is unfortunately true that in many cases

where a catering vehicle becomes defective and both stores and equipment need to be transferred into a replacement car, this can only be done during the train's journey.

It is not of course possible to make the transfer whilst vehicles are in the sidings and the intensity of coach workings is such that the train sets are not available to be put into a platform at other times to enable the transfer to be carried.[4]

We won't attempt a translation. This choice example won the top booby prize among the Plain English Awards in London in 1982. The judges called it "absolute tripe—official gibberish which no one could be expected to understand."

Why do people write gobbledygook? In some cases, they want to dodge an issue or confuse the reader. In other cases, they lack the skill to say what they mean or they simply don't know what they are talking about.

How to Spot Gobbledygook

Gobbledygookers usually prefer long words to short words. They "initiate" instead of "start," "modify" instead of "change," and use an "implement" instead of a "tool."

Oliver Hazard Perry at the Battle of Lake Erie: "Area accessed in combat mode; mission finished."

Gobbledygookers sprinkle their long and involved sentences with "–ize" words: optimize and channelize. They love "–wise" words: programwise and businesswise. They use such expressions as time frame, fast track, gear up, off load, and interface. Saying "at this point of time" sounds more impressive and official than saying "now."

A writer, just for fun, once translated some famous sayings into gobbledygook.

John Paul Jones, during the Revolutionary War:
"I have not yet begun to fight."
Gobbledygook:
"Combatwise, the time frame is upcoming."

Oliver Hazard Perry during the battle of Lake Erie, War of 1812:
"We have met the enemy, and they are ours."
Gobbledygook:
"Area accessed in combat mode; mission finished."

George Dewey at Manila Bay, Spanish-American War:
"You may fire when you are ready, Gridley."
Gobbledygook:
"Implementation of aggressive action approved; time frame to be selected by fire control officer."[5]

Give It a Try
Try your hand at translating these famous sayings into gobbledygook:

- Don't fire until you see the whites of their eyes.
- The only thing we have to fear is fear itself.
- There is Jackson standing like a stone wall.
- Ask not what your country can do for you—ask what you can do for your country.
- Prosperity is just around the corner.

Words, Phrases, and Expressions

We have looked at the kinds of words poor writers use and have suggested that you avoid them. Now, let's discuss how you can choose words that will help you write clearly.

Your Vocabulary

The English language currently contains more than a half million words. As life becomes increasingly complex, people will borrow or invent even more words to describe new ideas and activities. Words that are seldom used are gradually dropped from the language. Thus language is alive, constantly changing and growing.

We all have two different vocabularies: *use* and *recognition*. *Use* vocabulary consists of the words you use in writing or speaking. *Recognition* vocabulary is made up of the words you understand, but normally do not use when writing or speaking. If you are like most people, your recognition vocabulary is much larger than your use vocabulary. It is estimated that the average American has a use vocabulary of 10,000 words and a recognition vocabulary of 30,000 to 40,000 words.

The following word list can help you estimate the size of your recognition vocabulary. As you go through the list, note those words you are able to define. These should include the words you normally do not use when writing or speaking. Compare your total with the chart that follows to find your probable recognition vocabulary.[6]

abrasive	disembowel	lodgment	rotund
accent	doubloon	maelstrom	sampan
aegis	éclat	marinade	scraggy
alleviation	emblematical	melodramatic	shaveling
anise	equivocation	metamorphic	shelly
archenemy	exorcise	milliard	shillelagh
attribution	fascia	modicum	simulation
bambino	flabbergast	mossback	snuffle
beechen	forgather	nabob	spheroid
besprent	fructification	necromancer	stethoscope
bigamous	gaby	nonpareil	subservience
binomial	genital	offing	surrogate
buckram	gondolier	oubliette	tabard
calender	grunter	padrone	tannery
carom	hansom	participator	therapy
chaffer	herbivorous	perforation	tocsin
cloister	hornbeam	pickaback	trefoil
cochineal	hypotheses	plumbago	tyro
collusive	inadmissible	pottle	unchartered
complainant	indubitable	prioress	urbane
constitutionality	internationalist	psychiatry	vesicle
cosine	jamb	quiescent	waggle
daguerreotype	kapok	rearrangement	well-disposed
demagnetize	laminate	reimburse	wimple
devourer	leukocyte	revocation	yachting

Words You Know in Above List	Your Probable Vocabulary
100	50,000 or more
90	40,000
80	30,000
70	25,000
60	20,000
50	15,000
40	12,000
30	10,000

With such a large store of words from which to choose, how can you possibly select the words that will help you express your ideas clearly? Here are two rules to guide you.

Rule 1: Choose familiar words over unfamiliar words.
Choose words that the reader is likely to know, keeping in mind that these will vary depending on your audience. You would, for example, use different words when writing for children than when writing for adults. An engineer writing an article for the general public would probably use a different vocabulary than when writing an article on the same topic for other engineers.

You may not recognize some of the words in Shakespeare's plays because language changes with time. But Shakespeare, to appeal to a wide audience, both educated, and uneducated, wrote in the language of his day. *Huckleberry Finn*, written a hundred years ago, is still easily understood. Mark Twain wrote simply, employing everyday vocabulary. You are in good company when you choose familiar words over unfamiliar ones. This is not to suggest that you should never use big words. They give variety to your writing and can, occasionally, add precision and economy. You can, for example, save six words by using *caisson* instead of "a wagon in which to carry ammunition." "A feeling of well-being and happiness" can best be expressed with *euphoria.* "Hand on the hips and elbows turned outward" can be simply *arms akimbo.*

Do not be afraid to use words that exactly convey your meaning. Keep in mind, however, that few people read, or care to read, with a dictionary at hand. Use unfamiliar words, but use them sparingly. If you decide to use a word that the reader probably will not know, you may wish to subtly give the meaning: "Clara returned his stare with an *ingenuous* smile, a smile both simple and innocent."

Give It a Try
For each of the words below, substitute a more familiar word with the same meaning.

parsimonious	lugubrious	nebulous	luminous
endorsement	expostulate	erudite	enigmatic
encumbrance	ignominious	glutinous	countermand
debilitate	elucidate	ebullient	odium
obstreperous	opprobrium	portent	rectrocede

Rule 2: Choose concrete and specific words over general and abstract words.   Concrete and specific words paint a clear picture of what you are trying to express. They grab and hold the reader's attention. Abstract and general words, on the other hand, often confuse and annoy the reader. You can usually substitute or modify general words to achieve clarity.

Poor: Will you look at that *tree* on the *hill?* Which tree, which hill?

Better: Will you look at that *ancient oak tree* growing *half way up* the *higher hill?*
Yes, it's beautiful!

Abstract words—words that name ideas and qualities rather than objects or things—can also be made specific or concrete. This is usually done with examples or illustrations. You might, for example, define *inflation* as "too much money chasing too few goods." Although this definition is fairly specific, you can make it concrete by giving an illustration: "If apples are scarce and people really want apples and have the money to pay for them, they will pay a high price for them. This will cause inflation in apple prices."

We commonly use such abstractions as "democracy," "freedom," and "nation," but what do they mean to readers? The following definition by E. B. White appeared during World War II, when Americans were concerned about preserving democracy.

> We received a letter from the Writers' War Board the other day asking for a statement on "The Meaning of Democracy." It presumably is our duty to comply with such a request, and it certainly is our pleasure.
> Surely the Board knows what democracy is. It is the line that forms on the right. It is the don't in Don't shove. It is the hole in the stuffed shirt through which the sawdust slowly trickles; it is the dent in the high hat. Democracy is the recurrent suspicion that more than half the people are

right more than half of the time. It is the feeling of privacy in the voting booths, the feeling of communion in the libraries, the feeling of vitality everywhere. Democracy is a letter to the editor. Democracy is the score at the beginning of the ninth. It is an idea which hasn't been disproved yet, a song the words of which have not gone bad. It's the mustard on the hot dog and the cream in the rationed coffee. Democracy is a request from a War Board, in the middle of a morning in the middle of a war, wanting to know what democracy is.[7]

Give It a Try

Make each of the following abstract words more concrete by giving an example or illustration.

   love   freedom   fear   happiness

Words We Sometimes Confuse

The English language contains certain pairs and trios of words that are, at times, confusing.

accept, except.

Accept is a verb meaning "to receive willingly." The verb *except* means "to omit or exclude." When used as a preposition, *except* means "other than."

> I *accept* your gift with great appreciation. Students without written permission from their parents were *excepted* from the trip.
> She finished the entire book *except* the last chapter.

advice, advise.

Advice is a noun; *advise* is a verb.

> Jane was sorry that she didn't follow her father's *advice.*
> My lawyer *advised* me to remain silent.

affect, effect.

Affect is a verb that means "to influence." *Effect* can be used either as a verb or a noun. When used as a verb, *effect* means "to produce, accomplish, or cause." The noun *effect* means "a result or consequence."

> The teacher *affected* my decision to attend college.
> The new law will *effect* changes in the way police question suspects.
> Failing a test can be the *effect* of not studying for it.

aggravate, irritate.

Aggravate means "to make worse." *Irritate* means "to annoy."

Sunbathing *aggravates* my skin rash.

Phil's habit of popping his chewing gum *irritates* his friends.

among, between.

Use *among* to show the relation of three or more persons or things. Use *between* when discussing two things, or more than two things that are considered separately.

Among the four of us, we had enough money to pay the bill.

This is a secret *between* you and me.

The airline flies *between* Los Angeles, Chicago, and New York.

anxious, eager.

Anxious means "worried or troubled." *Eager* means "enthusiastic or looking forward to."

Mrs. Duke became *anxious* when her daughter did not come home on time.

He is *eager* to begin his new job with the railroad.

awhile, a while.

The first is an adverb; the second (*while*) is a noun.

Practice *awhile* longer, and then take a break.

I'll only be gone for *a while.*

bad, badly.

Bad is an adjective; *badly* is an adverb.

I felt *bad* about my behavior.

I had never behaved so *badly* before.

compose, comprise.

Compose means "to make up." *Comprise* means "to embrace, include, or take in."

Molecules are *composed* of atoms.

Our school *comprises* students, teachers, counselors, and the principal.

farther, further.

Use *farther* to indicate a distance that can be measured. *Further* suggests a greater quantity, degree, or extent.

We traveled *farther* than we had planned.

I need to do *further* research on the subject.

imply, infer.

Imply means "to hint or suggest." *Infer* means "to reason or draw a conclusion."

His boss *implied* that he wasn't doing a good job.

My car was gone; I *inferred* that someone had stolen it.

irregardless, disregardless, regardless.

The correct word is *regardless;* don't use *irregardless* or *disregardless.*

principal, principle.

Principal can be either a noun or an adjective. As a noun, it refers to the chief person or a sum of money. As an adjective, it means "main, most important, or chief." *Principle* is a noun meaning "rule, law, or belief."

Ms. Mendez hopes to become a school *principal.*

My principal goal is to get a good education.

Janet always sticks to her *principles.*

recur, reoccur.

Reoccur is not a word; *recur* means "to occur or happen again."

that, which.

Use *that* in restrictive clauses (clauses that are essential to the sentence's meaning). Use *which* in nonrestrictive clauses (clauses that are not essential to the sentence's meaning).

> The book *that* I borrowed from the library is now overdue.
>
> "Birches," *which* was written by Robert Frost, is my favorite poem.

Avoiding Redundancy

If you want to write clearly, avoid *redundancy*—saying the same thing twice. Redundancy usually results from an incomplete understanding of the meaning of common words. We often read that a new product is "highly unique." *Unique* means *one of a kind.* A new product cannot, therefore, be very one of a kind, highly one of a kind, or even somewhat one of a kind.

A magazine publisher may offer a "free gift" for renewing a subscription. The expression "free gift" is redundant; gifts, by definition, are free.

You may read of "end results" or "final outcomes." But, results always come at the end, and outcomes are always final.

Proximity means "closeness." You will agree that "close proximity" may be uncomfortably close.

"He shouted loudly." Does anyone shout quietly? "She whispered softly." How else would she whisper? "He is brave and courageous." Again, the same thing is being said twice.

"The minister preached a sermon." To give a sermon is to preach, and to preach is to give a sermon. It would be better to say that the minister "preached on sin" or "gave a sermon on sin."

The phrase "a moving stream" sounds nice. However, all streams move; water that does not move fills a pond. Thus, "still pond" is also redundant.

Redundancy can be avoided by frequently consulting the dictionary. Check out the exact meaning before using the word.

Give It a Try
Explain why each of the following phrases is redundant. If necessary, consult that dictionary.

rich opulence	sweetly saccharine
wild pandemonium	cascading waterfall
kamikaze suicide mission	large mansion
uniquely different	sharp, pungent odor
grateful thanks	everlasting eternity

Untouchables—Worlds Best Left Alone
Some words are best avoided—for example, *hopefully*. It means "in a hopeful way," but people often use it to mean "I am hoping," "I am hopeful," or simply "I hope." We mentioned earlier in the chapter that language is a living thing. It changes as usage changes. "Hopefully" is misused constantly: "Hopefully, I'll make my train" or "Hopefully, I'll get there on time." Has constant misuse made it acceptable? No, not yet. It may become acceptable in a generation or two. But, in the meantime, people who write and speak *clearly* do not catch trains or meet friends,

filled with hope. They hope they catch their train or hope they arrive on time. The difference is the difference between communicating *exactly* what you mean and communicating "hopefully."

Another phrase to avoid is "more importantly." Use either "more important" or "what's more." "Seldomly" falls into the same category; seldom is already an adverb, meaning "rarely."

You often see lists of items beginning with "first," followed by "secondly," thirdly," and so on. Why not "firstly," then? No one writes, or even says, onely, twoly, and threely. First, second, and third still work well, as do one, two, and three.

We mentioned *–wise* words earlier, in connection with gobbledygook. Avoid the temptation to hook *–wise* onto any and every noun. You will end up with such meaningless nonwords as *profitwise, businesswise, taxwise,* and *workwise.*

Very is a word that is often overworked. It is, besides, a weak word and usually unnecessary. "She was very happy." How much happier is "very happy" than just plain "happy"? "He ran very fast." How much faster than "fast" is "very fast"? "It was very cold." Why not be precise? "It was ten degrees below zero."

Clichés

A *cliché* is *an expression or idea that has been worn out by overuse.* You may be familiar with these clichés: "in the twinkling of an eye," "quick as a flash," "white as snow," "nipped in the bud," and "ignorance is bliss." Undoubtedly you can think of others. Try to avoid clichés in your writing. Instead, think carefully about what you want to say and use your own words to express your ideas.

Clichés can be fun, however. Try turning them around or using them to make puns or jokes: "Into every athlete's life a little sprain might fall." "If words fail to express your gratitude, why don't you try using money?" "When I didn't have time to drink my milk shake, it was the last straw."

Give It a Try

Read the following clichés. Then, use each one in an unusual way. You may wish to turn the clichés around or use them to make puns or jokes. Here are two possibilities: "A sturdy joke from a little corn grows." "Lack of need smothers invention."

- Bull in a china shop.
- Blood is thicker than water.
- A sturdy oak from a little acorn grows.
- Green with envy.
- Hungry as a bear.
- Get down to brass tacks.
- In one fell swoop.
- After all is said and done.
- Necessity is the mother of invention.
- Mad as a hornet.
- Time marches on.
- A wolf in sheep's clothing.

Sentences

Arranging ideas in sentences. Sentences, and the ideas they express, can be arranged in a variety of ways. In a *loose sentence,* the main idea is given first, with details added later to strengthen the statement.

Example: Jill wants to become a teacher because she likes both children and books.

A *periodic sentence* places the main idea at the end of the sentence.

Example: Because she likes both children and books, Jill wants to become a teacher.

A *balanced sentence* presents two or more ideas of equal importance. These ideas are presented in separate parts of the sentence.

Example: Jill wants to become a teacher; her sister Marilyn hopes to enter politics.

Loose sentences are direct and easy for the reader to follow. Too many loose sentences in a row, however, will bore the reader. Periodic sentences lend drama and suspense to your writing, since the main idea is placed at the end of the sentence. Balanced sentences, which have a definite beat, bring rhythm to your writing. Rhythm is an important element of writing, adding flow that keeps the audience interested and reading.

In much of your writing, you will probably use loose sentences as your main sentence pattern. But do remember to vary the pattern by including both periodic and balanced sentences.

Give It a Try

Rewrite these loose sentences as periodic sentences.

- I read *War and Peace* during my vacation last summer.
- Softball is Cindy's favorite sport, although she also likes volleyball and soccer.
- Most of my friends live close to me, although a few do not.
- I usually walk to shool, although it is all the way across town.
- I learned to eat snails while I was visiting in France.

Active Versus Passive Voice

Verbs have two voices: *active* and *passive.* A verb is active when the subject of the sentence acts: Mark won the race. A verb is passive when the subject of the sentence receives the action: the race was won by Mark.

In general, use the active rather than the passive voice. The active voice produces writing that is clear, direct, and forceful. Notice the difference between the following sentences.

Active voice: The detective gathered the evidence, arrested the suspects, and charged them with first-degree murder.

Passive voice: The evidence was gathered by the detective, and the suspects were arrested by her and were charged with first-degree murder.

There are, of course, times when you should use the passive rather than the active voice. Use the passive voice when the person or thing *receiving* the action is more important than the one *doing* it: "He was shocked by her refusal to marry him." You may also use the passive voice when you don't know who said or did something: "It's been said that there's no fool like an old fool."

You will, however, find that you can use the active voice in most of your sentences, even descriptive ones. "There were ten guards standing outside the palace entrance" can be changed to "Ten guards stood outside the palace entrance." Notice that the active voice is more forceful and direct; it also shortens and simplifies the sentence.

Give It a Try

Rewrite the following sentences using verbs in the active voice.

- A change in the ingredients was made.
- Evaporation of the liquid took place overnight.
- He has the intention of going.
- The spectator was struck by the basketball.
- The door was left unlocked by someone.
- The groceries were checked out by the clerk.
- The man was fired by the boss.
- Her income tax return was sent in two weeks late.

Omitting Unnecessary Words

Writing in the active voice usually leads to more concise sentences. Let's also look at other ways to eliminate words. Read the following sentence:

> Because at the present time we are ahead of schedule by a period of a week, a large number of us are of the opinion that, if we have a modicum of good fortune, there is a distinct possibility that we can complete an investigation of three instead of only two cases.[8]

This 52-word sentence leaves the reader breathless from wading through a bog of unnecessary words. Let's shorten and simplify it.

> We are now a week ahead of schedule, and, therefore, many of us think that, with luck, we might investigate three instead of two cases.

We have weeded out more than half the words; the message is expressed with greater speed and economy. But, let's try to do even better.

> We are a week early, which could mean three instead of two investigations.

We are now down to 13 words. But have we gone too far? Has any of the original meaning been lost?

Try your hand at the example below. Pare it down to the minimum without losing the original meaning.

> According to our agreement you are to furnish services periodically on alternate days of the week in amounts to be specified at irregular intervals. Due to circumstances beyond our control, we herewith ask you to interrupt your services for one period only, effective Monday, May 30. Please note that services are to be resumed as of Wednesday, June 1, in the same amount and manner as heretofore.[8]

How many words were you able to cut? The example above can actually be rewritten in two words—"Skip Monday."

Here is a list of clumsy, needless phrases that can clutter your writing. Each is followed by a word or phrase to use in its place.

owing to the fact that	because
the question as to whether	whether
there is no doubt that	no doubt, doubtless
in the amount of	for
this is a subject that	this subject
make inquiry regarding	inquire, ask
take into consideration	consider, think about
costs the sum of	costs
seldom ever	seldom
do not pay attention to	ignore
in the near future	soon
do not have much confidence in	distrust, lack confidence in
in order to	to
we call your attention to the fact	please note
each and every one of us	all of us
at this, that point in time	now, then
at the present time	now
I am of the opinion	I think

Give It a Try

Rewrite these sentences, eliminating all unnecessary words.

- We call your attention to the fact that your payment is at the present time overdue.
- I would like to make inquiry regarding the question as to whether I can buy a new car in the near future.
- I felt ill at that point in time owing to the fact that I had a cold.

More Unnecessary Words

Using "there" and "it is" can also add unnecessary words to your writing:

There is something wrong with this.
Something is wrong with this.

There are two things wrong here.
Two things are wrong here.

It is a trap that many people fall into.
Many people fall into the trap.

It is a pity he is so weak.
Too bad he is so weak.

Run-on Sentences

When two or more sentences are joined into a single sentence, they must be properly connected. The following examples illustrate improper connections, that is, run-on sentences:

Last Saturday we went out to dinner, then we saw a movie.

Melissa won first place, her prize was $100.

I want to buy a new suit, I can't afford it.

You can correct a run-on by making two separate sentences:

Last Saturday we went out to dinner. We then saw a movie.

You can join the two sentences with a semicolon:

Melissa won first place; her prize was $100.

You can also join the sentences with a conjunction:

I want to buy a new suit, *but* I can't afford it.

Avoid run-on sentences. They are occasionally used by professional writers to produce a particular effect. If you use them, however, your reader may consider them incorrect.

Give It a Try

Correct the following run-on sentences.

- Sinclair Lewis wrote *Main Street*, he also wrote *Babbitt*.
- The star pitcher was drafted by the Atlanta Braves, however, he decided to attend college first.
- I went to a movie on Friday night, I met friends in the lobby.
- Learning to write clearly can be difficult, learning to write clearly can also be rewarding.

Sentence Fragments

A sentence fragment is an incomplete sentence; it cannot stand alone and make sense. Here are some examples:

If I decide to go.

When I finish high school.

Swimming in the lake with his friends.

You can correct these sentence fragments by completing the thought or by rearranging or adding words.

If I decide to go, I'll let you know.

When I finish school, I plan to start my own business.

He went swimming in the lake with his friends.

You can occasionally use sentence fragments for emphasis. They may also be used in dialogue.

The crisis wasn't over. Not yet.

"Do you mind if I join you?"

"Not at all."

In general, however, avoid sentence fragments. Again, your reader might consider them errors and conclude you are a poor writer.

Parallel Construction

Parallel construction refers to using the same grammatical form to express related ideas. These sentences are examples of parallel structure:

The company ships goods *by land, by sea,* and *by air.*

Bill worries more *about having a good time* than *about making a living.*

Use parallel structure; the resulting balance and rhythm adds emphasis and interest to your writing. You can rewrite sentences with faulty parallelism, as in these examples.

Incorrect: Diana always does her best, both *at school* and *when working.*

Correct: Diana always does her best, both *at school* and *at work.*

Incorrect: Mr. Warner *teaches advanced physics* and *is the baseball team coach.*

Correct: Mr. Warner *teaches advanced physics* and *coaches the baseball team.*

Incorrect: *Having approved the new law* and *since they had finished all other business,* the city council adjourned.

Correct: Since they *had approved the new law* and *had finished all other business,* the city council adjourned.

Give It a Try

Rewrite the following sentences using parallel structure.

- She liked hiking and to swim.
- They were all athletic or chess players.
- The book is not only worthwhile, but a necessity.
- He hoped that she would come or the telephone would ring.
- One if by land, two if the British are coming by sea.

"I saw a deer driving down the street with my father." Allowing your modifiers to dangle may give the wrong impression. "Driving down the street with my father, I saw a deer."

Misplaced and Dangling Modifiers

Modifiers—phrases and clauses that give more information about other words in the sentence—can be troublesome. Like keys and gloves, they can be *misplaced:*

> She wore an old hat on her head that she bought at an auction.
> We watched the sun come up eating doughnuts and drinking coffee.
> He told his teacher with a red face that he had forgotten to do his homework.

Such sentences are corrected by placing the modifiers close to the words they modify.

> Sue wore on her head an old hat that she bought at an auction.
> Eating doughnuts and drinking coffee, we watched the sun come up.
> With a red face, he told his teacher that he had forgotten to do his homework.

Modifiers can also dangle, hopelessly seeking something to modify.

> Listening to the radio, her favorite song was being played.
> Tiptoeing through the woods, a bear suddenly appeared.
> Young and restless, her parents' farm was a boring place.

Dangling modifiers are corrected by adding the words or phrases to which the modifiers are related. It is sometimes also necessary to rearrange words to complete the thought.

> Listening to the radio, he heard his favorite song being played.
> As I was tiptoeing through the woods, a bear suddenly appeared before me.
> Young and restless, she thought her parents' farm was a boring place.

Give It a Try

The following sentences contain misplaced or dangling modifiers. Rewrite each sentence correctly.

- Speaking in a clear voice, the presidential address was a great success.
- Touring through Europe, the scenery was beautiful.
- Leaving a string of broken hearts, the ship sailed from port to port.

Sentence Length

The length of sentences should vary to create interesting, lively prose that will hold a reader's attention. Short sentences are, generally, the easiest to understand. However, too many short sentences in succession can be boring:

> I felt tired. I got into my nightclothes. I went to bed. I hoped my dreams would be pleasant.

Short, choppy sentences can be combined into a single sentence:

> Feeling tired, I got into my nightclothes and went to bed, hoping for pleasant dreams.

The reverse, however, can also be true. Longer, more complicated sentences may need to be divided into two or more shorter ones:

> Being chosen to become a congressional page was the greatest thrill of my life because it meant that I would have the honor of serving in our nation's capital.

Although the sentence is grammatically correct, the following is clearer and less complicated:

> Being chosen to become a congressional page was the greatest thrill of my life. Now I would have the honor of serving in our nation's capital.

When writing sentences, whether short or long, always aim for clarity. Even very long sentences can be clear. Consider this sentence from E. B. White's *Stuart Little*, a children's classic:

> In the loveliest town of all, where the houses were white and high and the elm trees were green and higher than the houses, where the front yards were wide and pleasant and the back yards were bushy and worth finding out about, where the streets sloped down to the stream and the stream flowed quietly under the bridge, where the lawns ended in orchards and the orchards ended in fields and the fields ended in pastures and the pastures climbed the hill and disappeared over the top toward the wonderful wide sky, in this loveliest of all towns Stuart stopped to get a drink of sarsaparilla.[9]

Although you probably will not write sentences as long as White's—107 words—do remember to vary the length of your sentences. If you read *Stuart Little*, you will find that White followed this advice. The seven sentences preceding the long one have 2, 8, 7, 8, 3, 34, and 14 words, respectively. The seven sentences that follow have 43, 15, 60, 19, 19, 9, and 5 words, respectively.

E. B. White, a master of the English language, influenced a generation of American writers with his clean, direct prose.

Paragraphs

The paragraph is the basic unit of composition. A well-written paragraph consists of sentences that develop or explain one main idea. This idea, called a topic, may be stated in a *topic sentence.*

Topic Sentences

A topic sentence tells the reader exactly what the paragraph is about. As in the following example, it is most often the first sentence of the paragraph.

> I'll always remember the day I started my first job. The weather never seemed more pleasant, the sky more blue, the sun more friendly. The trees were budding, Canada geese headed north overhead, and here and there patches of slightly green grass contrasted with the dirty snow. I had a feeling things were going to go well.

The topic sentence does not, however, have to be the first sentence of the paragraph. You might place it at the end to sum up the paragraph's main idea; or you can place it in the middle of the paragraph. Although it is often best for the inexperienced writer to include a topic sentence in every paragraph, it is not essential. Read the following paragraph:

> You can't breathe through your nose. Your lungs are congested, your throat is gravelly, and your eyes are red. Your nose runs all the time. You ache. And nothing seems to make you feel any better.

Notice that although the paragraph does not have a topic sentence, it is still developed around a single main idea: the common cold. Descriptive passages, such as the paragraph above, often work best if the topic is not spelled out, but left to the reader's imagination.

Unity

A paragraph must include more than just a good topic sentence. It should also include sentences that develop and explain the main idea. When all of the sentences in a paragraph are directly related to the main idea, the paragraph has *unity,* as in the following example:

> Summertime is the best time of all. The weather is warm, you can go biking, and you can wear light clothing. It's pleasant to hear insects humming, see

birds flying, and lie around lazily on soft, green grass. At night, you can sit outside and sip lemonade while listening to a baseball game on the radio.

Keep in mind that a unified paragraph should *develop* the main idea. Some paragraphs fail to do this. Notice that the main idea of the following paragraph, which is stated in the first sentence, is never developed.

Interviewers judge a job applicant on the basis of two chief factors, the person's achievement and personality. Of course, some interviewers consider other factors as well. Try to learn as much as you can about the job before the interview.

After you write a paragraph, reread it to make sure you have not included details unrelated to the main idea. Which sentence in the following paragraph is unrelated to the main idea?

On the way back from the movie, we passed the scene of a terrible accident. We learned later that a car had hit a deer that had wandered onto the road. After hitting the deer, the car swerved out of control and hit a tree. The driver and two passengers were seriously injured. We had never driven down this road before.

The last sentence, of course, is unrelated. The others all describe the main topic, the accident.

Paragraph Development

We have learned that the topic sentence must state the main idea of the paragraph and that the other sentences must develop and explain the main idea. Now, let's discuss some specific methods you can use to develop paragraphs.

Method: Illustrations or examples.

In every culture, spring brings a renewal of hope, and people celebrate the change of seasons in different ways. In ancient Inca society, priests blessed seeds, and the emperor symbolically plowed the first furrow. Pastoral Indian groups mark especially the arrival of the first lamb. In Christian societies, people celebrate Easter.

Method: Listing of details.

Soft soap lathers easily, smells good, refreshes the skin, and cleans well. *Soft* costs less, too. That's why many people prefer *Soft* to any other soap.

Method: Define by example.

The word *run* suggests rapid motion, but it has other meanings, too. A clock that runs is simply operating. A sore that runs is oozing. You find sheep in a run, run butter is melted, and run-down means exhausted.

Method: Define by attribute or personal quality.

My little boy is more than snips and snails and puppy-dog tails. He is also dirty fingernails, torn trouser knees, sloppy sneakers, and smudged forehead. He's a large bump of curiosity, too. At times he's a whirl-wind; at other times, he's buried deep in thought.

Method: Cause and effect.

Interchangeable parts and the assembly line increased auto production while decreasing the cost of manufac-turing. This brought car prices down. The installment plan helped people who could afford to buy a car only by making piecemeal payments. New oil discoveries kept the price of gasoline low. Responding to popular demand, states began extensive road-building pro-grams. By the 1920's, America was a nation on wheels. This, in turn, stimulated growth in auto serv-ice businesses, and created motels, roadside restau-rants and dance halls, and the drive-in movie.

Method: Comparison and contrast.

The pistons in your car's engine behave like a row of people doing knee bends in an exercise class, moving up and down. But unlike the people, pistons do not move in unison. While some are going down, others are going up, and no two pistons start up or down at precisely the same time.

Method: Giving reasons.

We live in the worst of times. The unemployment rate is high. Governments cannot be trusted. The high crime rate makes us fearful even in our own homes. Worst of all, the possibility of nuclear war hangs over our heads.

Method: Analogy.   An analogy points out similarities be-tween things that are otherwise unlike each other.

A computer is very much like a bank. Bits of informa-tion are deposited, like money, into the machine, transformed into a numerical language, tabulated, and stored. And like money on account, the informa-tion patiently sits there until, when needed, it is with-drawn.

Give It a Try

Try your hand at developing paragraphs for at least two of the following topic sentences. You may use the method given in parentheses or any of the methods discussed above. Make sure all sentences in each paragraph are directly related to the main idea.

- There is just no accounting for taste. (illustration)
- Grandparents are wonderful people to have around. (define by attribute or personal quality)
- The size of the average American house shrinks as the cost of labor increases. (cause and effect)
- The United States is, compared with Britain, a violent nation. (comparison and contrast)
- We are not going on a vacation this year. (giving reasons)

Transitions Between Paragraphs

Transitions are needed between two or more related paragraphs if writing is to flow smoothly. Words and phrases are needed that show the reader the relationships between the ideas in the paragraphs. Notice the transitions at the beginning of the second and third paragraphs:

> Writing is a skill, an art that needs to be practiced regularly by those who wish to maintain their skill. Since the paragraph is the smallest unit of composition, you are asked to practice writing paragraphs to perfect your skill in writing longer compositions.
>
> Writing paragraphs is especially important in this day of speed and time-saving devices. Newspapers, magazines, and business reports have adopted the capsule means of coverage; the long editorials, articles, and reports of former days have been replaced by brief pointed editorials and articles and one-page reports. Think of the value the concise paragraph has for government officials, business people, and all others who must rely on hundreds of reports each day.
>
> In view of the importance of the independent paragraph as a unit of composition and as a step in learning to write longer papers, a great deal of practice in independent paragraphs is necessary. As you perfect your skill in writing paragraphs, you will, in a way, be performing the exercises of the accomplished pianist and the sports star. Your goal, of course, is success in writing a long composition.[10]

Notice how the writer used transitions to show the relationships between the ideas in the three paragraphs. The first paragraph talks about how important it is to practice writing paragraphs. The second paragraph gives other examples of the importance and value of writing paragraphs. In the third paragraph, readers are told what they must do as a result of the ideas presented in the first two paragraphs.

Transitions between paragraphs can sometimes be made by using words and phrases like the following: *so, therefore, thus, in conclusion, to this point, nevertheless, first, second, next, however, still, to sum up, as a result, on the other hand.*

Revision

We have discussed how you can use words, sentences, paragraphs, and transitions to express your thoughts on a particular topic. Once you finish your first draft, however, you still have work to do. You must *revise* your writing, always with the aim of making it clearer, more direct, and more expressive.

Almost all successful writers spend hours revising. According to James Thurber, his work rarely came out right the first time: "For me it's mostly a question of rewriting," he said. "It's part of a constant attempt on my part to make the finished version smooth, to make it seem effortless."[11]

Aldous Huxley said: "Generally, I write everything many times over. All my thoughts are second thoughts. And I correct each page a great deal, or rewrite it several times as I go along."[12]

About his short stories, Frank O'Connor remarked that he rewrote "endlessly, endlessly, endlessly . . . and then after it's published in book form, I usually rewrite it again."[11]

As you can see, you are in good company when you spend time revising your writing. But what exactly does the revision process involve?

Revise literally means "to look again." So, after you have finished writing, whether it's a single paragraph or a lengthy composition, you need to take another look. Ask yourself these questions as you reread:

- Does every paragraph have a main idea?
- If I wrote a topic sentence, does it state the main idea of the paragraph clearly?

Effective writing can be learned with practice and with exposure to good writing. William Faulkner's "stream of consciousness" style redefined what could be expressed with the written word.

- Do all the sentences in the paragraph explain and support the main idea?
- Have I used transitions to make clear the relationships between paragraphs?
- Have I avoided gobbledygook, clichés, and expressions that say the same thing twice?
- Have I chosen words that the reader is likely to know?
- Have I used a variety of sentence types—loose, periodic, and balanced?
- Have I used the active voice in most of my sentences?
- Have I avoided run-on sentences and sentence fragments?
- Have I used parallel construction?
- Have I varied the length of my sentences?
- Have I corrected any errors in grammar, spelling, and punctuation?

If the answer to any of these questions is *no* revise your writing according to these guidelines. For certain points, you may also wish to consult a book on grammar and style. The appendices, which begin on page 359, contain additional information on spelling rules and parts of speech. Appendix B shows how the use of proofreaders' and editors' marks can speed up the revision of your writing.

Style

You may have heard or read statements like these: "I always read her column because I like her writing style"; "He writes in a style similar to that of F. Scott Fitzgerald"; "Few people write in the style of Jane Austen anymore. But I love her novels." But what, exactly, is writing *style?*

E. B. White says that style is the sound a writer's words make on paper. Style is the words a writer chooses and the way he or she arranges them in sentences and paragraphs. It is certainly mysterious—style cannot be seen or touched. It can, however, be felt. Consider a famous sentence written by Thomas Paine: "These are the times that try men's souls." Paine's style—the words he chose and the way he arranged them—produced a sentence that inspired the Continental Army during the difficult days of the Revolutionary War. E. B. White offers some variations on Paine's famous statement:

How trying it is to live in these times!
These are trying times for men's souls!
Soulwise, these are trying times![13]

The thought is the same, but the inspiration is missing. Style and inspiration, both in writing and speech, are often inseparable. How a thought is expressed can be as important as the thought itself. If Shakespeare had written, "I wonder if I should go on living" instead of "To be or not to be, that is the question," would we still read Shakespeare? If Churchill, after the Battle of Britain, had said, "And I want to thank the boys of the Royal Air Force. We really owe you fellows a great deal" instead of "Never in the field of human conflict was so much owed by so many to so few," would the RAF, as well as the English nation, have been inspired to keep going? Style, in writing as well as in speaking, can be everything.

Although each writer's style is unique, it does, to a certain extent, reflect the age in which the writer lives. Jane Austen's style differs from Joyce Carol Oates's, in part, be-

Ernest Hemingway created a unique writing style—hard-hitting, terse, razor sharp—which reflected the content of his stories as well as his image as a man of action.

cause speech and manners today are far less formal. Austen's parents addressed each other as Mr. and Mrs: "Mr. Austen, will you. . ." or "Mrs. Austen, may I. . ." Ms. Oates's characters, although similiar in position to Miss Austen's, speak the language of middle-class Americans, and her prose reflects the informality of the day. However, when Oates writes novels that take place in the era of Jane Austen, her style assumes the formality common to the early nineteenth century.

As a writer, you already have a style, whether you realize it or not. The question, however, is whether your style of writing is appropriate for what you wish to convey to your reader. The style Churchill used to thank the men of the RAF after the Battle of Britain was heroic and highly appropriate given the extreme situation. But, the same style, however eloquent, would be ridiculous in a thank-you note for dinner. Writing style, to be effective, must be appropriate and based upon intent. If your intent is heroic, the style should be heroic; if your intent is to charm, the style should be light, perhaps whimsical.

If you wish to further develop and refine your own writing style, begin by reading the works of fine writers. Listen to the sounds their words make as you read. Notice how the writer's words move, delight, bore, amuse, and inspire you. Think about the way the writer arranges words into sentences, sentences into paragraphs, and paragraphs into compositions. Notice how the pace of your reading can be speeded up or slowed down depending upon how the author manipulates you with his words.

Writers such as Theodore Dreiser or F. Scott Fitzgerald can, with their style, transport you as a reader into a world of their own making. Dreiser forces his reader through slow, muddy prose that fits perfectly the unhappy, corrupt world he portrays; the reader feels as trapped and caught as the characters about which Dreiser writes. Fitzgerald, on the other hand, sails the reader into a beautiful world of light and color. The reader understands the characters' weaknesses because the reader, just as Fitzgerald intends, is drawn toward the same romantic light.

Every new writer produces a new and different style. It comes, to some extent, from within, from an inner ear that judges each word, sentence, and paragraph against a standard evolved through practice and exposure to good writing. But there are, of course, some basics:

- Use familiar words. Use words that the reader is likely to know. Avoid the ten-dollar word when a simpler one will do.
- Aim for clarity. The point of all writing is communication. The reader must understand what you are saying if your writing is to be effective.

- Avoid clichés. Do not rely on old sayings to express your ideas. Use your own words to communicate your own thoughts.
- Know your audience and know your purpose. Keep them always in mind as you write.
- Revise. Be ruthless about omitting needless words and redundant phrases. Rewrite what is awkward or unclear. Listen to the sounds your words make as you reread them. Keep reworking your writing until the sounds are those you want to hear.

References

1. Maury Maverick. "The Case Against 'Gobbledygook'." *The New York Times Magazine*, May 21, 1944, p. 11.

2. Robert Gunning. *The Technique of Clear Writing*, 2nd ed. New York: McGraw-Hill, 1968, p. 73.

3. Sheridan Baker. *The Complete Stylist and Handbook.* New York: Harper & Row, 1976, p. 194.

4. *The World Almanac and Book of Facts.* New York: Newspaper Enterprises Association, Inc., p. 54.

5. Bruce L. Felknor. "Intelligencewise," *The New York Times.* Nov. 8, 1983, sec. 1, p. 28.

6. Robert Gunning. *The Technique of Clear Writing*, 2nd ed. New York: McGraw-Hill, 1968.

7. E. B. White. "Notes and Comments." *The New Yorker*, July 3, 1943.

8. Rudolf Flesch. *How to Write, Speak, and Think More Effectively.* New York: The New American Library, Inc., 1951.

9. E. B. White. *Stuart Little.* New York: Harper Row, 1945.

10. Wallace Stenger, ed. *Modern Composition, Book 5.* New York: Holt, Rinehart, & Winston, 1964, p. 166.

11. Malcolm Cowley, editor. *Writers at Work, The Paris Review Interviews.* New York: Viking Penguin Inc., 1958, p. 88.

12. George Plimpton, editor. *Writers at Work, The Paris Review Interviews*, 2nd series. New York: Viking Penguin Inc. 1963.

13. William Strunk, Jr. and E. B. White. *The Elements of Style.* New York: The Macmillan Company, 1959, p. 53.

Writing Creatively

If you want to write creatively, first stand on your head. It may not stimulate your brain, but it will surely change your point of view. Looking at something from a different point of view may just be the essence of creativity.

Bruce Feirstein stood on his head for a time, at least figuratively, and came up with what he called "The Definitive Word" for *The New York Times Magazine.* Feirstein wrote that people have debated and discussed certain questions and bits of common wisdom since the beginning of time, and yet, they have never reached an agreement. He decided, therefore, to give the definitive, or final, word on such matters.

Common wisdom says that a bird in the hand is worth two in the bush. But according to Feirstein, "It all depends on how much the bird in your hand is worth."[1] You may have heard that if you dig straight down, you will come out in China. Feirstein disagrees: "This is a popular misconception. If you dig straight down, you'd probably come out somewhere in Nepal."[2]

Here are more of Feirstein's "final words." See if you can figure out the popular saying or question to which he refers in each. Answers appear on page 83 at the end of the chapter.

- No. They actually only have six lives. The exaggeration was a marketing ploy when they weren't moving well as house pets.
- Not always last; sometimes those guys finish next to last.
- No. Sometimes he who hesitates is only pausing to ask for directions.
- They won't spoil the broth—but too many will, in fact, absolutely mangle a chicken.
- This used to be true, but today, with good publicity and a large enough advertising budget, you can fool everyone all of the time.
- It honestly doesn't matter whether you starve it or feed it. Just do everyone else a favor and stay home.
- If he could chuck wood, he would chuck exactly two cords.
- It's nine-tenths of the law everywhere except in states with joint property clauses, and Discount, N. J., where it's been marked down to seven-tenths.

- Healthy, maybe. Wealthy, possibly. Wise, perhaps. Boring, definitely.
- This is false. Given enough typewriters, the monkeys would probably not be able to produce anything much better than a made-for-television movie.
- Yes, all is fair—except declaring war on a former girl-friend or boyfriend.
- When P. T. Barnum made the original calculation in 1890, the figure was accurate. Given the exponential growth rate of the populace, however, at best estimates today there's one born every 27½ seconds.[3]

Give It a Try

Stand on your head for a bit and, then, try your hand at writing the definitive word on these:

- Spare the rod and spoil the child.
- An apple a day keeps the doctor away.
- Into each life a little rain must fall.
- Two heads are better than one.
- A fool and his money are soon parted.
- Every cloud has a silver lining.
- The pen is mightier than the sword.
- All work and no play makes Jack a dull boy.
- A word to the wise is sufficient.
- Pride goes before a fall.

Bruce Feirstein gave different interpretations to old sayings and thought of new answers to old questions. You did the same thing in the exercise you just completed. Was this creativity? Certainly. To understand why, let's discuss the nature of creativity.

What Is Creativity?

If we define creativity as the act of making something that did not exist before, then we are hard pressed to name even one act of creation. We might list the invention of the wheel and fire making and argue that all modern civilization rests on these two acts. Even if one agrees to this argument, it should be pointed out that all of the ingredients necessary to invent the wheel and to make fire existed long before their discovery.

We really have no idea how many generations of observation and experimentation took place before the invention of the wheel or the discovery of how to make fire. Perhaps the realization that two pieces of wood vigorously rubbed together will generate enough friction to produce a flame was entirely accidental. And humans probably used logs as rollers for thousands of years before the idea of detaching two pieces from a log to serve as wheels occurred to someone. In other words, one thing led to another.

We tend to think of creativity as rearranging the familiar, rather than making something entirely new. And that, of course, is what standing on your head is all about. Judging from what creative people have to say, a creative act results from some new insight, fresh approach, different slant, or unusual point of view. Shakespeare's plots and themes, for example, were not new. His insights into character and motivation, his ability with simile and metaphor, rather than his ability to plot a story, mark him as an unusually creative writer.

Now that we have a feel for what creativity is, let's examine one theory of creativity in detail.

A Theory of Creativity

Theories help us organize our thoughts and understand things. The most useful theories are those that stimulate further exploration in search of greater understanding. Numerous theories on creativity exist; but let's consider one that Albert Rothenberg, a psychiatrist at Austen Riggs Center in Stockbridge, Massachusetts, offers.[4] Rothenberg bases his theory on the way certain people who are considered creative respond to word association tests.

A word association test is simple. All you do is respond with the first word that comes to mind as the tester reads stimulus words, such as *sweet, beautiful, light, soft, smooth,* or *tall.* You are not supposed to think it over; you simply respond as quickly as possible. The interval between each stimulus and your response is timed. Timing is considered as important as response.

Common responses in word association tests indicate that most people treat the stimulus words as characteristics of something, for example, *beautiful/girl, light/ feather, smooth/cheek.* Rothenberg and others who analyze the results of word association tests found, however, that certain people generally give the opposite of the stimulus word. Examples include *sweet/sour, beautiful/ugly, high/low, soft/hard,* and *smooth/rough.* Thus, some people stand on their heads more often than others. Rothenberg, from this evidence, developed a hypothesis on creativity: the more creative the person, the more likely he or she will be of giving an opposite response.

Rothenberg tested this hypothesis in several ways. In one case, a 99-item word association test was given to 12 Nobel Prize winners in chemistry, physics, and medicine; to 18 mental patients; and to 113 Yale University students. Rothenberg found that the Nobel Prize winners gave opposite responses with greater frequency than did the other groups. He found that students judged to be creative in their thinking and performance gave opposite-type responses more often than those not considered creative.

The timing of the response, as mentioned previously, was of great importance. Rothenberg pointed out that even if a person knew that he or she was to respond with an opposite, the individual could not do so as quickly as the Nobel Prize winners.

Upon completion of the experiment, Rothenberg concluded that word association tests can identify people with the potential for creative thinking; that it is a myth that genius and mental instability are related; and that creativity can be learned. The creative thinker, he claims, displays "a consistent tendency to formulate opposites very rapidly and to conceptualize them simultaneously, [going] beyond ordinary logic into the realms of the unexpected and unknown."[5]

Albert Einstein, thinking in opposites, came up with what he called his "happiest thought": that a man falling from the roof of a house is both in motion and at rest simultaneously. This realization provided the foundation for his general theory of relativity.

The creative process, however, involves more than simply responding with opposites in word association tests. An ability to examine both sides of an issue and to react either positively or negatively to both sides of that issue *may* be the heart of the matter. According to Rothenberg, it may come down to the old saw: not everything is black or white. It is possible that if one side of an issue is black, the opposite side may also be black. The reality may also be that both sides are gray. Do not assume the obvious. Keep an open mind and look at everything very carefully.

Rothenberg points out that Albert Einstein used opposite thoughts to develop the theory of relativity. Einstein came up with the idea that a man falling from a roof was, at the same time, both in motion and at rest. How can this be? To a person observing the fall, the man falling is moving toward earth. The man who is falling, however, feels himself motionless—the *earth* is moving toward *him.*[6] Holding these opposites in mind, Einstein mentally grasped the possibility that movement in space is relative to the observer; that is, reality, like beauty, is in the eye of the beholder. What you see is not, necessarily, what I see.

Another example.   For centuries, light was thought to be composed of waves. Later evidence suggested that it was composed of particles. The physicist Nels Bohr asked himself if both theories could be true. Out of this contradictory thought grew the quantum theory, the basis of modern physics.

"Highly creative people see things more complexly," says Dr. Edward Sheridan of the Northwestern University Medical School. "Responding in opposites is one of the first things that they might do in order to explore other possibilities. There is other research that has been done that shows quite clearly that that's what happens: that they go off in different directions and then bring all their ideas together."[7]

Rothenberg tells of a poet who reported getting an idea for a line in a poem while thinking of the words *price* and *praise.* These words were the same in the area where he grew up. In the context of the poem he wrote, price and praise formed opposites: paying a price was a punishment and earning praise was a reward.

Rothenberg calls this tendency to think in opposites, "Janusian," after the ancient Roman god Janus. Janus had two faces and could look in opposite directions at the same time. He was the god of doorways and oversaw daybreak and other such beginnings.

Rothenberg acknowledges that Janusian thinking does not account for all aspects of creativity. Creativity often involves the putting together of contrasting ideas that are not necessarily opposites. Obviously, much more than thinking in opposites went into Einstein's theory of relativity and Bohr's quantum theory. Even if an idea appears in a flash, the need to work it out remains: the individual must revise, refashion, and refine.

Nevertheless, the concept of thinking in opposites as an avenue to creativity is stimulating. According to Rothenberg, evidence suggests that some people do learn to be creative from their environment and experience. "If that's the case," he concludes, "I think it [creativity] can be learned by others."[8]

Exercises in Creativity

Creative thoughts usually do not simply spring from the mind. In most cases, you must be aiming at something and you must work at it. Einstein and Bohr were not musing idly when those important thoughts occurred to them. They were looking for something. And so it is with nearly every creative thought and act.

The remainder of this chapter consists of projects with which you can exercise your creativity. Some of what we suggest comes from children's games. Approach these games as a child would, free from preconceived notions and built-in ways of thinking that might inhibit your responses. Unleash your imagination and float in the world of the upside down. Allow yourself to be stimulated.

Some Sense Contradictions

What is the sound of one hand clapping? To answer such a question, you must free your mind from its usual way of thinking. Buddhists use such questions or statements, called *koans,* as subjects for meditation. See if you can break out of your usual thought patterns and sharpen your powers of description as you complete the following exercise.

Give It a Try

Use as many words or sentences as you wish to answer the following questions.

- What is the sound of grass on a windless summer day?
- What is the feel of a foghorn's sound?
- What is the taste of the color green?
- What is the smell of a rock?
- What is the sound of granite?
- What is the smell of pain?
- What is the color of sadness?
- What is the taste of joy?
- What is the sound of falling feathers?
- What is the feel of a baby's cry?

Swifties

Now let's try a common word game: Swifties. The idea is to think of an adverb that is related to a noun in the sen-

What is the sound of grass on a windless summer day?

HAVE A CRACKER, HE SAID SALTILY.

tence. This adverb should describe how the speaker might have said the words. Here are two examples:

"Give me some ginger," she said *snappishly;*

"Have a cracker," he said *saltily.*

Give It a Try

Complete each sentence by filling in the blank with an adverb that is related to a noun in the sentence.

- "Listen to the sound of that jet engine," he said ＿＿＿.
- "Lend me your ballpoint pen," she said ＿＿＿.
- "The smoke detector isn't working," he said ＿＿＿.
- "Listen to that horse nicker," he said ＿＿＿.
- "Try some cold cream," she said ＿＿＿.
- "That fish is out of water," he said ＿＿＿.
- "You're squeezing my neck," he said ＿＿＿.
- "Be careful with that razor blade," she said ＿＿＿.
- "I operate a bulldozer," she said ＿＿＿.
- "This letter is for you," he said ＿＿＿.
- "This is a great apple," he said ＿＿＿.
- "I'm a nervous wreck," she said ＿＿＿.

- "Stop biting your nails," she said _____.
- "You're as skinny as a pencil," he said _____.
- "Here, catch this piano," he said _____.

Try making up swifties of your own.

The Question Man

Let's try the Question Man, a favorite parlor game. You begin with an answer for which you must supply a question. As you will see, there is a strong reliance on puns. Here are some examples.

A. Doughnation.
Q. What's a gift of money called?

A. Tolerance.
Q. Which ants are different from short ants?

A. Arrears.
Q. What do we kids often forget to wash behind?

A. Hamicide.
Q. What do you call it when a pig self-destructs?

Give It a Try

Supply a question for each of the following answers.

- Chop talk
- Lighthouse
- Polka dots
- Hamlet
- A lawn mooer

Nonsense Words

Now we will go way back to that old standby, Lewis Carroll's "Jabberwocky."

Jabberwocky

Twas brillig, and the slithy toves
 Did gyre and gimble in the wabe:
All mimsy were the borogroves,
 And the mome raths outgrabe.

"Beware the Jabberwock, my son!
 The jaws that bite, the claws that catch!
Beware the Jubjub bird, and shun
 The frumious Bandersnatch!"

He took his vorpal sword in hand:
 Long time the manxome foe he sought—
So rested he by the Tumtum tree,
 And stood awhile in thought.

And, as in uffish thought he stood,
 The Jabberwock, with eyes of flame,
Came whiffling through the tulgey wood,
 And burbled as it came!

One, two! One, two! And through and through
 The vorpal blade went snicker-snack!
He left it dead, and with its head
 He went galumphing back.

"And hast thou slain the Jabberwock?
 Come to my arms, my beamish boy!
O frabjous day! Callooh! Callay!"
 He chortled in his joy.

Twas brillig, and the slithy toves
 Did gyre and gimble in the wabe:
All mimsy were the borogroves,
 And the mome raths outgrabe.

After reading "Jabberwocky" to a class, a teacher asked the students to respond to three questions:

1. If there were brillig outside, would you be glad or sorry?

2. Describe a slithy tove.

3. List three of the Jabberwock's physical characteristics and three words describing its personality.

Beware the Jabberwock, my son! The jaws that bite, the claws that catch!

Here is how one student responded:

1. I would be glad. Brillig is like snow made out of feathers. It only falls about once a year and when it happens, everyone gets a holiday.

2. Slithy toves are wet round worms. Nobody likes to touch them. Brillig sticks to them, and they like the feeling.

3. The Jabberwock is powerful with a strong beak and a huge head. He is cruel, impatient, and jealous.[9]

How would you respond to the questions? Write out your answers and be creative.

Give It a Try

Explain what the following nonsense words from "Jabberwocky" mean. Let your imagination roam. Write out your answers.

- gyre
- gimble
- wabe
- mimsy
- borogroves
- mome
- raths
- outgrabe

You may also want to try translating a few stanzas of "Jabberwocky" into a poem of your own. Here is an example:

Snatcherwocky

Twas raining, and commuting hordes
    Did push and scramble to the train.
Slippery were the platform boards,
    Drippy the umbrella canes.

Beware the cool cutpurse, my son!
    The hand that glides, on dough to latch!
Beware that rub-rub bird, and shun
    That woeful money snatch!

What If?

Now let's play the "What If?" game. Think about how you would respond to these questions.

What if things never got dirty?
What if there were no more wars?
What if there were no peanut butter?
What if we used only one-ounce pieces of lead for money?

"Yes, it is true. I was born without a trunk. Fortunately, an elderly aunt left me her Samsonite.® Now, I 'pack all I derm' want to."

What if Cinderella had had big feet?
What if the wheel had never been invented?
What if the day were 48 hours long?
What if there were no schools?
Let's play with one of these for a moment. What if there were no more wars? A number of thoughts come to mind immediately.

- We would no longer need the armed services, the Pentagon, arms and supplies manufacturers, and military bases. Millions of people would be looking for jobs.
- The billions of dollars spent on defense every year could be spent on other things or could be saved.
- We would have a great deal of military hardware to dispose of, from tiny replacement screws and washers to huge aircraft carriers.
- Veterans' organizations would gradually disappear.
- We might need to change our definition of patriotism.

Give It a Try
Write answers for at least three of the "what if" questions above. Then make up several questions of your own.

What If Stories
"What if stories" are another twist to the "what if" idea. These stories grow out of "what if" questions, such as "what if a shark did not have teeth?" The title of such a story might be "The Shark That Lost Its Teeth."

Give It a Try
Write a story about one or more of the following topics.
- The lion that could not roar.
- The monkey that never got the hang of swinging from limb to limb.
- The elephant born without a trunk.
- The dog that could not bark.
- The beaver that could not swim under water.
- The antelope that could not play.
- The skunk that gave off an odor of delightful perfume.
- The billy goat that refused to be gruff.
- The worm that refused to turn.
- The dog that refused to have its day.

What Is It Like?

Study the object pictured below for about five minutes. Look at it as it appears; turn the book to see the object sideways and upside down. What do you think the object is? What does it make you think of? Jot down your responses. You should be able to list at least six.

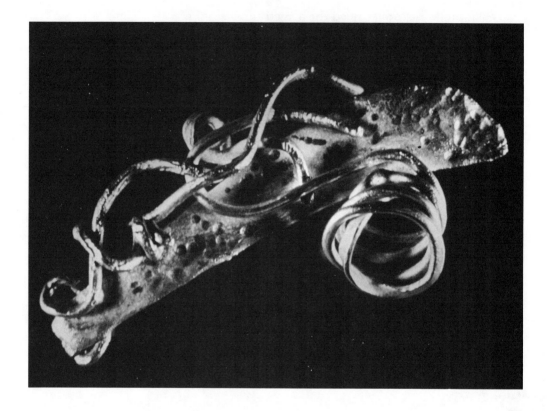

Listed below are responses from people who have performed this exercise:

The object represents

- the cross of the lives of two snakes and the path of fate upon which they are meeting.
- a man's tie whose owner had been eating spaghetti, spilling it all over himself.
- a snake coiled around a woman.
- a sword cutting an octopus.
- a very old sword that has been found on the beach, entangled in seaweed.

- a saxophone, which seems to vibrate and come alive like the music that comes out of it.
- an oar with the water from a lake swirling against it and around it.
- a broken ski with the ski bindings coming apart after a downhill race.
- an overstressed person in need of an Alka-Seltzer.®
- a hurricane hitting the coast of Florida.
- a baseball pitcher about to toss the ball to first base; the bound-up wire is the dust rising up after the runner ran to first base.
- a toothless comb snagged in hair.
- a treble clef on a musical staff line. [10]

Give It a Try

Study the objects pictured below for about five minutes each. Jot down all the thoughts that occur to you. Don't reject any because they seem too wild or fanciful; they might be the best kind.

Much of the art of the 20th century is abstract, that is, it does not represent or reproduce. Like music, it is a pure expression of the artist's creativity. Instead of recognizing the familiar, the viewer responds to the art, as a listener responds to music.

Cause and Effect from Pictures

Another creative exercise involves looking at a picture, describing the action, and listing causes and effects.

Give It a Try

Study the picture below for a few minutes. Write a paragraph describing what you think is going on in the picture. List factors that might have caused the action. Finally, list *effects* that may result from the action.

Interpreting Shapes

What do you see when you look at this shape? Let your imagination go. Jot down your answers. (It might represent a sunrise, a sunset, a turned-down mouth, a finger-nail seen from the edge, and a crescent moon.)

Give It a Try

Look at the shapes below. Write down at least five things each shape might represent.

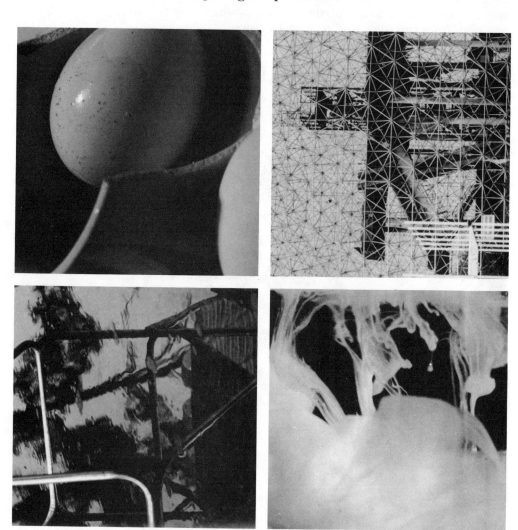

Conclusion

There are many sides to creativity. We have, in Chapter 3, examined only one of these: how to look at the familiar with a fresh and different point of view. We discussed opposites in detail, but remember that creativity is not simply a matter of looking at both sides. It is looking at opposite sides of an issue with a new and unprejudiced eye.

And this, of course, is only a beginning. Keep in mind the point made in Dr. Rothenberg's study: creativity *can be learned.* It is not an attribute with which only a few are born. Like effective writing, creativity can be mastered with practice and hard work.

Answers to exercises on pages 64—65

Cats have nine lives.

Nice guys finish last.

He who hesitates is lost.

Too many cooks spoil the broth.

You can't fool all of the people all of the time.

Feed a cold, starve a fever.

How much wood would a woodchuck chuck if a wood-chuck would chuck wood?

Possession is nine-tenths of the law.

Early to bed and early to rise makes a man healthy, wealthy, and wise.

All's fair in love and war.

Could a room full of monkeys, given enough time, paper, and a typewriter, eventually stumble into writing *The Complete Shakespeare?*

There's a sucker born every minute.

Which came first, the chicken or the egg?

References

1. Bruce Feirstein. "The Definitive Word." *The New York Times Magazine,* Sept. 25, 1983.
2. Bruce Feirstein. "The Definitive Word." *The New York Times Magazine,* Sept. 25, 1983.
3. Bruce Feirstein. "The Definitive Word." *The New York Times Magazine,* Sept. 25, 1983.
4. Albert Rothenberg, "Psychopathology and Creative Cognition." Archives of General Psychiatry, Sept. 1983, pp. 937-942.
5. Albert Rothenberg, "Psychopathology and Creative Cognition." Archives of General Psychiatry, Sept. 1983, p. 941.
6. Ronald Kotulak, "Word Association Test Used to Spot Creative Geniuses." *Chicago Tribune,* Oct. 2, 1983.
7. Ronald Kotulak, "Word Association Test Used to Spot Creative Geniuses." *Chicago Tribune,* Oct. 2, 1983.
8. Albert Rothenberg, "Psychopathology and Creative Cognition." Archives of General Psychiatry, Sept. 1983, pp. 937-942.
9. Priscilla L. Vail. *Clear and Lively Writing: Language Games and Activities for Everyone.* New York: Walker & Co., 1981.
10. Gabriele Lusser Rico. *Writing the Natural Way.* Los Angeles: J. P. Tarcher, 1983, pp. 195-197.

Selecting a Topic
for a Narrative

Writing for School

*G*raphophobia—from *grapho*, meaning "writing," and *phobia*, meaning "fear"—is a made-up, but useful, term. It describes a kind of anxiety that strikes students in particular. Graphophobia leaves sufferers trembling and sweaty, fearful at the thought of putting pen to paper. A teacher making a simple statement can bring on an attack of graphophobia: "Class, for tomorrow I want you to write . . . " This anxiety can, of course, be overcome.

When faced with a school writing assignment, say to yourself: "I'm going to have a conversation with a friend." And then say to yourself: "But first I'll consider the conversation carefully. I'll plan it and try it out a few times." You will, then, be able to think over your topic, gather the information you need, make an outline, and write, revise, and rewrite.

The Composition

Writing for school usually means writing compositions, which are also called themes. A *composition* is a piece of writing that develops an idea or a topic in an organized, unified way. Each paragraph must be related to the idea or topic. The paragraphs themselves must be logically developed and connected. (Review the section on writing paragraphs on pages 52–56.)

When you write for school, your teacher is usually your audience. Although every teacher you write for wants to help you learn to write better, teachers differ in their standards.

One teacher might be highly critical of any spelling or grammatical error, deducting points for each. Another teacher may pay more attention to your ideas and how they are expressed. A teacher might insist that a composition be 300 words long. Another may give you leeway—200 to 400 words or no limits. One teacher might want the topic sentence always to appear as the first sentence in a paragraph. Another might be more flexible on the matter, insisting only that there be a topic sentence. A teacher might frown on contractions (*I'm, can't, we're,* for example), insisting that you spell these out *(I am, cannot, we are)*. Another might permit contractions, especially when you write informally.

Undoubtedly you can think of other teacher requirements. Always keep these in mind when you are writing to fulfill school assignments.

A "Most" Composition

"Most" compositions are common school assignments. A teacher, for example, might ask you to write a composition on your "most" frustrating experience. How might you handle such an assignment? Here is one way.

My Most Frustrating Experience

I had an assignment in geography. It was important to my grade. I did not start on the assignment until after dinner the night before it was due. Then I found out that I had the wrong volume of a book I badly needed. Then I remembered that the public library had the book. I started out for the library on my bicycle. I had a flat tire. I walked the rest of the way. The library was closed. I was mad. I got a lower grade in the course. The whole thing was my fault. I did not look at the book carefully when I borrowed it from the school library. I waited too long to begin the assignment.

Does that sound like a conversation with a friend? There are bones, but not much flesh. Did the composition make you yawn? Did it bore you? Suppose it were written like this:

My Most Frustrating Experience

Frustration can bring change. A good grade in geography depended upon a certain assignment, and I settled down to work on it the night before it was due. I then discovered I had brought home the wrong volume of an important book. I started to panic, but then I remembered that the public library had a copy of the book. Time was short, but I set off, peddling furiously, on my bicycle; and—you guessed it—I had a flat tire. So I walked the rest of the way, foolishly hoping that the library would not close on time that night. It did. I am not ashamed to admit that I cried. My stupidity cost me a letter grade in the course. I read book titles more carefully now. And, as added insurance, I no longer wait until the last minute to start an assignment.

The second version sounds more like the way such an experience would be told to a friend. It has life and emotion. This composition would most likely earn a better grade than the first.

Forms of Writing

There are four forms of writing: narration, description, exposition, and argument. All four will be examined in this chapter. The writing form used in the above sample composition was narration.

Narration

Narration is essentially storytelling: it relates a series of connected happenings, moving from one to the next in an organized way. Like a news story, narration explains *who, what, when, where,* and often *why.* Narration frequently focuses upon a problem or the achievement of a goal. This produces conflict and suspense. Narration is found in many types of writing: novels, short stories, fables, histories, biographies, and autobiographies.

Good narration, like any effective writing, has a clear beginning, middle, and end. In outline form the parts look like this:

I. Beginning
   A. Arouses reader interest
   B. Presents problem or theme
II. Middle
   A. Adds detail on problem or theme
   B. Action moves toward solution or outcome
III. End
   A. Climax—high point, or turning point, in action
   B. Solution
   C. Resolution

Beginnings

The events in a narrative are often chronologically related; that is, they are told in the order in which they happen. But must a story always begin at the beginning?

We have looked at two compositions. Both relate a student's experience while doing an assignment. The first composition opens at the beginning of the story: "I had an assignment in geography." The second composition begins with the resolution: "Frustration can bring change." Look back at the narrative outline. The second composition really begins at the end (III.C.).

A story can start at almost any point if the writer fills in the needed details. To show how this works, we will look

A good narrative has a clear beginning, middle, and end. The first step, however, is selecting the subject about which you will write.

at three versions of the same fable, "The Hare and the Tortoise." The first version is told chronologically—it begins at the beginning.

The Hare and the Tortoise

The Hare boasted of his speed before the other animals. "I have never yet been beaten when I put forth my full speed," said he. "I challenge anyone here to race with me."

The Tortoise replied quietly, "I accept your challenge."

"That is a good joke," said the Hare. "I could dance round you all the way."

"Keep your boasting till you've beaten," answered the Tortoise. "Shall we race?"

So a course was fixed and a start was made. The Hare, at once, darted almost out of sight. But the Hare, to show his contempt for the Tortoise, soon stopped and stretched out for a nap.

The Tortoise plodded on and on. When the Hare awoke, he saw the Tortoise nearing the finish line, but could not run fast enough, soon enough, to save the race.

And the Tortoise said, *"Slow but sure wins the race."*

This version is straightforward, clear, and easy to follow. In the next version of the old fable the story begins at the middle. Notice how the wording changes to fit the change in chronology.

The Hare and the Tortoise

"Keep your boasting till you've beaten. Shall we race?" So answered the Tortoise to the Hare, who had bragged of his speed on that day of the great race.

"I have never yet been beaten when I put forth my full speed," the Hare had boasted before the other animals. I challenge anyone here to race with me."

And the Tortoise had replied quietly, "*I accept your challenge.*"

"That is a good joke," the Hare had said. "I could dance round you all the way."

Now the time for the race had come. The course was fixed, and a start was made. The Hare, at once, darted almost out of sight. But, the Hare, to show his contempt for the Tortoise, soon stopped and stretched out for a nap.

The Tortoise plodded on and on. When the Hare awoke, he saw the Tortoise nearing the finish line, but could not run fast enough, soon enough, to save the race.

And the Tortoise said, *"Slow but sure wins the race."*

This version of the fable is less straightforward than the first version, but more suspenseful. Note how little the vocabulary and sentence construction was changed.

The final version of Aesop's fable begins at the end of the story. As you read, try to pinpoint the effect the changes in order bring to the story.

The Hare and the Tortoise

"Slow but sure wins the race." So the Tortoise proved to the animals one day by beating the Hare in that great race.

The Hare, proud of his speed, had boasted of it before the other animals. "I have never yet been beaten when I put forth my full speed," said he. "I challenge anyone here to race with me."

The Tortoise had replied quietly, "I accept your challenge."

"That is a good joke," the Hare had said. "I could dance round you all the way."

"Keep your boasting till you've been beaten," answered the Tortoise. "Shall we race?"

So a course was fixed and a start was made. The Hare, at once, darted almost out of sight. But the Hare, to show his contempt for the Tortoise, soon stopped and stretched out for a nap.

The Tortoise plodded on and on. When the Hare awoke, he saw the Tortoise nearing the finish line, but he could not run fast enough, soon enough, to save the race.

Slow but sure won the race for the Tortoise. And this lesson the animals—but especially the Hare—have never forgotten.

This version begins with the end or the moral of the fable. As you may have guessed, the technique of starting a story at the end is an excellent way of teaching something, of making a point. People sometimes learn better if they know the point of their lessons before they begin to work on them. The chapters of a textbook are often organized with an introduction first, a list of contents second, the body of the text following, and a summary at the end. The introduction and summary contain roughly the same material; thus, textbooks often begin at the end. The technique is, at times, used in fiction as well. *Treasure Island,* the Robert Louis Stevenson classic, is an example of a novel that reveals the ending at the onset.

Try experimenting wtih different stories you know, moving the parts of the stories around. You will find that the same move will not always produce the same effect. Keep in mind that you may begin the narrative wherever you wish. But if you do not start at the beginning, you must fill in what has already happened. The reader, to appreciate the story, must understand the order in which the events took place.

Give It a Try

Read the following version of "The Shepherd Boy and the Wolf," another of Aesop's fables. Rewrite the first paragraph of the story, beginning with either the middle or with the end of the original tale.

The Shepherd Boy and the Wolf

Day after day, a young shepherd boy watched over his sheep while they grazed. He passed the time by seeing how far he could throw a rock or by looking at the clouds to see how many animal shapes he could find.

He liked his job well enough, but he longed for a little excitement. So, one day he decided to play a trick on the people of the village.

"Wolf! Wolf! Help!" he shouted as loud as he could.

Hearing the shepherd boy's cry, the people in the village, armed with pitchforks and clubs, ran to help save the sheep. But, when they arrived, they found no wolf. They saw only the shepherd boy, doubled with laughter.

"I fooled you. I fooled you," he said, laughing.

The people of the village did not take the joke at all well, and they warned him not to call again, unless he was certain he saw a wolf.

But a week later, the boy again played his trick on the villagers.

"Wolf! Wolf!" he cried out.

Once again, the people ran to his aid; and once again, they found no wolf—only the boy, laughing at them.

The next day, a wolf, ferocious and hungry, came down from the hills to help itself to a few fat sheep.

"Wolf! Wolf!" yelled the shepherd boy with all the power in his lungs. The people of the village heard his shouts for help and smiled: "He's trying to trick us again, but we won't be fooled this time."

Finally, the boy stopped shouting. The villagers did not believe him. He knew they would not come. And so, the boy returned to his usual seat on a rock, and watched, instead of clouds rolling by, the wolf killing and devouring his precious sheep, one by one.

People who tell lies are, eventually, not believed, even when they do tell the truth.

Developing a Narrative

Choosing Details.   The details given in a narrative offer the reader more information about the theme or problem. Details also add interest and keep the story moving. Look again at the "frustration" composition on page 86.

If you were to write such a composition, could you add more details? Why, for example, did the narrator wait until the last minute to begin the assignment? After discovering that he or she had picked up the wrong book, how much time was left before the library closed? How would it feel, exactly, to arrive at the library, after so much trouble, and find the doors closed? The inclusion of details, such as these, adds suspense and interest to the story. If the reader knows how much time is left, he or she is aware of the minutes ticking away and feels the same anguish felt by the narrator.

When choosing details, however, be careful to include only necessary details. Leave out those that do nothing for the story; they distract and sometimes irritate the reader. Think again about the "frustration" composition. Before beginning the story, the writer probably sat down at a desk, turned on a lamp, and took out pen and paper. But are those details important to the story? Perhaps the writer owns a 10-speed bicycle. Would adding that detail give more information about the theme or problem? Would it move the story along? The answer, of course, is no.

Give It a Try

Rewrite the "frustration" composition on page 86, adding at least three details to the story to make it more interesting or suspenseful.

Give It a Try

Weed out the unnecessary details in the following composition. The first part has been done for you.

My moment of glory came in the Glenview game last year, on a cold December night. I had warmed the bench up till then. But that night only eight members of the team could play. Our team won the state championship last year. With one minute to play, and with our team behind 52 to 51, our fourth player fouled out. I think this happened because the referee was against us. Our coach had no choice but to put me in. He's a giant of a man. With three seconds left, the ball fell into my hands, and I was fouled as I tried to shoot. That meant I would get two free throws. I shot and missed the first one. Oh well, I thought as the referee handed me the ball again, I can still tie the score. I noticed then that my shoelace was untied. I shot the ball and missed again. Some moment of glory.

Choosing Verbs

As you develop narrative writing, pay attention to the verbs you choose. Whenever possible, use verbs in the active rather than the passive voice. Narration thrives on action. (Active and passive verbs were discussed on pages 44–45; you may wish to review these pages.) The following story uses verbs in the active voice to create movement and suspense. As you read notice how the verbs affect the narrative.

The street lamps popped, and a purple gloom settled between the rows of houses. Why did the lights go out? I quickened my step and continued up the street. Boughs from large trees hung over the walk, forcing me to duck here and there. As I crouched to walk under a branch, my jacket snagged on a thorn. Why did I go for a walk tonight? Bending back under the tree, I tugged and worked the material to free myself. Finally, in exasperation, I yanked the jacket loose. The material ripped. Just my luck, I thought, as I straightened myself and smoothed down the jacket, which had twisted around me.

I could see, up ahead, two men walking toward me. Or were they boys? What were they doing out at this time of night? A vague feeling of unease came over me. Should I turn back? No, that's ridiculous. I marched on. The boys slowed their pace as I increased mine. We would meet in a few seconds. Were they going to divide and allow me to pass?

I could see their faces. They certainly didn't look as if they had any intention of stepping aside. Without breaking stride, I pulled to the left to step around them. Bam! A fist slammed against my head, and I reeled, trying to regain my senses.

Bam! Another fist. Stars burst across my eyes, and I tripped, landing in the wet grass.

Out of the corner of my eye I could see a man, standing at his front window. Slowly he pulled the window shade down. I watched him, in silhouette, turn away and leave the window. My stomach wrenched.

"Gimme your money," one of the boys said in a voice that sounded unnaturally low.

"You little punk!" As soon as the words were out, I realized my mistake. The silver blade of a knife flashed in the yellow light from the shaded window.

"Gimme your money, you creep." His voice shook, and I realized the whole drama was being played for the benefit of the other boy, who remained silent.

"Look, put away the knife, and I'll give you the money," I said. Time had slowed down, and we stared at each other for seconds that moved like hours. He suddenly lunged toward me with the knife. I knew I was well out of range, but instinctively rolled through the grass toward the curb.

Tires rumbled on the brick pavement, and I looked up the street. Long beams of light rocked up and down as the car sped along the irregular pavers. A spotlight cut through the dark, and we heard the siren scream. A police car!

"A police car!" I yelled.

"You're lucky," the kid said. I agree, I thought. I agree.

He calmly and expertly bent the blade of the knife back into its handle and squeezed it into his jeans pocket. And they were gone, immediately lost in the shadows of the overhanging tree branches. The police car pulled up.

"Where did they go?" the driver asked.

"Down the street," I said. I looked up. The man across the street again stood at the window. Almost imperceptively, he waved. I nodded. And slowly the window shade came down, and I watched him, in silhouette, turn away.

The author's use of active verbs paints a scene. You picture the action: the street lights pop; the jacket snags; stars burst; the knife flashes; and the boy lunges. After you finish a narrative, reread it and check the verbs. If you did not use active verbs, revise your sentences. Give them life with lively verbs.

Using Dialogue

Dialogue—which, in this context, is written conversation —adds variety, liveliness, and authenticity to a narrative. Dialogue also breaks up large blocks of type, which is important; professional writers are very aware that long, unbroken paragraphs of straight type can be boring and difficult to read. So, whenever possible, allow your characters to speak for themselves.

In nonfiction writing, dialogue is, of course, not simply "made up." It is quoted from sources, which may include interviews, speeches, biographies, autobiographies, letters, and diaries.

In fiction, dialogue is a product of the writer's imagination. Keep in mind, however, that invented speech must ring true; it must sound natural and appropriate.

Speech is a subtle indication of background: geographic, professional, and social. In George Bernard Shaw's play *Pygmalion,* retitled *My Fair Lady* in the American musical, the main character, Professor Higgins, claims he can identify, within a block or two, where anyone in London was born simply by listening to the man or woman's speech. His claim is not as far-fetched as it may sound.

Each of us speaks in a distinct manner and uses speech patterns and vocabulary that reflect where we were born and raised, how we were educated, and our position in the community. A Midwesterner, giving directions, might say: "The Smith home is two blocks down the street." An Easterner, on the other hand, might say: "The Smith house is two squares south." An English teacher, conscious of grammar, might state: "If I were you, I would study the sections on Byron and Keats." A fellow student, translating the message, might say: "If I was you, I'd check out the chapter on Byron and Keats. I think there's going to be a pop quiz. I mean she didn't really say for sure, but that was the idea. Ya know how Miss Miller works."

The differences in speech are subtle, but real. We all have an ear for realistic dialogue and can usually catch speech that does not sound true to life. As you write dialogue, read it to yourself. Does it sound realistic? Are the words right? Is the pattern or rhythm correct? If you try to tackle a certain dialect, make sure you know that dialect very well yourself. Check out the masters of dialect— Mark Twain, for example. Notice how he only sprinkles the dialect through the conversation. Too many "cute" words or spellings can ruin the effect.

Dialogue is set off by enclosing it in quotation marks. It is identified with the correct speaker by using *dialogue carriers: he said* or *she said.* If dialogue is to work, the reader *must* know which character is speaking. If your composition contains much dialogue, you may get tired of using *said* and search for substitutes. Be careful, however. "He replied," "she answered," and "they responded" work, but may be unnecessary. Dialogue carriers should not draw attention to themselves. The conversation, not the speaker's identification, should be given the focus.

Avoid carriers that describe how a speech is said:

"I hate you," she hissed.

"I've got a cold," she sniffed.

"You're funny," he giggled.

Carriers, such as hissed, sniffed, and giggled, do not actually describe speech. A sniffle is a sniffle; a giggle is a giggle; and only snakes truly hiss. People speak, say, and, occasionally, state. If you need to describe how a character said something, use modifiers with *said*.

"I hate you," she said in an angry voice.

"I've got a cold," she said while blowing her nose.

"You're funny," he said between bouts of laughter.

Dialogue is arranged by beginning a new paragraph each time a different character speaks.

"Dad, you should have seen the big fish I caught," said Rita.

"Well, where is it? What did you do with it?" said Dad.

"I threw it back after it begged for its life. And besides it was much too big to eat," said Rita.

"Sounds like a fish story to me," said Dad.

Punctuation and quotation marks are sometimes troublesome. Periods and commas *always* go within quotation marks, even if the punctuation is not part of the dialogue: *When she said,"I love you," I was shocked.* Semicolons, unless an integral part of the dialogue, go outside the quotation mark. Colons are placed outside the quotation mark.

Give It a Try

Add dialogue to the "frustration" composition on page 86. Make sure that characters speak naturally and that their conversation gives additional information about the theme or problem.

Endings

The ending of a narration consists of three parts: the climax, the solution, and the resolution. The resolution is a summary, stating the outcome and relating that outcome back to the beginning. This unifies the narrative.

In the "frustration" composition, the climax, or turning point, was the flat tire episode. This made it impossible to get to the library before it closed. The solution, or outcome, of course, was the writer's inability to get the needed book to complete the assignment, which resulted in a lower grade in the course. This result is connected to the beginning of the narrative when the writer tells how it has changed his or her behavior: the writer now reads book titles more carefully, and he or she no longer waits until the last minute to start an assignment.

You may wish to experiment with changing the endings of some familiar stories. For example, in "The Hare and the Tortoise," the climax occurs when the Hare awakes from his nap too late to beat the Tortoise. The solution is the outcome of the race. But what would the outcome have been if the Hare had only been pretending to be asleep? How would this change the resolution, the moral of the story *("Slow but sure wins the race")*, which summarizes the outcome and connects the ending of the story to the beginning?

Give It a Try

Write a new ending for the "frustration" composition, "The Hare and the Tortoise," or "The Shepherd Boy and the Wolf." Change both the climax and the outcome. Be sure to summarize the outcome and connect it to the beginning of the story.

Writing Your Own Narrative

Choosing a Topic.   Now that you have practiced writing narrative beginnings, middles, and endings, it is time to write a brief narrative of your own. You may wish to write a "most" composition; or you may want to tell a story about an interesting experience you or someone else had. Keep in mind that your purpose is to entertain and interest the reader. Your narrative can be either nonfiction or fiction.

Listed below are possible topics for a narrative paragraph or composition.

- My most embarrassing experience
- I was our town's mayor for a day
- The cat with ten lives
- My encounter with a UFO
- How I became a hero
- How a clever scheme backfired
- The day I witnessed a bank robbery
- The April Fool's Day tragedy
- The boy who did not read signs

Outlining the Narrative

After you have selected a topic, make a brief outline of your narrative. The basic form is reviewed below:

I. Beginning
   A. Arouses reader interest
   B. Presents problem or theme

II. Middle
   A. Adds detail on problem or theme
   B. Action moves toward solution or outcome

III. Ending
   A. Climax—high point, or turning point, in the action
   B. Solution or outcome
   C. Resolution—results stated or suggested and connected to beginning

Here is how one student outlined a story about how a clever scheme backfired:

I. Beginning
   A. Clever schemes sometimes backfire
   B. Wanted to get out of doing laundry

II. Middle
   A. Decided to "accidentally" ruin some clothes
   B. Purposely washed dark and light colors together

III. Ending
   A. Accidentally ruined my best white sweater
   B. Would have to earn the money for a new sweater
   C. My clever scheme backfired

Give It a Try

Follow the procedure just described to outline a narrative. Choose one of the topics on page 98 or think of one of your own.

Writing the First Draft

After completing an outline, you are ready to write the first draft of your narrative. Use your outline. Follow it as you write. Present the theme or problem in a way that will arouse a reader's interest. Remember to include details that will give your reader more information about the theme or problem. Use verbs in the active voice and include dialogue whenever possible. After you finish the climax and solution, be sure to resolve the story by relating the ending to the beginning.

Give It a Try

Follow the procedure just described to write the first draft of your narrative.

Revising and Rewriting

Although you have worked hard up to this point, you still have work to do: revise and rewrite your narrative. Check to see that all the ideas in your outline are covered. Make sure that you have included enough details about the problem or theme. Delete details that are not related to your topic.

Where possible, use verbs in the active rather than passive voice. Look carefully at the words and phrases used. Can some of them be replaced with words and phrases that will make your writing livelier and more interesting? Finally, correct errors in spelling, word usage, grammar, punctuation, and capitalization.

Here is a revised first draft of the story about the scheme that backfired. Changes between the outline and the narrative were made to improve the story.

The Scheme That Backfired

Clever schemes sometimes backfire, as I found out recently. I decided to think up a way to get out of doing the family's laundry each week. I was given this chore when my parents decided I should help out more around the house. My scheme was to "accidentally" ruin a few of my parents' old clothes by washing light and dark colors together.

But my plan backfired. As I removed the laundry from the washer, I saw my white sweater. It was now a muddy gray.

Just then my father walked in the room. "What a shame. I guess you'll have to buy a new sweater," he said.

So much for my scheme to avoid work. I'll have to work very hard to earn enough money to replace the sweater. And I still have to do the laundry.

Give It a Try

Revise the first draft of your narrative. Then, recopy it on a fresh sheet of paper.

Description

A *description* is a word picture that tells about a particular person, place, thing, or event. Description always appeals to one or more of the reader's senses—sight, smell, taste, touch, or hearing. A description may also appeal to the reader's emotions.

In the following description, the writer appeals to the senses of sight and hearing.

> We reached the top of the hill, dropped our backpacks, and stretched out on the soft grass that covered the cool earth. The air was filled with the fragrance of hundreds of brilliant wildflowers, their dense patterns and colors— purple, pink, red, orange, and blue—spread out like Oriental carpets laid at a bazaar. The air was still around us; not a sound filled the air. But from down below in the valley came the sharp, clear chime of a church bell and the duller clank of cowbells.

The following descriptive passage appeals to emotions as well as to the senses.

> I saw him standing outside the train station, clutching his white cane and rattling the coins in his battered tin cup. His clothes were old and tattered, and he wore a thin coat even though it was the dead of winter. The tempting odors of bacon and eggs drifted from a restaurant a few doors away, where customers sat eating their fill in comfortable booths near the window. I wondered if the beggar had eaten breakfast. As I approached him I fished a few coins out of my pocket and dropped them in his cup. His face lit up, and he nodded his head in appreciation. He then began rattling the coins back and forth again.

The passage appeals to the senses of sight, hearing, and smell. But it also appeals to emotion. Did you feel sorry for the man and wonder what it would be like to be in his situation?

Choosing Details

Descriptive writing appeals to the senses and, sometimes, to the emotions. But how can you choose details that will produce a clear picture in the reader's mind or that will evoke the feelings you wish to convey?

An Important Rule. Choose specific and concrete details over general and abstract ones. Look again at the passage above. Notice the use of these specific, concrete details: "soft grass," "cool earth," "brilliant wildflowers," "sharp, clear chime of a church bell," "duller clank of cowbells."

The specific, concrete details you choose will depend upon which of the senses you want to appeal to. For example, if you were describing a visit to a chocolate factory, you would include details that appeal to the senses of smell and taste. If you were describing a musical performance, you would concentrate on details appealing to the sense of hearing. You might also appeal to the sense of sight in describing how the musicians looked and acted.

Give It a Try

Choose two items from the following list.Write two or three sentences, using specific, concrete details, describing the items you chose. In your description, appeal to the sense or senses listed in parentheses.

- Your favorite dessert (taste)
- A busy intersection (sight, hearing)
- A turkey roasting in the oven (smell, sight)
- Scraping your fingernail on a chalkboard (touch, hearing)
- A school pep rally (sight, hearing)

Point of View

Once the details of a description have been chosen, the point of view from which to present these details must be established. There are basically two: a *fixed point of view* or a *moving point of view*.

The wildflower description on page 101 uses a fixed point of view; the writer describes the scene from a single vantage point. A moving point of view is used in the description of the beggar (page 101). The writer first observes the man from a short distance away, detailing his appearance and actions. The description then moves briefly to a nearby restaurant. Finally, the writer describes walking up to the man and giving him some coins.

Give It a Try

Use either a fixed or a moving point of view to develop a descriptive paragraph on one of the following topics. If you wish, you may use an idea of your own. Appeal to at least two senses in your description.

- Fishing on a lake in the predawn hours
- Visiting the Grand Canyon (or Pike's Peak, Niagara Falls, Redwood National Park) for the first time
- A basketball game
- Eating at a fast-food restaurant
- A bus or train ride

The point of view from which a description is written is often dictated by the subject matter. A description of a giant redwood might include how the writer feels as he or she stands at the foot of the tree. The point of view would, thus, be fixed, rather than moving.

Exposition

Exposition is the writing form used to explain things, ideas, and processes. The reader learns *who, what, why,* or *how.* You will probably use exposition more than any other type of writing, both in school and throughout life. Definite techniques are used to develop effective expository writing: explaining a process; defining; explaining cause and effect; using examples; and using comparisons.

Explaining a Process

Step-by-step instructions are a form of exposition. The following paragraph explains how to build a particular kind of campfire.

> The hunter-trapper fire is built by placing two logs side by side, a little farther apart at one end than at the other. The fire is built between them. The logs should be 6 to 8 inches (15 to 20 centimeters) thick and 3 feet (91 centimeters) or more long. The wide end should be placed towards the wind. When starting the fire, a damper stick may be placed under one of the logs at the wide end. Later this stick may be removed.

These instructions are complete and clearly written. After reading them, you should understand how to build a hunter-trapper fire.

Expository writing can also tell how something works. The following explains how a player piano produces music.

> A player piano is operated by a roll of paper with patterns of holes that correspond to different notes. The roll moves over a cylinder, which also has small holes. A system consisting of a pump, bellows, and valves creates a vacuum in the cylinder. This vacuum sucks a stream of pressurized air through matching holes in the moving roll and the cylinder. The pressurized air causes the piano's hammers to move and strike the strings, producing music.

Give It a Try

Write instructions on one of the following topics, or choose a topic of your own. Make sure your instructions are clear and take the reader through the process step by step.

■ How to teach a dog to sit

- How to tie shoelaces
- How to get from your house to your school
- How to make chocolate chip cookies
- How to hit a baseball or softball

Defining

Definition is another form of exposition. A definition explains the nature of something; it tells what it is and what it does. In a paragraph, the topic sentence—the sentence that tells what the paragraph is about—usually states the definition. The other sentences give facts and details that make the definition clearer. Can you find the topic sentence in this paragraph?

A tornado is a powerful, twisting windstorm. The winds of a tornado are the most violent winds that occur on the earth. They may whirl around the center of the storm at speeds of more than 300 miles (480 kilometers) per hour. Most tornadoes measure several hundred yards or meters in diameter, and many have caused widespread death and destruction.

Notice how the other sentences in the paragraph give additional facts and details to support the definition given in the topic sentence (the first sentence).

Give It a Try

Write a paragraph that defines one of the following topics. State the definition in a topic sentence, and then, write at least two more sentences with facts and details that make the definition clearer.

- diary
- canoe
- salamander
- pentagon
- carburetor

- mathematics
- pizza
- fable
- pneumonia
- molecule

Explaining Cause and Effect

Another technique of exposition uses cause-and-effect relationships to explain a topic. The following paragraphs explain some of the causes and effects of the Great Depression, which began in October 1929.

Many causes contributed to the severity of the Great Depression. During the 1920's, numerous bank failures, together with low incomes among farmers and factory workers, helped set the stage. Uneven distribution of income among workers also contributed to the slump. Most economists agree that the stock market crash of 1929 triggered the Depression.

The Depression had lasting effects on the United States government and on many Americans. The government assumed more responsibility for the nation's economy. In addition, many Americans who lived during the Depression later put greater emphasis on material security and comforts.

Give It a Try

Here are some notes a student made listing causes and effects. Use them to develop a paragraph explaining why the student did poorly on a final exam.

Causes
- Waited until the day before the exam to begin studying
- Stayed up past midnight cramming for the exam
- Was so exhausted I forgot to set my alarm clock

Effects
- Overslept because alarm did not go off

- Got to class too late to take the exam
- Had to stay after school to take the exam
- Was so tired I could hardly keep my eyes open
- Could not remember most of what I had learned the night before

Using Examples

Writers often use examples to help the reader understand a topic. In the following paragraph, the first sentence states the main idea. The other sentences offer examples that support the main idea.

Dogs use their keen senses to help people. A sharp sense of smell enables beagles and many other hunting dogs to track wild animals. Police rely on the bloodhound's sensitive nose to find criminals and lost people. Law enforcement officials also train German shepherds and other dogs to sniff out illegal drugs and hidden explosives. Guide dogs lead blind people. Other specially trained dogs serve as "ears" for deaf people.

Give It a Try

Choose one of the following topic sentences. Develop a paragraph in which at least three examples are used to support the main idea expressed in the topic sentence.

- Working a part-time job can benefit a young person in many ways.
- Pioneer women played a vital role in pushing the frontier westward.
- Computers can perform a wide variety of tasks.
- Encyclopedias are storehouses of information.
- Petroleum, a valuable natural resource, is used to make thousands of products.

Using Comparisons

Comparisons are also used in expository writing. In the following paragraph, the writer uses personal experience to explain similarities and differences between high school and college.

High school and college are alike in certain ways, but very different in other ways. Both involve attending classes, reading textbooks, writing papers, and taking exams. In high school, teachers take attendance, assign homework, collect and grade it, and call your parents if

you goof off. But in college, you are on your own.
Professors rarely take attendance. They may assign
reading or other types of homework, but whether you do
these assignments or not is up to you. And professors
certainly do not call your parents if you goof off.

Similes and metaphors are specific types of comparisons
that can be used to develop an exposition A *simile is a
comparison that uses* **like** *or* **as** *to show similarities between two basically unlike things:* "Planning and playing
a football game *is like* waging war." A *metaphor also com-
pares two basically unlike things, but does not use like
or as:* "The night *is* a menacing stranger." The writer of
the following paragraph uses metaphors to explain his
idea of a cat.

What is a cat? It is more than just a four-legged, furry
creature. A cat asleep in your lap is warmth, peace, and
comfort. A cat playing with a ball or string is a clown. A cat
sitting in the window in the sunlight is a decoration. A cat
trotting out to greet you when you come home is a joy.

Give It a Try
Use comparisons to explain one of the following topics in
one or more paragraphs. Label any similes or metaphors
that you use.
- What getting out of bed in the morning is like
- How baseball and softball are alike

- The similarities and differences between a typewriter keyboard and a computer keyboard
- How women's roles today compare with women's roles in the 1950's
- How you feel on the first day of spring

Argument

Argumentative exposition is written to persuade the reader to agree with a particular opinion, idea, or attitude. An argument may also attempt to convince the reader to follow a particular course of action.

Arguing a Position

Writers use a variety of techniques when constructing arguments: giving reasons and examples; stating facts; relating incidents; and presenting opposing views. In the following argument, the writer gives reasons and facts to support her opinion.

Employers should be allowed to pay teen-agers less than the minimum wage. Minimum wage laws were passed to protect workers trying to support themselves and a family. However, most teen-agers are not self-supporting. Many employers are willing to hire teen-agers, but cannot afford to pay them minimum wage because of their inexperience. But how can young people get job experience if no one is willing to hire them? Permitting teen-agers to work for less than minimum wage would allow them to gain valuable job experience. It would also reduce the high level of youth unemployment.

A written argument must be supported with evidence. It is *not* enough to simply give an opinion.

Cultural exchange programs between countries are in my opinion, of little value. This sending of a lot of singers, dancers, and musicians back and forth is not going to solve any problems. Maybe some good feeling is created, but the stage cannot take the place of the conference table. And just try to sing away a stockpile of atomic bombs. When the Russians see our entertainers—and our sports stars, too—they realize how much better we are, and this makes them jealous.[1]

This example of argument is unconvincing because it does not offer proof to support the writer's opinions. It does not relate a specific incident or present and then disprove an opposing view.

Give It a Try

Construct an argument for or against one of the following opinions, or use an opinion of your own. Be sure to support your opinion with facts. You may also wish to give reasons or examples, relate an incident, or present and then disprove an opposing view.

- Typing should be a required course for every high-school student.
- Playing video games is a waste of time.
- The school year is too long.
- Small cars are better for the environment than large cars.
- U.S. Presidents should be allowed to serve more than two terms.

Arguing for a Course of Action

Some arguments attempt more than simply trying to persuade the reader to accept a particular opinion. They might urge the reader to follow a particular course of action. When constructing such an argument, writers use many of the same techniques that are used when arguing a position: giving reasons and examples; stating facts; relating incidents; and presenting opposing views.

Persuading people to do something is, however, usually more difficult than persuading them to agree with an idea or an opinion. Thus, arguing for a course of action involves giving special consideration to the audience and to the organization of the argument.

Avoid offending the audience. Insults do not win arguments; they prolong them. Use language that the audience can understand. Neither talk down to or confuse the reader with unfamiliar words. Facts are the most convincing evidence. Be sure you are armed with the facts to back your opinion. Organize your argument: give the least important facts first and the most important facts last. The argument will, thus, end on a high note; it will end with the most convincing evidence. Finally, sum up by stating the course of action you feel the reader should take.

The following argument urges parents not to allow their children to go trick-or-treating on Halloween.

You may want to think twice before allowing your children to go trick-or-treating this Halloween. Do you really want them to gorge themselves for days on sugary treats that have little nutritional value? In addition, the danger of traffic accidents increases as excited trick-or-treaters dart across streets without looking. Of course, you can accompany your children on the trick-or-treat adventure. You can guide them across streets and make sure that strangers do not harass them. However, you cannot prevent the possibility that certain disturbed or misguided persons may give your children treats that have been tampered with. Police have reported an alarming increase in such incidents in recent years. Do you really want to inspect each and every piece of candy to make sure it's safe to eat? Probably not. We strongly urge you to keep your children at home this Halloween. It will be much easier, and safer, for everyone.

The argument is convincing because it is based on sound reasons and facts. These reasons and facts are ones to which the audience—parents—can relate and understand. The argument is organized with the least convincing facts first and the most convincing facts last. Finally, it ends by stating the action the reader should take.

Give It a Try

Use one of the following topics or a topic of your own to develop a paragraph that argues for a course of action. Choose an audience and list facts that support your position before you begin writing. Give the least important facts first and the most important facts last. Conclude by stating the action you want the reader to take.

- Stopping industrial pollution
- Raising or lowering the voting age
- Requiring all high school students to learn about computers
- Dealing with the problem of stray dogs
- Ensuring that all family members do their fair share of household chores

Combining Different Writing Forms

We have discussed the four types of writing—narration, description, exposition, and argument—and have given examples of each. You have practiced producing each type of writing in its pure form. Keep in mind, however, that any of the four types of writing may be combined in a single piece. For example, narration may contain passages of description and exposition. Description may include expository passages. Writers sometimes narrate an incident to make a point in an argument.

Do not hesitate to combine various types of writing. Remember that the aim of all writing is communication. Use whatever form or forms that will help you communicate with your audience.

You will find that the various forms, or combination of forms, can be employed for school assignments regardless of subject matter. A report on a science project may include narration to describe the procedures of an experiment; description to give a realistic picture of the results of the experiment; and argument to convince the reader that the experiment proves an hypothesis.

The same combination of writing forms might be employed for a history report: expository writing can set the stage of the period of history about which you are reporting—the who, what, and where of the French Revolution, for example; narration is used to fill in the details—"The people of Paris rose up on July 14 and stormed the Bastille, a fortress-prison, in an effort to secure arms and to free many political prisoners"; description gives life and color to what might, otherwise, be a dry subject—"And when the severed head of Marie Antoinette, a woman hated for her extravagance, rolled down the chute and tumbled into the waiting basket, an ecstatic cry went through the unruly mob"; and argument is used to convince the reader that your interpretation of history is valid—"For all its excesses and terror, the French Revolution, like all revolutions, was rooted in idealism and the belief that the world could be made a better place in which to live."

Any subject, if effectively written about, can be fascinating. Narration, description, exposition, and argument are the building blocks. A nuclear physicist writing a book must, if he or she wants to be understood, use the same building blocks that you use when completing a writing assignment for school. "Writing for School" continues with how these forms, these building blocks of writing, can be combined to successfully complete book reports, short research reports, and term papers.

Book Reports

The book report is a standard school assignment from junior high through college. The expected level of sophistication increases, of course, as you graduate from grade to grade. And in college, a report is simply called "a paper." But the basic form of the book report remains the same.

Your teacher may assign a specific book for you to read and report on, or you may be allowed to choose the book. In either case, read the entire book shortly before you begin writing. Do not attempt to report on a book that was read months, or years, ago without first rereading.

Do not try to take notes for your report as you read. Doing so may distract from your enjoyment and understanding of the book. Allow yourself enough time to skim or reread sections if this becomes necessary as you write the report.

Once you have finished reading, you are ready to take the notes from which the first draft of your report is written. Begin by listing the title, the author's full name, and the date the book was first published. Describe the *setting*, the time and place in which the story takes place. Then list the major characters and briefly describe each one. Finally, summarize the important events in the story's plot. (In the higher grades, an interpretation and discussion of the meaning of the book may be requested by the teacher.)

Refer to your notes as you write the first draft. Your teacher may give you a specific format to use when writing book reports. If not, you may follow the format used in this sample book report.

Treasure Island

Treasure Island, by Robert Louis Stevenson, was first published in 1883. The story takes place in the 1700's. The setting is England and the Spanish Main, which was the name English sailors gave to the northern coast of South America.

The main characters in the story are Jim Hawkins, Squire Trelawney, Dr. Livesey, Long John Silver, Captain Smollett, and Ben Gunn. Jim Hawkins, the story's hero, narrates most of the story in the first person. He is a young boy who serves as cabin boy on the *Hispaniola*, the ship that sails for Treasure Island. The *Hispaniola* is purchased and outfitted by Squire Trelawney, a wealthy man drawn by the romance and adventure of sailing in search of hidden treasure. Dr. Livesey, a physician who cared for Jim's father until his death, also joins the expedition and narrates part of the story. Long John Silver, hired as the ship's cook, later becomes the leader of the mutineers. Mr. Smollett is the man hired by Squire Trelawney to be

captain of the *Hispaniola*. Ben Gunn is a sailor who has
been marooned on Treasure Island for three years.

The story begins when Bill Bones, an old sailor, arrives
at the inn owned by Jim's father. Bones stays at the inn
until his death, which occurs after a blind man comes to
the inn and gives him the Black Spot, a symbol that
pirates used as a death notice to their enemies.

After Bones dies, Jim and his mother search his sea
chest. From it Jim takes a packet that he later gives to Dr.
Livesey and Squire Trelawney. The packet contains a map
showing the location of a treasure hidden by a bloodthirsty
pirate named Captain Flint. Trelawney decides to go after
the treasure, and Dr. Livesey and Jim agree to join him.

Trouble begins shortly after the voyage starts. Captain
Smollett does not like the crew and feels that Silver has
too much influence over them. Jim accidentally learns that
Silver is planning a mutiny with some of the crew.

When the island is sighted, Smollett permits some crew
members, including Silver, to go ashore. Silver kills two
men who will not join the mutiny. Dr. Livesey, who has
gone ashore and found the stockade used by Captain
Flint, returns to the ship and tells the others what Silver

is doing. A decision is made to leave the *Hispaniola* and take refuge in the stockade.

Earlier, Jim had smuggled himself ashore with Silver and his men to spy on them. While on the island, Jim meets Ben Gunn, a sailor who has been marooned there for three years. After leaving Gunn, Jim goes to the stockade. A fierce battle soon takes place between the pirates led by Silver and the men still loyal to Captain Smollett.

The stockade later falls into the pirates' hands. The pirates capture Jim, and one of them tries to kill him. Silver, who by now has the chart showing the location of the treasure, saves Jim's life. The pirates go to find the treasure, only to discover that it is gone.

The treasure is in Ben Gunn's cave, where he has kept it since discovering it several years before. Jim, Dr. Livesey, Squire Trelawney, Captain Smollett, Long John Silver, and Ben Gunn leave the island with the treasure. Silver, the only pirate in the group, escapes the *Hispaniola* during the return journey. Those remaining divide the treasure.

After completing the first draft of your book report, re-read it to make sure it contains all the parts listed on page 113. Then put it aside for a day or two before rereading and revising it. Ask yourself these questions as you re-read:

- Did I include both the time and the place in which the story happens?
- Are the descriptions of the main characters brief and to the point?
- Do these descriptions help the reader better understand the plot summary?
- Does the plot summary include only the most important events in the story?
- Have I included enough details so that the reader can understand the plot summary?

Finally, check your book report for errors in spelling, word usage, grammar, punctuation, and capitalization. Either neatly type the report or rewrite it in your best handwriting. Before submitting it, read it one more time for any errors you may have missed.

Give It a Try

Write a report on a book of your choice. Be sure to revise and recopy your first draft.

Short Research Papers

Many teachers assign research papers. As the name implies, a research paper is always based on research, rather than personal experience. Books, magazines, and encyclopedias are consulted for the information with which the paper is written.

The average short research paper may range in length from 300 words (1½ typewritten pages) to 3,000 words (about 15 typewritten pages). Longer research papers are called *term* papers. These will be discussed later in the chapter. Regardless of the paper's length, certain steps are necessary in the planning and organizing of a research paper: choosing a topic; limiting the scope of that topic; analyzing the subject; researching the topic; and outlining the research paper.

Choosing a Topic

The topic of a research paper may be assigned, may be chosen from a prepared list, or left up to the writer. If you are allowed to choose a topic, be sure to take the time to choose wisely. Select a topic that interests you. You are not likely to enjoy writing about a topic that you find boring.

When choosing a topic, consider the length of your paper and how much time you have to complete it. In general, a topic for a short paper should be narrower than one for a longer paper. Even for longer papers, however, avoid topics that are too broad or complex. If your paper is due in a short time, you may wish to choose a topic with which you are already familiar. Such a topic will require less time to research than one about which you know nothing.

Once you have decided on a general topic, go to the library to determine if enough sources are available on your topic. Begin by looking in the card catalog under your subject. If you were writing about pollution in the Great Lakes, for example, you would look under "Pollution" and "Great Lakes."

The *Readers' Guide to Periodical Literature* contains listings of articles that have appeared in magazines and journals. Check recent issues of the *Readers' Guide* to see if there are articles available on your topic. A sample *Readers' Guide* entry follows.

Great Lakes
Lake Ontario's fish—how they almost got
away. S.
Peterson. bibl f il *Environment* 25:25—32
N'83

If you find that there is not enough material available on
your topic, choose another and follow the same procedure
for checking sources.

Limiting the Topic

Students sometimes make the mistake of choosing topics
that are too broad to be covered in a research paper. Keep
in mind that your paper should focus on one main idea or
event.

A topic such as "Nuclear Power" is much too broad to be
covered in a research paper, even a long one. Topics such
as "The Presidency" and "Computers" are also too broad.
You might narrow these topics as follows:
- The Hazards of Nuclear Power
- The Roles of the Presidency
- Home Computers

For shorter reports, these topics can be narrowed further:
- Managing Radioactive Wastes
- The President as Commander in Chief
- Using a Home Computer to Budget Household Expenses

In general, the shorter your paper, the narrower your
topic should be. But regardless of length, it is always better to cover a smaller topic in detail than to give only general ideas on a larger topic.

Give It a Try

Limit each of the following general topics twice: the first
time for a long paper, the second time for a shorter paper.
- Automobiles
- Space Exploration
- Popular Music
- Life in Colonial America
- Gardening

Analyzing the Subject

After selecting and limiting a topic, do some background reading on your subject. Encyclopedia articles offer a general idea of what a subject is about. You may want to consult other sources as well.

When you have finished your background reading, make up a preliminary outline. This outline may consist of a list of ideas you might include in your paper; it may also be a list of questions you intend to answer in your paper. If your topic were "The President as Commander in Chief," your list of ideas might include the following:

I. President helps determine the size of armed forces
II. President appoints top military officers subject to approval of Congress
III. President decides whether to use nuclear weapons
IV. President keeps country strong during peacetime
V. President cannot declare war, but can send troops into military conflicts

This preliminary outline will serve as a guide in your research. It may also provide a foundation for the working outline, which you will write later.

Give It a Try

Do some background reading on one of the topics you limited for a shorter report (page 117). If you prefer, you may choose and limit a different topic. Then prepare a preliminary outline by listing questions or ideas about that subject.

Researching the Topic

The first step in researching a topic is finding relevant sources. When you choose your topic, you checked the card catalog and the *Readers' Guide to Periodical Literature* to make sure there were enough available sources. Now gather all the materials that may help you research the topic.

For sources of information on current events, check *The New York Times Index* and *Facts on File.* Also check the library's vertical file, which contains pictures, pamphlets, and maps. Radio or television programs and personal interviews are also possible sources of information about your topic.

Make a bibliography card for each source gathered.
Sample bibliography cards for a book, a magazine article,
a newspaper article, and an encyclopedia article are given
below:

Book

> Bookchin, Murray. *Our Synthetic
> Environment.* New York: Harper and
> Row, 1974.

Magazine Article

> Hyde, Nina. "The Queen of Textiles."
> *National Geographic,* vol. 165, Jan-
> uary 1984, pp.2-49.

Newspaper Article

> Tyner, Howard A. "Soviets Cry Foul
> Over Olympics." *Chicago Tribune,*
> April 10, 1984, sec. 1, p. 2.

Encyclopedia Article

> "Pioneer Life in America." *The World
> Book Encyclopedia* (1984), Vol. 15,
> pp. 428-442.

These cards will be used later to make up the bibliography that must be submitted with your paper. Completing
these cards correctly now can save a great deal of time
later on.

Once sources are gathered and a bibliography card
made for each, begin reading and taking notes. *Note cards*
should be a different size or color than bibliography cards.
This will help to keep the two sets of cards separate.

Write only one fact, idea, or quotation on each note
card. By doing this, the cards can be arranged and rear-
ranged in any order. Each note card should contain the
following information:

- *A heading.* A heading, placed at the top of the note card, identifies what the note is about. You might use an idea from your preliminary outline as a heading. The headings on your note cards may later be used as headings or subheadings in your actual outline.
- *The source.* Write the author's last name, an abbreviated form of the title, and the page number on which you found the information. Doing so will allow you to recheck the source if necessary. It will also allow you to write a footnote if you quoted or paraphrased the author.
- *The body of the note.* The actual note may be a few words, a sentence, or a brief summary. Write the note in your own words unless you intend to quote the author directly. Use direct quotations sparingly, however. Always enclose the author's words in quotation marks so you will remember to give credit for the quote.

Heading	History of silk making
Source	Hyde, Jan. 1984, National Geographic, p. 13
Body of note	For more than 4,000 years, people have been using silk to make a variety of products.

Give It a Try

Find at least five sources for a topic of your choice and make bibliography cards for each. Then read these sources and make at least four note cards for each source.

Outlining the Topic

It is time to outline your topic. Although your teacher may not require you to make an outline, doing so will help organize your notes. You will also use the outline as the foundation or basis for first draft of the paper.

Begin by separating note cards into piles according to their headings. (Also refer back to the headings in your preliminary outline.) Use the piles of note cards to decide what the main headings should be. An outline on the topic of the President as commander in chief might have these main headings:

- Powers shared with Congress
- Wartime powers and duties
- Peacetime power and duties

Arrange these headings in a logical order. Number each with a roman numeral.

    I. Peacetime powers and duties
   II. Wartime powers and duties
  III. Powers shared with Congress

Refer to your note cards for possible subheadings to place under the main headings. Write a capital letter in front of each subheading.

  III. Powers shared with Congress
      A. Sending troops into combat
      B. Major military expenditures
      C. Expansion of armed forces

Subheadings are not necessary under every main heading. But if subheadings are used, always include two or more. Sub-subheadings may, at times, also be necessary. Again, always use two or more.

  III. Powers shared with Congress
      A. Sending troops into combat
        1. Only Congress can declare war
        2. President can send troops into military conflicts
      B. Major military expenditures
      C. Expansion of armed forces

Give It a Try

Use the preliminary outline and the note cards you prepared earlier to outline your topic. Include at least two main headings in your outline. Write two or more subheadings under at least one main heading. If necessary use sub-subheadings as well.

Planning the First Draft

You have chosen, limited, analyzed, researched, and outlined a topic. Now it is time to plan the first draft.

First, consider your audience. Although your teacher is usually your only audience, the paper may be read by other members of your class as well. Research papers may also be used as the basis for class discussion.

Plan how you can capture and hold the audience's interest. State your ideas clearly and support them with facts. Review your note cards to make sure you have enough facts to back up the main headings in your outline.

Decide on a purpose for your paper. You may choose to write a summary paper or a critical paper. A *summary paper* presents the information you found in your research, but does not include your opinions and judgments. A *critical paper* both summarizes the research and presents your evaluation of these findings. In a critical paper, you must take a position and justify it.

The next step in the planning process is to write a *thesis sentence,* which states the main idea of the paper. Review the outline and note cards to decide on the main idea uncovered in the research. If you were writing a summary paper about the President as commander in chief, the thesis sentence might be—

> The President's main responsibility as commander in chief of the armed forces is to defend the country during wartime and to keep it strong during peacetime.

If you were writing a critical paper on the same topic, the thesis sentence might be—

> Congress should take a stronger stand against Presidents who send American troops to fight in undeclared wars.

Be sure you have documented facts to support the thesis sentence. If your facts are skimpy, return to the library.

The last step in planning the first draft is to check your outline against your thesis sentence. You may discover that you want to emphasize certain ideas and delete others.

Give It a Try

Decide whether you will use the notes and outline you prepared earlier to write a summary paper or a critical paper. Review your notes and outline and write a thesis sentence. Make sure you have enough facts to support your thesis sentence. Finally, check your outline against your thesis sentence. If necessary, revise your outline.

Writing the First Draft

The outline is the foundation upon which the paper is built. Keep it and your notes in front of you as you write. If you compose at a typewriter, double-space your copy so that you will have room to make later revisions. If you write in longhand, write on every other line to leave space for revisions. Leave wide margins so that you can make notes to yourself as you write.

As you write, do not worry about errors in grammar, spelling, or sentence and paragraph structure. These can be corrected during revision. Your goal at this point is to get all your ideas on paper.

Put the thesis sentence in the first paragraph. Your purpose is either to inform or persuade the reader about the main idea in your thesis sentence. To do this, state your facts, ideas, and opinions clearly and in logical order. Omit any information that is not related to your thesis sentence.

Use footnotes when you give direct quotations or when you paraphrase the ideas of other writers. Also use footnotes when you present facts or figures that the reader might question. Footnotes are numbered consecutively and are placed at the bottom of the page. Sample footnotes for a book[1], magazine article[2], newspaper article[3], and encyclopedia article[4] follow:

[1]Clifford Geertz, *Islam Observed*, p. 49.

[2]Donald Vining, "Main Street Revisited," *Metropolitan Home*, vol. 15, May 1983, p. 53.

[3]"Mayors Seek Greater U.S. Effort Against Drugs," *The New York Times*, May 6, 1971, p. 19.

[4]"Fallout," *The World Book Encyclopedia, vol. 7, 1984.*

Some teachers may ask for end notes, rather than footnotes. *End notes* are placed in a single list at the end of your paper. They are written exactly like footnotes except the number before each end note is not raised about the line and is followed by a period.[5]

5. William Strunk, Jr., and E. B. White, *The Elements of Style*, p. 25.

Prepare the bibliography after you have finished writing the first draft. The bibliography should include *all* the sources you used while preparing the paper. Arrange your bibliography cards alphabetically by author—last names first. (If you made a card for a particular source but did not actually use the source, do not include it in the bibliography.) If no author is listed, alphabetize by article or book title. If you used two or more sources by the same author, put the cards together and order them alphabetically by title. On your bibliography, use a long line to represent the author's name after the first entry. A sample bibliography follows. Use this format as you copy information from your bibliography cards into your bibliography.

Bernstein, Theodore M. *Bernstein's Reverse Diction-ary.* New York: Quadrangle/The New York Times Book Co., 1975.

_____ *The Careful Writer: A Modern Guide to English Usage.* New York: Atheneum, 1978.

Ellis, William S. "Canada's Highway to the Sea." *National Geographic,* vol. 157, May 1980, pp. 594–623.

"The Righting of Writing." *Time,* vol. 115, May 19, 1980, pp. 88–91.

Strunk, William, Jr., and White, E. B. *The Elements of Style.* 2d ed. New York: Macmillan Publishing Co., 1972.

Give It a Try

Write the first draft of your paper, following the procedure outlined in this chapter. Include footnotes and a bibliography.

Revising the First Draft

After you have finished the first draft of your paper, put it aside for a day or two before you begin revisions. This will allow you to look at it with a "fresh eye." Begin the revision process by reading the thesis sentence. Then read the entire paper, circling any sentences that do not relate to the thesis sentence. If possible, rephrase these sentences. Delete sentences that cannot be rephrased in this manner.

Check the paper against your original or revised outline to make sure that all important ideas are included. Use a separate paragraph for each important idea. Be sure you gave evidence to support your major points. If you are writing a critical paper, check that your position is clearly stated and justified.

Find the weak points of the paper and improve them. This may involve rewording sentences, rearranging sentences in a paragraph, or adding details to complete an explanation. Read the following paragraph, keeping in mind how it might be improved.

When the President appoints someone to an important military job, Congress has to approve it. Congress also has to approve when the President wants to spend money on the military or make the armed forces bigger. So as you can see, the President and Congress share certain military powers.

In the following version, the writer has improved the paragraph by rewording sentences and moving the topic sentence to the beginning of the paragraph.

The President shares some military powers with Congress. Top appointments in the armed services require congressional approval. Major military expenses and plans to expand the armed forces also need the consent of Congress.

Maintain coherence in each paragraph. *Cohere* means "to stick together." All the sentences in a paragraph should "stick together," that is, they all should be related to one main idea. The main idea of each paragraph should be stated in the topic sentence.

Coherence should also be maintained between paragraphs. Make sure that paragraphs are presented in a logical manner—that they flow smoothly into one another. If necessary, add *transition words* to show the relationships between paragraphs. Commonly used transition words include *however, therefore, nevertheless, on the other hand, thus, first, second, next,* and *finally.*

Decide whether to use the present or past tense as your primary verb tense. Check to make sure you have used it consistently. Also check the *person* used in the paper— first, second, or third—and make sure you used it consistently.

I will demonstrate in this paper that . . . (first person)
You will learn from this paper that . . . (second person)
This paper demonstrates that . . . (third person)

Omit unnecessary words and phrases. Rewrite sentence fragments as complete sentences. Sentences that are too long should be broken into two or more sentences. Combine, when possible, two or more short, choppy sentences into a larger sentence.

Finally, read the paper one more time to find errors in spelling, capitalization, punctuation, and word usage that you may have missed.

Give It a Try
Follow the procedure described above to revise the first draft of your paper.

Preparing the Final Copy
Prepare the final copy of your paper using the revised first draft. Type the copy double-spaced on good quality typing paper. Be sure to incorporate all the changes and corrections from the first draft.

If you cannot type your paper, write it in your best handwriting. Use a good pen and white paper with wide lines.

Finally, proofread your paper and neatly correct any errors. Now you are ready to submit your paper.

Give It a Try
Follow the procedure just described to prepare the final copy of your paper.

Term Papers
Writing a term paper is similar to preparing a short research paper. There are, however, some important differences. Term papers are longer than short research papers and deal with broader topics. Term papers usually range in length from 1,600 words (about 8 typewritten pages) to 3,000 words (about 15 typewritten pages) or more. Term papers require more sources and more detailed research than the typical research paper. Teachers usually require that the final or working outline be submitted with the completed term paper.

Planning a Term Paper
Review pages 116–121 on how topics are chosen, limited, analyzed, researched, and outlined. Also review the section on how to plan the first draft. Follow the same steps as you plan your term paper. The following sections give additional suggestions.

Preparing a Schedule.   Writing a term paper is a lengthy undertaking. It *cannot* be done overnight. If you wish to minimize the "painful" aspects of the experience, *prepare a schedule.* This will help identify the tasks involved and allow you to budget enough time for each task.

Get out a calendar. Note the date the term paper is due. Set up a schedule by counting backward from the due date. Assume you have eight weeks to complete a ten-page term paper. You will most probably also need to submit an outline and a bibliography. The complete assignment, therefore, calls for twelve pages.

- Plan on an hour per page to type, correct, and proof-read the final copy. Thus, you will spend about 12 hours over several days completing this step.
- Allow an hour per page, or a total of 12 hours, to re-vise the first draft. If you work 3 hours each day, this step will take 4 days to complete.
- Count on 1½ hours per page, or a total of 18 hours, to write the first draft. If you work 3 hours each day, you will finish in 6 days.

This schedule shows that it will take approximately 42 hours to write the first draft, revise it, and prepare the final copy. If you work 3 hours each day, you should be able to finish in 14 days—about 3 school weeks. This leaves you 5 weeks for choosing, analyzing, researching, taking notes, and outlining. If you will not be able to work three hours each day, you must adjust your schedule accordingly.

Choosing and Limiting a Topic

Your teacher may assign the topic for your term paper. If you, however, must choose and limit a topic, follow the steps described on pages 116–117. Keep in mind that it is always better to cover a smaller topic in detail than to give only general ideas on a topic that is too large or too complex. Also remember to choose a topic that interests you.

Analyzing and Researching the Topic

Refer to pages 118–120 for guidelines on analyzing and researching a topic. Remember that a term paper requires more detailed research than a short research paper. Additional sources of information that you may find useful are listed below:

- *Questionnaires and surveys* can be distributed to a large number of people. The answers can provide information on lifestyles, trends in public opinion, and so on.
- *Family records* can be valuable sources of information. These include photographs, scrapbooks, home movies, and records of births, deaths, and marriages.
- *Personal interviews* allow you to ask individual people about a topic. Before an interview, prepare ques-

tions that focus on the information you need for your paper.
- *Historical societies and government record offices* can provide information unavailable elsewhere.

Outlining and Planning the First Draft

Refer to pages 120–122 for instructions on outlining and planning the first draft. Pay special attention to the procedures for outlining, as you will probably have to submit a final outline with your term paper. The final outline will be based on the working outline you develop now.

Preparing a Term Paper

Review pages 122–126 on how to write and revise the first draft and prepare the final copy. The following sections offer additional suggestions for preparing a term paper.

Writing the First Draft.   Follow the procedures described on pages 122–124 for writing a first draft. Carefully review the guidelines for preparing footnotes or end notes. After you have finished writing the first draft, prepare the bibliography.

Revising the First Draft.   If you delete or rearrange material as you revise, note these changes on the working outline. Doing so will make preparing the final outline much easier.

Preparing the Final Outline

The amount of time it takes to prepare the final outline depends upon how carefully you constructed the working outline, wrote the thesis sentence, and checked the outline against the thesis sentence. Whether or not you made necessary changes in the outline during the writing and revision of the first draft is another factor.

If you followed these procedures carefully, most of the work is done. Reread the outline for errors in form, grammar, spelling, capitalization, and punctuation. If you have more than five main headings, you may be able to combine two or more that cover the same idea. Check to see that you do not have single subheadings—an *A* without a *B* or a *1* without a *2*.

You will need to choose a title for the term paper. A good title tells the reader exactly wht the paper is about. Be as specific as possible.

An example of a final outline follows. Make sure your outline is in this form before submitting it.

NATIONAL SERVICE: ALTERNATIVES TO THE DRAFT IN PEACETIME
Outline

Thesis sentence: A program of national service that would enable all Americans to actively serve their country should be considered as an alternative to the military draft in peacetime.

I. Purposes of national service
   A. Unite Americans in a common goal
   B. Create positive aspects of patriotism
   C. Give citizens opportunities to solve their country's problems

II. Kinds of national service
   A. VISTA
   B. Peace Corps
   C. Conservation programs
   D. Research and development programs

III. Requirements of national service
   A. Two years of service
   B. No deferments
IV. Pay for national service
   A. Based on minimum wage
   B. Not taxed

Preparing the Final Copy

Type and proofread the final copy of the term paper. (Review instructions on page 126.) If you cannot type, pay someone to type the paper for you.

Remember to type a clean copy of the final outline and bibliography. Also type a title page. This should include the title of the paper, your name, the date, the name of the course, and the teacher's name.

Assemble the parts of the term paper in this order: title page, final outline, text, end notes (if footnotes are not at the bottom of the pages), and bibliography. Enclose the paper in a folder or binder before submitting it.

Writing for the School Newspaper

Writing for the school newspaper can be a challenging and rewarding experience. You will, in the process, learn more about your teachers, classmates, school, and community. Working on the school newspaper may also spark a life-long interest in journalism. Many professional journalists began their career on this way. This section covers news stories, sport stories, and features.

News Stories

The steps involved in writing a news story include gathering the facts, writing the lead, writing the body of the story, and revising and rewriting.

Gathering the Facts

Assume that the editor of your school newspaper has assigned you to write a story about the work-study program, which began at your school six months ago. To gather the facts you will need to interview Ms. Lawson, the program director. Contact her promptly to schedule an interview.

When gathering facts for a story, keep in mind that a delay in setting up interviews may result in missing a deadline. People you need to interview may be busy and unable to meet with you on short notice.

Before conducting the interview, look at past issues of the school newspaper to see if other articles on the work-study program have been published over the last year or so. You may find articles that were written while the program was being planned. Or an article may have appeared when the program started. Take careful notes on any information you find. You may use these notes as you plan the interview questions and write the story.

Next prepare a list of interview questions. Sample questions designed to get the important facts from Ms. Lawson about the work-study program follow:

- How many students currently are enrolled in the work-study program?
- How many were enrolled when the program began?
- What kind of students are enrolled in the program?
- Why do students enroll in the program?
- Will the program be expanded further? If so, when?
- Has the school board approved funding to expand the program?
- How can interested students learn more about the program?

Joining the staff of a student newspaper can provide both writing and editorial experience as well as exposure to a wider variety of students and faculty. It can also be that first step toward a career in journalism.

Notice that these questions cover the fundamentals of expository writing: who, what, why, or how.

After preparing a similar list of questions, you are ready to conduct the interview. Try to arrive five to ten minutes before the scheduled time. This will allow you to get out your notebook and briefly review the prepared questions.

Begin the interview by briefly describing the topic of your article and what you hope to learn from the person you are interviewing. Then ask the questions you prepared. Take careful notes of the person's answers. Do not, however, bury your head in the notebook. Maintain frequent eye contact with the person so he or she will know you are listening carefully.

Notes can be written faster by using abbreviations, *wsp* for *work-study program* and *sb* for *school board*. Ask for the correct spelling of important names. Try to distinguish between important and unimportant information, taking notes only on facts you will need for your story. If a response is confusing or evasive, ask that the answer be clarified. You may be able to record the interview on tape, thus eliminating the need to take notes. However, be sure to ask permission in advance.

Organize and recopy your notes as soon as possible after the interview. Expand on the notes, adding facts and details that you did not have time to write down during the interview. If you used a tape recorder, take notes as you play back the tape. Then organize and recopy the notes.

You may discover, as you organize the notes, that you need additional information. If so, do research or background reading on the topic. Or you may find that you need to call or request a second interview to get more information.

Once you have organized your notes and gathered any additional information, you are ready to write the story. Begin with the lead.

Writing the Lead

The *lead* is the first paragraph of a news story. A well-written lead is short; it briefly summarizes the important information in the story. The reader should be able to grasp the main idea from the first paragraph. The lead must be able to stand alone, since some or even all of the other paragraphs of the story may have to be cut when pages are made up. Also, many readers skim a newspaper, catching lead paragraphs only.

An interview can be one of the most effective ways to gather the facts before writing a news article. Prepare for an interview by developing a complete list of questions. Take along paper and pencils to record the answers.

Stories, of course, are all different, but a good lead should include *who, what, when, where, why,* or *how.* The lead for the story on the work-study program might be written as follows.

Enrollment has nearly doubled in Central High School's work-study program since it began six months ago. Plans are being made to further expand the program next September, according to Ms. Patricia Lawson, program director.

Note that the lead summarizes the important facts in the story by telling *what, when,* and *who.*

What: Enrollment has nearly doubled in the work-study program.

When: over the past six months

Who: according to Ms. Patricia Lawson, program director

The following lead tells *how* in addition to *who, what,* and *when.*

Philip Melendez was, by a narrow margin, elected president of the Student Council last Tuesday.

This lead tells *who, what, when, where,* and *how.*

Police located two stolen cars in the North Shore High School parking lot yesterday after receiving an anonymous telephone tip.

You have learned that leads should be short and should include only the important information in the story. But how should the information in a lead be arranged? In general, the most important information should be placed first. Read the two leads that follow and decide which places the most important information first.

The senior class raised a total of $800 to help pay for their trip to Washington, D.C. Homeroom 213 raised $285, the highest total among the four homerooms.

Homeroom 213 raised $285, the highest total among the four homerooms, for the senior class trip to Washington, D.C. A total of $800 was raised for the trip.

The answer, of course, is the first lead. Which homeroom raised the most money is less important than information about the total amount raised.

Word order within the sentences in the lead is also important. Look again at the leads on page 133 and above. Note that all the sentences begin with the subject and verb: "Enrollment has doubled," "Plans are being made," "Philip Melendez was elected," "Police located," "The senior class raised," and "Homeroom 213 raised." In general, stick to subject-verb word order when writing leads. This order tells the reader immediately who or what acted and what happened.

Avoid expressing an opinion in the lead to a news story. Present the facts and let the reader decide on their meaning.

Principal A. N. Foley announced Monday that students may no longer leave school grounds during the lunch hour. Many students have protested this unfair rule.

Note that the reporter expresses an opinion by calling the rule "unfair." To avoid expressing an opinion, the second sentence can be rewritten as follows: "Many students have protested the new rule, which they consider unfair."

Give It a Try

Use the information in each of the following items to write the lead for a news story. Give the most important facts first. Use subject-verb word order in each sentence.

- When: during the lunch hour on Thursday, October 10
  Where: the school cafeteria
  What: a bake sale will be held
  Who: student council is sponsoring the sale
  Why: to raise money for new gym equipment

- What: mayor spoke to students about summer jobs in village parks and forest preserves
  When: last Thursday
  Who: Mayor Packwood
  How: students can fill out job applications at village hall beginning May 1

Writing the Body

The body of a news story gives more information about the facts presented in the lead. This information adds to the reader's understanding of the main idea of the story.

The first step in writing the body is to review the lead. Look again at the lead on page 133 for the story about the work-study program. Note the important facts: (1) enrollment in the program has nearly doubled, and (2) plans are being made to further expand the program. The body of the story will give more information about these facts, using a separate paragraph for each. As you write the body paragraphs for a story, refer to the notes you took when gathering the facts.

The body paragraphs for the story about the work-study program might be written as follows.

Enrollment now stands at 30 students, up from 16 students when the program began. Ten students are currently on a waiting list.

Ms. Lawson hopes to expand the program to include 45 students by next September. School board members have already approved the necessary funds for the expansion.

After more information on the important facts in the lead have been given, you may, if space allows, include additional related information. The following paragraphs could be added to the work-study story.

Students in the work-study program spend mornings attending classes and afternoons working in various businesses throughout the community.
    Ms. Lawson suggests that interested students arrange an appointment with her to discuss the program.

When news stories have to be shortened, cutting is done from the bottom up. In the work-study story, both the last and second-to-last body paragraphs could be eliminated. If further cutting were necessary, the editor could eliminate the second sentence in each of the first and second body paragraphs. In certain situations, the editor might even cut all the body paragraphs, leaving only the lead.

Because of the way news stories are generally shortened, remember to always arrange the body paragraphs from most important to least important. Even within each paragraph, give the most important information first.

Use subject-verb word order in most of your sentences. The presentation of information is, thus, direct and easy for the reader to understand.

Maintain coherence within paragraphs and in the story as a whole. *Cohere* means "to stick together." Check that all the sentences in each paragraph relate to the paragraph's main idea. Make sure that all the paragraphs in the story relate to the main idea or ideas expressed in the lead.

The paragraphs in the story on the work-study program stick together because all are related to the main ideas expressed in the lead. Also, certain key words or names are repeated throughout the story. These include *enrollment, program, Ms. Lawson,* and *expand.* Repeating key words helps paragraphs flow smoothly into one another.

Use of transition words and phrases—*now, then, soon, meanwhile, at the same time, finally,* and *later*—can also help to give a story coherence.

As in the lead, avoid giving your opinions in the body paragraphs. However, you may quote others giving an opinion on a topic:

Dorothy Williams has this opinion about study halls: "I think that study halls are a waste of time. They are usually so noisy that it is impossible to get any studying done."

Revising and Rewriting

After the body paragraphs have been written, reread the entire story, including the lead, and make any necessary corrections and revisions. Ask yourself these questions:

- Does the lead briefly summarize the important information in the story?
- Could the lead stand alone if all the body paragraphs were cut?
- Does the lead give the most important information first and the least important information last?
- Do most of the sentences in the story use subject-verb word order?
- Does the story stick to the facts and avoid injecting the reporter's opinions?
- Does the body of the story give more information about the important facts in the lead?
- Are the body paragraphs arranged from most important to least important?
- Are the sentences within each body paragraph arranged from most important to least important?
- Do all the sentences in each body paragraph cohere, or stick together?
- Do all the paragraphs in the body relate to the main idea or ideas expressed in the lead?
- Are devices such as key words and transition words and phrases used to make paragraphs flow smoothly into one another?
- Are there factual errors or errors in spelling, grammar, word usage, capitalization, or punctuation?

Once you have corrected and revised your story, make a clean copy by neatly typing it or recopying it in your best handwriting. Read it one last time for any errors you may have missed. Then, submit it to the editor of your school newspaper.

Give It a Try

Practice writing your own news story. Choose a topic and gather the facts about the story. Then write the lead and the body paragraphs. Revise and correct the story. Finally, make a clean copy of your story. You may wish to submit it to the editor of your school newspaper.

Sports Stories

Sports stories are in many ways similar to news stories. A sports reporter gathers the facts, writes the lead, writes the body, and revises and rewrites the story.

The typical sports story differs from a news story only in its informality, color, and variety of writing styles. Sports writing explodes with active, lively verbs that quicken the pace and attempt to recapture the excitement of the original event: teams *destroy* their opponents; coaches *bully, cajole,* and *inspire* their teams toward victory; players *pout* and *fume* at decisions; and cheerleaders *sparkle* with youth and enthusiasm. No other breed of newspaper reporter enjoys the same opportunity to breathe life into his or her copy.

The basic form of a good sports story is the basic form of the news story: a lead that condenses all the important information into one or two sentences—the who, what, when, where, why, or how; and supporting body paragraphs that provide additional information in descending order of importance.

A sports lead, like a news lead, focuses on the funda-

Good sports writing explodes with active, lively verbs that quicken the pace and attempt to recapture the excitement of the sporting event.

mentals. Who won? What was the score? When was the game held? Where was the event held? What was the turning point in the game? Who was the hero? And why did the winner win and the loser lose? But the sports writer has more freedom in deciding what information to include in the lead and how to present that information. Notice how the following lead emphasizes the significance of an individual player's achievement while giving the important facts about the story.

> **Batting in 10 runs in last Saturday's 15–6 victory over West High has won a spot in the record books for Main High's Matthew Sanders.**

The body paragraphs in a sports story give additional information about the facts presented in the lead. As in a news story, they are also arranged in order of decreasing importance to allow the editor to cut the story from the bottom up.

Give It a Try

Write a sports story. Use information from an event you have recently attended or from a television sports program. Remember to use active, lively verbs to enrich the narrative.

Feature Stories

Feature stories, like news stories, are based on fact. But they differ from news stories in several important ways. While news stories seek to inform the reader, the primary purpose of a feature story is to entertain. News stories are written so they can be cut from the bottom up; feature stories are not usually cut. News stories must contain a lead that summarizes the important information in the story. Feature stories, on the other hand, usually begin with a lead designed to grab the reader's attention or stimulate the reader's curiosity.

As you read the following feature story, think about how it differs from a news story.

> **"Sure, it gets depressing sometimes. But if I can help just one older person feel less sad and less alone, it's worth it."**
>
> **That is how Melanie Cowell, sophomore at East End**

A human interest
story appeals to the
reader's emotions
and is written in an
interesting manner.

High School, sums up her volunteer job at Golden Sunset
Nursing Home.

For the past two years, Melanie has spent three hours
each Sunday afternoon at the Home. Like most teen-agers,
Melanie used to spend Sunday afternoons going out with
friends, talking on the telephone, shopping, or listening
to records. Now she spends that time talking, walking, or
just sitting with the patients in Ward G at the Home.

"Sunday afternoons are lonely times for people whose
families don't come to visit, or for those who don't have
families. These people feel more alone when they see all
the visitors. So I visit with them and become almost like
family to them."

Melanie admits that some Sundays she doesn't feel like
going to the Home.

"But I always go whether I feel like it or not. The patients
count on me and are really disappointed if I don't show up.
And—I know this sounds corny—I always end up receiving
a lot more than I give."

This type of feature is called a human interest story. Although the story has little or no news value, it appeals to

the reader's emotions and is written in an interesting manner. Like many human interest stories, it quotes the person who is the subject of the story. These quotations help the reader understand the person's thoughts and feelings and also bring the story to a more personal level.

Note that the lead captures the readers' attention, inducing him or her to read on, to learn more about the person being quoted. The important facts are spread throughout the rest of the story, presented in the style and in the order the writer considered most effective.

Although feature stories are based on facts, writers sometimes use the techniques of fiction to present such stories. These techniques include description, narration, dialogue, and suspense. A feature writer may, in fact, use any form or style of fiction or nonfiction writing that he or she considers appropriate. The narrow form of the news story does not apply to feature writing.

Other types of features include news feature stories, which are related to events in the news, but written with a human interest slant; stories about personal experiences or achievements; stories about holidays or seasonal events; and personality sketches.

Give It a Try

Write a feature story based upon one of the following topics. Remember that the lead paragraph should attract and hold the reader's attention. Use a variety of writing techniques, including narration, description, and exposition, to give the story an interesting, but informative, appeal.

- What punk rock is all about
- How television has changed baseball
- What ever happened to New Math
- How teaching school has changed in the last 30 years
- Are today's teen-agers more materialistic than they were in the 1960's
- Why are horror movies so popular with teen-agers

References

1. Wallace E. Stegner. *Modern Composition,* vol. 5. New York: Holt, Rinehart & Winston, Inc., 1964, p. 121.

Writing for Work

We live in an era that has been called the "age of anxiety." The times might, with equal propriety, be dubbed the "age of relevancy." The second description is, perhaps, an outgrowth of the first. If one questions the possibility of a future, the present becomes all-important. Anything that cannot be applied to the here and now is examined and discarded as superfluous. Time-honored traditions—the teaching of the classics, the teaching of Latin—have been dropped for lack of relevancy. Who needs it? What good is it? What's the bottom line?

Chapter 5, "Writing for Work," is the bottom line. It deals, specifically, with how to get a job and how to keep a job. And that is relevant.

You may ask what writing has to do with getting and keeping a job. Our answer is concise: résumés, cover letters, office memoranda, business letters, business reports, and business proposals.

Technology and instantaneous communication are changing American business. The United States is now the world's bookkeeper. With computers and sophisticated telecommunication systems, we keep track of a world economy. Across the nation, vast amounts of paper dealing with oil from Saudi Arabia, shoes made in Taiwan, and corn grown in Iowa is shuffled across thousands of desks. It all ends up in a computer. But computers only count up numbers and store them away. People still write the information down and that information begins as a memo or a report.

Mastering the skills of effective writing is now more important than ever for a successful career. And effective writing in today's marketplace is "relevant"; it is precise, concise, to the point. Chapter 5 demonstrates how and why.

Résumés and Cover Letters

Writing a résumé and cover letter is the first step toward finding a job. Accompanied by a cover letter, a résumé is normally a mailed request for an interview. It is the first impression you give to a prospective employer and should, therefore, be a neat and efficient review of your background, both educational and professional. A good résumé will not get you a job, but it may get you an interview, which can be an all-important first step.

Cover letters accompany a résumé and fulfill three functions: they include a statement of purpose, that is, you state that you are seeking a job, usually a specific job that has been advertised; they include a polite request for an interview; and they include an explanation of why your background qualifies you for the position. A résumé is general; it broadly covers experience and education. A cover letter is specific; the format allows you the freedom to tailor your experience to fit the requirements of the prospective job. The same résumé is mailed to a number of possible employers; but each cover letter is individually written, individually fitted to the description of a specific job.

Résumés

A résumé follows a fairly rigid format. Certain information is *always* included: your name; your address; your telephone number; the position or type of position in which you are interested; your work experience; and your educational background. Depending upon the situation, other information may also be included: foreign languages spoken; and outside activities. It is not necessary to date a résumé. As long as your work experience and educational background data are up-to-date and your address and telephone number are current, your résumé is in good order.

It is not necessary on a résumé to give your age, your marital status, or establish that you may have children. It is also not necessary to list physical handicaps. It is reasonable to assume that you would not apply for a job if you were physically unable to perform. If you are handicapped in any way, it will be apparent during an interview and should not be a factor in employment.

It is not necessary to list references. A sentence can be included on the cover letter stating that references can be furnished upon request.

Do *not* include salary requirements on a résumé. Salary requirements are discussed at an interview.

Name and Address

The physical make-up of a résumé is also fairly rigid. Your name, address, and telephone number are placed, in a block, at the top of the page. They may either be centered or placed flush against the left or right margins. It is not necessary to include your middle name or initial if you normally do not use it. A résumé is not a job application. If you do not have a permanent address, use an address where you can be reached or at which a responsible adult will take messages and relay information. You need not explain that an address is not permanent.

JAMES MORGAN
33 East 7th Street
Pottsville, Illinois 61531

Objective

Your objective, or the type of position you are seeking, is placed after your name and address. The objective can be either specific or general. This usually depends upon your work experience or training. If you are just entering the job market and your training is general, your objective should be general. If you were trained for a specific kind of job or if you already have a position and are looking for a specific kind of job, your résumé objective can be specific. A heading is used with this category of the résumé, as well as with the "experience" and "education" categories. The heading is usually placed flush left.

Objective: Secondary teaching position

or

Type of Position Sought: Secondary teaching position

Experience

The next category entered on your résumé is your employment record or work experience. (If you have had only part-time or no work experience, you may wish to place your educational record directly after the employment objective listing.) Work experience is listed after a heading—Experience. Begin with your latest job. Include the dates of employment, the name and address of your employer, a job title, and a job description or a brief list of responsibilities. On a separate sheet of paper, work at developing a succinct, or brief and to-the-point, job description. Try to pare it down to a brief statement of facts. A prospective employer is not interested in every minute detail, only the general range of your responsibilities. The description need not be written in full sentences. Cut the subject of the sentence and begin with the verb: managed department of twelve technicians; developed program for hearing impaired; interviewed prospective clients.

After describing your latest position, follow the same procedure for previous jobs. Again list your jobs in reverse order—last job first and first job last. If you have a complete employment record of full-time jobs, you do not need to list part-time work or summer employment.

As you make out your employment record, try to account for all working experiences. If, for a period of time, you did free-lance work, research, or were self-employed, list it. However, do not try to fill in gaps in your employment record with nonworking information. Do not list time at home, keeping house or raising children. Also, do not list extended vacations. If an employer is interested in the gaps, he or she will question you about them at the interview.

Experience:

7/74 to 11/77	**Office of Evaluation Research** **University of Illinois, Chicago Circle** **Campus** **P.O. Box 4348** **Chicago, Illinois 60680** **Interviewed children and parents for** **evaluation study (2/77–11/77)**
9/70 to 6/74	**Michael Reese Hospital and Medical** **Center,** **School of Nursing** **2929 South Ellis** **Chicago, Illinois 60616** **Psychology instructor**

Note the arrangement of the heading, dates, and information in the example above. Also note how the descriptions of the various positions were cut to a simple verb and object: interviewed children and researched methods.

Give It a Try

Writing a job description in brief, concise sentences is the most difficult part of a résumé. Practice by describing your present work responsibilities, or job duties you once held, following the guidelines outlined above. Remember a job description can be written in sentence fragments.

Education

Under education, list the schools and training programs you have attended; the locations of the schools; the degrees you have earned; major areas of study; and the dates of attendance. If you have graduated from college, do not list your high school. The reader will assume you have completed 12 grades before entering college. However, if you have done graduate work, *do* list undergraduate data as well. Again, keep all listings simple and to-the-point.

Education	
1975 to 1977	De Paul University, Chicago, Illinois Received Master of Science degree (June, 1977) Major in clinical psychology
1966 to 1970	Southern Illinois University, Carbondale, Illinois Received Bachelor of Arts degree (June, 1970) Major in psychology

Note that education, like work experience, was listed in reverse order—the latest school first and the first school last.

Languages

List foreign language proficiency on a résumé if you are truly proficient and if you believe that the ability may have a bearing on landing the job. Proficiency is, in most cases, more than the obligatory two years of a foreign language required to graduate from high school or college.

Under a "languages" heading, list the language and your proficiency.

Languages:	**German (spoken and read)**

Outside Activities

Activities outside of work-related experiences might be listed on a résumé in two situations. If you are newly graduated from school and you have little work experience directly related to a full-time position, you may wish to list activities and organizations to which you belong or in which you once participated. However, list those activities that may have some bearing on the kind of work you are seeking. If, for example, you are looking for a position teaching music, by all means, list the musical activities in which you have participated.

Activities may also be listed on a résumé if you belong to a professional organization, either voluntary or honorary, within the discipline in which you are seeking employment. If you belong to the American Psychological Association and are applying for a position as a clinical psychologist, list your membership.

Outside Activities:	**Member of American Psychological Association**
Outside Activities:	**University Drama Club**
	Phi Mu Alpha (professional music fraternity)
	City Orchestra

Brevity

Brevity, besides being the soul of wit, is the essence of a good résumé. If you follow the suggestions outlined in this chapter, you will find that your résumé is concise and fairly brief. If you are lucky, it will fit on a single sheet of 8½- by 11-inch paper. If it does not fit on a single sheet of typing paper, you may wish to go back and pare down your job descriptions or list of schools and training programs.

Why should a résumé be brief? Won't a prospective employer be impressed by a long list of work experience?

Contrary to common opinion, prospective employers are not impressed by three-page résumés. The average manager who is looking for a new employee is busy. If he or she were not busy, another employee would not be necessary. If the new job is advertised, dozens, perhaps even hundreds, of letters and résumés are reviewed. That long résumé, which looked so impressive to the writer as it was slipped into a Manila envelope, will never be read in its entirety. A busy manager will give up halfway through the second page. The résumé on a single sheet, however, produces an impression of concise organization, a quality highly valued in a busy company. So keep it brief. Question if every entry is absolutely necessary. Will anyone care about your summer job experience during college if you have been holding full-time positions for three or four years? Does the seminar you attended at night have any bearing on the responsibilities of the prospective job? If yes, then list the seminar. If not, then drop it. Figure out what is and what is not important. Work for brevity and the best possible first impression.

Printing and Paper

Can a résumé be handwritten? No. Type your résumé and type it perfectly. Do not send a résumé with errors or even sloppy typing. If you cannot type a perfect copy, hire someone to type it for you.

Should résumés be set into type? It is not absolutely necessary to typeset a résumé, but the result is a highly professional appearance. It is also relatively inexpensive to have a single page of type set. The $15 to $20 you spend may be a good investment. A professional appearance and good first impression are important in certain fields.

Should a résumé be printed or photocopied? Photocopying is probably sufficient. Find a photocopy shop, rather than a machine available to the general public. Ask the manager to show you what paper stocks are available. Choose a good quality paper. The machines in a private photocopy shop are well maintained and will produce a clean, neat copy. Your résumé can be photocopied from either typed or typeset copy. But, again choose a paper of good quality. A prospective employer will recognize the extra effort you have made to supply him or her with a perfectly typed (or typeset), clean, easy-to-read résumé.

Examples of Résumés

Joan Wetcher
101 Sun Boulevard
Arlington, Arizona 00022
859–123–4567

OBJECTIVE:	Secretarial Position

EXPERIENCE:

Summer 1983 & 1982	Acme Manufacturing Company
	2112 Sand Street
	Arlington, Arizona
	general typing
Summer 1981	Sunshine Ice Cream Parlor
	320 South Main Street
	Arlington, Arizona
	soda jerk

EDUCATION:

1980– 1984	Arlington High School
	Arlington, Arizona
	graduated June, 1984
	significant courses: Typing I and
	II; Business typing; Shorthand I
	and II; Office practices

OUTSIDE ACTIVITIES:	Student Council
	Arlington Times Newspaper
	(typing and editorial for
	four years)

WILLIAM RODGERS
11 East Wall Street
Farmerstown, Illinois 61531
309–712–8333

OBJECTIVE:
Teaching position in secondary school
English and/or history

EDUCATION:
1980–1984   Western Illinois University
Macomb, Illinois
Bachelor of Arts
English major/history minor

EXPERIENCE:
Summer 1983   Farmerstown, Illinois, Park District
Summer 1982   Summer Recreation Program
supervised athletic and play activities for
children ranging in ages from six to sixteen

Summer 1981   Lester Screen Factory
1122 North Maple Street
Macomb, Illinois
worked drill press

Summer 1980   Myers Farm
Farmerstown, Illinois
detasseled corn
general farm work

OUTSIDE ACTIVITIES:
Writer's workshop (four years)
Student newspaper (four years)
Student yearbook (four years)

Examples of Résumés (Cont.)

ELIZABETH ROLLINS
900 Lake Shore Drive
Chicago, Illinois 60613
217–301–1414

OBJECTIVE:
    Food and beverage manager
    Major airline

EXPERIENCE:
    1980–1983
    Prairie Airline
    10 East Monroe Street, Chicago, Illinois
    Assistant food and beverage manager
      supervised department of thirty employees
      purchased daily supplies for a fleet of 100 planes
      completed menus and supervised meal planning
        and preparation
    1975–1980
    Prairie Airline
      purchased supplies in general purchasing department

    1970–1980
    Apex Manufacturing
    110 East 32nd Street
    New York, New York
      Purchasing agent

EDUCATION:
    1966–1970
    Columbia University
    New York, New York
      Bachelor of Arts
      Business major

LANGUAGES:
    French (spoken and written)
    German (spoken and written)

W. Charles Rightwood
3742 North Clark
Chicago, Illinois 60613
217–211–1330

OBJECTIVE: Department manager—contract design company

EXPERIENCE:
  1975–1984   Office Furniture Corporation
                       100 North Wells Street, Chicago, Illinois
                       Interior design and space planning for over
                       100 major clients, totaling 1,000,000 square
                       feet of office space. Major clients included

                           The Boston Store—Chicago
                           Capron, Capron & Capron—New York
                           Lestor Williams & Associates—New York
                           North American Telephone Co.—Chicago
                           Governor's Office—Springfield, Ill.
                           The Bateman Club—Boston
                           William James Associates—Chicago
                           Frazier & McWilliams—Los Angeles

  1971–1974   Edward Fieldstone Corp.
                       Merchandise Mart Plaza—Chicago, Illinois
                       Designed custom furniture and display equipment
                       Major clients included

                           Marshall Field—Chicago
                           Wanamaker's—Philadelphia
                           Bloomingdale's—New York
                           Macy's—New York
                           Jordan Marsh—Boston

EDUCATION:
  1970–1974   The Lexington School of Design
                       Chicago, Illinois

  1969–1970   The School of the Art Institute of Chicago
                       Chicago, Illinois
                       general art studies

Give It a Try

Following the guidelines suggested in this chapter, write a résumé of your own. Remember to include your name, address, telephone number, work objective, work experience, and educational background. Keep it concise and include headings.

Résumés for Part-Time or Summer Jobs

Many high school and college students look for part-time and summer jobs. The objective is usually not to begin or advance a career, but simply to earn money. A particular kind of job, consequently, is not the aim. Still, it is possible to fit skills to a certain range of jobs, and a résumé will help bring out skills that are marketable.

The response to an application for a part-time job is often negative or evasive: "We don't have anything right now, but fill out an application form and if something turns up, we'll call you." If you have a résumé to present along with the application form, a prospective employer will have a more complete picture of you and your skills.

To develop a résumé for part-time work, think back over your achievements. Write the achievements down. Consider what skills were necessary to attain those achievements. Next match these skills to the kinds of skills necessary and valuable for various kinds of jobs.

You may, for example, like to cook, have experience cooking, and have experience buying food and planning menus. These skills might interest a restaurant manager. You may not be hired as a cook, but the skills may get you through the door and into a summer job as a waiter or waitress.

Perhaps you have experience taking care of younger brothers or sisters. You know how to care for children, how to feed them, how to change their clothes, how to keep them occupied and happy. Playing up these skills might open the door to a summer job or part-time job in a day-care center or as a camp counselor.

You may, for example, have successfully solicited funds for a school organization or a charity. You have, thus, had experience meeting strangers, conducting sales talks, and concluding a "sale" of a particular kind. These are characteristics for which employers of all kinds of salespeople look.

Examine your experiences and skills and describe them in the format of a résumé. As you might lack work experience and your education is incomplete, use "Skills" and "Evidence" for headings.

Jane Drummond
14 Elm Street
Jackson, Illinois 61531
309–221–1314

SKILLS:

> Good communication with children; patience and firmness in dealing with children; calmness in emergencies; capable of planning, following directions, completing tasks.

EVIDENCE:

> Have, from the age of 12, cared for younger brother and sister; have been in demand as a babysitter in the neighborhood; have taken charge of planning, buying, and cooking at least one family meal per week; have kept school marks at B average.

If you enter an interview with a résumé of this kind, you will impress your prospective employer with your seriousness, give him or her subjects about which to ask questions, and arm yourself with points you wish to cover. The résumé will also assure you of a feeling of self-confidence, an important ingredient when trying to find a job.

Later Résumés

During the first years of a person's working life, it is not unusual for him or her to move from one job to another, seeking more responsible positions, higher pay, more congenial working conditions. A résumé grows with experience, and a person revises it to emphasize that experience over other elements. Education and school activities become less important.

The résumé of a person who has established himself or herself in a particular career is also not as brief, although it should be just as concise. Armed with a good deal of first-rate experience, the job applicant in this category has less trouble getting his or her résumé read. The résumé can, thus, be fuller. Experience is important, and it is described in detail.

PAUL CLARK
206 South Main Street
Pearl River, N.Y. 10965
(914) 735–8150

EXPERIENCE:

Editorial
Writing
Writing Staff Management
Copywriting

Editorial

Evaluated, rewrote and prepared for publication short and full-length feature articles for two quarterly magazines. Also in charge of proofreading galleys, final page makeup, and dummies.

Assumed charge as editor in chief and principal writer of newspaper published for 200 employee company. Assigned and edited feature and filler stories, photos, illustrations. Supervised/coordinated page design, typesetting, printing, and distribution.

Free lance copy editor for author of secondary world history textbooks and educational materials developed for secondary and college level history and political science courses.

Free lance proofreader for <u>Newsweek</u>.

Writing

Feature and filler story writer for company newspaper—personal and department profiles, companywide events, annual sales meeting reports, restaurant and movie reviews, and humor stories.

Researched and authored two units of secondary Latin American history text.

2

Writing Staff Management	Senior writer/copy chief managing five member copywriting staff plus free lance writers and graphic designers. Responsible for scheduling, project assignments, copyediting, rewrite, research, author contact, design approval, traffic and media advertising for book and magazine publishers.
	Heavy convention attendance entailing direct sales, public relations and exhibit booth management.
Copywriting	Promotion writer of direct response, catalogs, one, two, three, and four color brochures, subscription promotion, book club promotion, press releases, sales letters, space advertising, media kits, convention handouts and posters, blow and bind-in cards, and other promotion projects for book and magazine publishers.
Publications associated with	Newsweek World Broadcast News BM/E Broadcast Management/Engineering Nursing Forum Perspectives in Psychiatric Care A wide variety of scholarly magazines and journals

JOB HISTORY:

present	CREATIVE CONSULTANT Billboard Publications 1515 Broadway, New York, N.Y.
1982–1983	PROMOTION MANAGER Broadband Information Service, Inc. 295 Madison Avenue, New York, N.Y.

3

1982	PROMOTION MANAGER S. Karger Publishers, Inc. 150 Fifth Avenue, New York, N.Y.
1978 1979 1979–1981	COPYWRITER SENIOR WRITER COPY CHIEF Springer-Verlag New York, Inc. 175 Fifth Avenue, New York, N.Y.
1977–1978	COPYWRITER Executive Reports Corporation Prentice-Hall Englewood Cliffs, N.J.
1976–1977	ASSOCIATE PUBLISHER Nursing Publications, Inc. Park Ridge, N.J.
EDUCATION:	Michigan State University East Lansing, Mich., 1975 B.A. Russian language, with heavy coursework in writing, English, history and journalism
PROFESSIONAL MEMBERSHIPS:	National Writers Club
WRITING PORTFOLIO:	Available on request

Cover Letters

You might, when applying for a job, be one of several, perhaps one of dozens, of people submitting a résumé. The other applicants, in most cases, will possess the same academic background as you. How do you make yourself outstanding? How do you persuade a prospective employer that it would be to his or her advantage to interview you? Getting your résumé up to the top of the pile can be accomplished with a first-class cover letter.

The cover letter is your opportunity to convince a prospective employer that your qualifications, however slim, perfectly fit his or her needs. How is this done?

It is done by tailoring your qualifications and skills to his needs. Begin by studying the job description published in the newspaper or posted on an announcement board. Make a list of the qualifications noted in the job description. Then, match, point-by-point, your professional and academic experiences to the list of job requirements. If you cannot think of a work experience to match one of the job requirements, try to think of a scholastic or personal experience to meet the need. Your experiences might involve school courses or even extracurricular activities. These experiences might already be listed on your résumé. It is acceptable to relist them on the cover letter. Simply make sure that you have supplied a solid response to each of the job requirements. As you write the cover letter, keep the list of job requirements and your matching list of personal qualifications next to you.

A cover letter is written in the usual business letter format. Place your address, including ZIP code, and telephone number in a block, either flush left or right. Place the date of the letter under your address.

Next type the name, title, and address of the person to whom you are writing. This should be typed in a block against the left margin. Advertisements for jobs are often blind, that is, they are listed without company identification. A post office box is given for responses. Address your cover letter, in this instance, to the box number.

Box 124 B
Pittsburg Daily News
Pittsburg, Vermont 12345

The salutation in a cover letter is simply "Dear Mr. Smith" or "Dear Ms. Jones." The salutation is typed flush with the left margin and is punctuated with a colon. If you are answering a blind ad, the salutation should read "Dear Sir or Madam." This salutation has a somewhat old-fashioned ring, but covers all possibilities without sounding as blunt as "To Whom It May Concern."

Begin your letter with a statement of why you are writing: "I am writing in response to your *Tribune* advertisement of July 31, describing a sales position for which I should like to apply." This kind of opening sentence immediately gets down to business. Although a single sentence, it is a perfectly adequate first paragraph. Remember the reader is busy and is only interested in the facts.

The second paragraph should immediately address that list of job requirements and your qualifications. You need not list the requirements. Simply note your qualifications and how they apply to the job: "I have had experience in direct sales, working door to door while in college. I have for the past year been employed with Procter and Gamble's telephone marketing department and have experience in management and with the public." End your description of qualifications with a note that directs the reader's attention to your résumé: "A complete résumé is enclosed."

Newspaper advertisements for jobs often request that a salary history be submitted with the cover letter. A "salary history" is a euphemistic phrase for salary requirement—"how much do you expect?" It is probably best, even if requested to do so, not to specify in a cover letter what you expect to be paid. If you ask for more than the established salary range, you may not be granted an interview. If you ask for less than the base pay, you may be given less. It happens. If the ad requests a salary history, include a sentence that reads "salary is negotiable."

Conclude the cover letter with a statement on references: "References will be furnished upon request." This tells the prospective employer that you have references. It also tells the reader that you know that references are not checked unless a candidate is being seriously considered for the job. However, do line up references. Before you go to an interview, make up a list that includes names, positions, addresses, and telephone numbers of references. Ask permission before listing anyone as a reference. It is both common courtesy and your assurance that the person will furnish you with a positive endorsement.

A sample cover letter follows. Note the form of the letter as well as the pattern in the second paragraph.

1492 Columbus Street
Newtown, Alabama 12344

March 8, 1984

Box 123 X
Montgomery Advertiser
Montgomery, Alabama 12345

Dear Sir or Madam:

I am writing in response to your Montgomery Advertiser
advertisement of March 7, describing a bookkeeper position for which
I should like to apply.

I have had three years experience as a bookkeeper. I am familiar with
the details of accounts payable/receivable, bank reconciliation, and
interest billings. My typing speed is 65 words per minute, and I have
taken a 20-hour course in word processing. A résumé is enclosed.

My salary requirements are negotiable.

Professional references will be furnished upon request. I would
welcome the opportunity for an interview at your convenience.

Sincerely yours,

George Tydings

Enclosure

Note in the second paragraph of the sample letter how the writer fulfilled the various requirements listed in the original newspaper ad. The ad obviously specified that typing and word processing skills were required. Although the writer had not personally worked with a word processor, he mentioned that he had taken a course on the subject. The letter ended with the writer's signature above his typed name. Signatures can be difficult to read. Remember to type as well as write your name.

Give It a Try

Find a job ad, which interests you, in the want-ad section of the newspaper and write a cover letter in answer to it. Remember to list the specified requirements and to list your qualification to those requirements.

Writing Business Letters

The writing of a business letter is, for many people, a daily routine and a daily challenge. Writing effectively is, of course, always a challenge, but the writing of an effective business letter is a responsibility as well. The writer represents, with every letter, both himself and his company. He is responsible to the company and to himself to communicate clearly—with precision and economy—and to communicate effectively—in a manner that leaves the reader with a favorable impression.

This responsibility must also be accomplished in as short a time as possible, another challenge. Business letters are a very expensive form of communication. The average business letter, written, typed, posted, and delivered in the U.S., costs $15. A telephone call, even at long-distance rates, is obviously cheaper. A telephone call, however, is usually less effective than a letter.

A well-written letter—one that is thought out and moves in a logical progression—is, in the business world, an invaluable form of communication. Even if written in a hurry, a business letter allows time for reflection, for thought. Telephone and face-to-face communication demand immediate response. There is no time to carefully compose an answer. The letter, however slow and expensive, does allow for consideration and for a carefully composed response.

Business Letter Format

A business letter is written in a rigid format that includes six parts: the heading, the inside address, the salutation, the body, the complimentary close, and the signature.

Heading. The heading consists of the name of the business, the address of the business, and city, state, and ZIP code. If you are not using stationery with a letterhead, arrange the heading in block form, and place it in the upper right-hand corner of the letter. Note that abbreviations are not used in the heading, except for the state abbreviation used with the ZIP code. If you are using letterhead stationery, the date should be placed two or three lines below the letterhead, flush with either the right-hand margin or the left-hand margin.

Inside Address. The inside address includes the recipient's name and title; the name of the office or department, if any; the name of the company or institution; and the street address, city, state, and ZIP code. Use the block form for the inside address. Place it flush with the left-hand margin, four lines below the heading.

Always include the proper title before a recipient's name. Examples include *Mr., Ms., Mrs., Dr.,* or *Professor.* If the recipient has a job title, place it after the person's name. Use a separate line if the job title is long.

> Dr. John W. Stanton
> Vice President of Sales
> Wilmington Corporation
> 4401 South Shore Drive
> Chicago, Illinois 60671

Salutation. The salutation, also called the greeting, is placed two lines below the inside address. Use a colon, rather than a comma, after the salutation in a business letter. Address the recipient using the appropriate title and last name—for example, *Dear Dr. Stanton.* If you are not writing to a specific person in a company, you may use *Dear Sir* or *Madam* or *Ladies and Gentlemen* as a salutation, since most companies have both male and female employees.

Body. The body, which contains the message of the letter, begins two lines below the salutation. A block style for the body of the letter is appropriate for a business letter.

Do not indent the first word of each paragraph, but leave extra space between paragraphs.

Complimentary close.   The complimentary close is placed two lines below the body of the letter. It can be aligned with the heading or with the left-hand margin. The following complimentary closes are appropriate for business letters:
Sincerely yours, Yours very sincerely, Respectfully yours, Yours truly, Yours very truly, and *Cordially yours.*

Signature.   The signature is written in ink below the complimentary close. The name is typed below the signature, about four lines below the complimentary close.

Enclosures.   If you are enclosing something in a letter, indicate this by placing the word *Enclosure* or *Enclosures* flush with the left-hand margin, two lines below your typed name. Examples of enclosures include checks, money orders, and copies of a bill.

Carbon Copies.   You may sometimes send a carbon copy or a photocopy of a letter to another person. Indicate this by writing cc:, which stands for carbon copy, followed by that person's name. Place this notation flush with the left-hand margin, two lines below your typed name. If an Enclosure notation was used, place the cc: notation two lines below it.

The First Step—Planning the Letter

A well-written letter, as mentioned earlier, is planned and moves in a logical progression. The second characteristic—the logical progression—is a direct result of the first—planning. If you plan your letter before you sit down to write it, your thoughts will progress logically through the letter. A good business letter is mapped out before pen is put to paper. Every business letter has a message, a point or points to be made; a good writer knows exactly what those points are before he or she begins.

Planning a letter is a mental process, which, like any kind of thinking, improves with practice. The first time around is difficult. The hundredth time around is easier and faster. It comes with experience. Begin by asking yourself the following questions and answering the questions on a piece of scratch paper:

- What is the purpose of the letter? What is the message?

A well-written business letter is planned before pen is put to paper. Multiple drafts are unnecessary if the writer asks himself a series of questions before beginning: Who is the audience? What points should be made? What tone should be used?

- Is there an additional purpose to the letter? Are there additional points, besides the main one, that need or can be covered in the letter?
- Will the reader benefit from the communication?
- Who is the audience? To whom are you writing? What do you know about your audience that will effect how the letter is worded?
- What approach should be taken as the letter is written? How should the letter be worded to best communicate the message and to best represent the company?

If, before beginning to write, you ask and, then, answer these questions, either on paper or in your mind, you will find that writing the actual letter is a fairly simple process. You know exactly what the message of the letter is to be, that is, you know exactly what point you are going to make; you know if there are auxiliary points to be made; you know to whom you are writing and how the letter should be worded to best communicate your points to that reader; and you know that a certain tone, which will leave the reader with a certain impression of you, the writer, and of your company, should be written into the letter.

If you habitually use this question and answer method of letter planning, you will find that it becomes second nature, automatic. Instead of making notes before beginning a letter, you will make mental notes, which will speed up the process considerably. You will, before long, be able to dictate business letters either directly to a typist or via a dictation machine. Dictating letters in this fashion expedites business correspondence. You can breeze through piles of correspondence in a fraction of the time it would take to either write out or type the letters. The question and answer method of planning ensures a thoughtful and logical letter whether written out by hand or dictated.

An example of a letter you might receive and need to answer is given below. As you read it, ask yourself how you would respond.

The Georgia Paper Company
412 North Graceland
Winchester, Georgia 12345
April 9, 1984

James Williams, Vice President
The Wellington Corporation
21 North Wellington Place
Wainwright, Michigan 54321

Dear Mr. Williams:

As you know, Georgia Paper has a contract to supply The Wellington Corporation with our #10 Packing Cases at the rate of 10,000 a month at a price of $.1200 per case. Due to increased labor costs and increases in the cost of our supplies, we are unable to maintain our unit price. Effective the first of May, 1984, the unit price of the #10 packing case will increase to $.1400.

However, we do find that if you increase your monthly purchase from 10,000 to 15,000 cases, we will be able to maintain the original figure of $.1200 per case. Is this feasible?

We are sure you understand our position. Holding costs steady for orders of relatively small number is becoming increasingly difficult.

If we can offer any additional information, please feel free to call us.

Sincerely,

Wilbert Lane

Wilbert Lane
Sales Manager

ET:cc

Mr. James Williams, Vice President of the Wellington Corporation, must now answer Mr. Lane's notification of an increase in prices. He begins by asking the usual series of questions, which he answers on a separate sheet of paper before actually beginning his letter.

■ What is my message to Mr. Lane?

To inform him that his increase in rates is unacceptable under the terms of the contract.

■ What other points need to be made in the letter?

1. That the contract between Wellington and Georgia Paper is legally in effect for another two months; 2. that Wellington Corporation expects Georgia Paper to deliver 10,000 packing cases per month at the agreed-upon price for another two months; 3. that Wellington is not interested in increasing its order to maintain the original price; 4. that when the contract expires, Wellington will renegotiate the price.

■ Who is the audience for the letter?

Mr. Wilbert Lane, sales manager for Georgia Paper Company.

■ Will the reader benefit from the communication?

It is important that Mr. Lane and the Georgia Paper Company know that Wellington expects the terms of the contract to be met.

■ What approach should be taken with Mr. Lane?

The letter should be written in a way that allows Mr. Lane to acknowledge the mistaken expiration date of the contract.

THE WELLINGTON CORPORATION
21 North Wellington Place
Wainwright, Michigan 54321

April 15, 1984

Mr. Wilbert Lane, Sales Manager
The Georgia Paper Company
412 Graceland Street
Winchester, Georgia 12345

Dear Wilbert:

I have received your letter of April 9 notifying us that the price of #10 Packing Cases will increase effective May 1, 1984.

Wilbert, you may want to check the original agreement we signed on June 1, 1983. I believe we still have two months before that contract expires. Our copy states that 10,000 #10 packing cases will be shipped per month at a unit price of $.1200 beginning June 15, 1983, and ending June 15, 1984. Can we assume we will receive two more monthly shipments at the agreed-upon price?

Wilbert, I'd love to help you out by taking an additional 5,000 cases per month, but I'm afraid, at least for the time being, we can't really use more than the contracted 10,000 cases per month.

Why don't you plan a trip up here in the next month or so. We can talk about a new contract.

Wilbert, it is always good to hear from you. I look forward to seeing you in the next few weeks.

With kindest regards,

James Williams
Vice President

Mr. Williams' letter, although friendly, is all business. The first sentence acknowledges Mr. Lane's letter and reviews the situation.

The second paragraph covers Williams' main point: he reviews the terms of the contract; he gently reminds Lane of those terms; and he informs Lane, with a rhetorical question, that The Wellington Corporation expects Georgia Paper to fulfill the terms of the contract.

The third paragraph covers an additional point that Williams wants to make: he is not interested in increasing his order from 10,000 to 15,000 cases per month.

The fourth paragraph subtly informs Mr. Lane that Mr. Williams may not accept the price increase after the old contract has expired. He asks that Lane meet him for negotiation.

The final paragraph is more than simple pleasantry. With the phrase "I look forward to seeing you," Williams informs Lane that he fully expects Mr. Lane to travel to Michigan to discuss the terms of a new contract.

Notice how Williams' letter covers, point-by-point, the various notes jotted down before the letter was written. Notice also the tone Williams uses throughout the letter. While making his point, he does not insult Lane or back him into the wall.

Planning Sheets

The question and answer method of planning a letter is not new or unusual. Companies throughout the country have for some time helped their employees write letters by providing planning sheets to guide them. The writer fills out the appropriate sheet and then bases his or her letter on it. A typical planning sheet is produced below. If you think this aid would be helpful, construct one of your own. Type up a master and photocopy a few dozen copies. Whenever you begin a letter, pull out a planning sheet and fill in the appropriate responses.

Letter Planning Sheet

1. What is the purpose of the letter?

2. What message needs to be conveyed?

3. What additional points can be made in the letter?

   _____

4. How will the reader benefit from the letter?

   _____

5. Who is the audience?

   _____

6. What approach should the letter take? Should the letter, for example, be appreciative, friendly, apologetic, humorous, urgent, positive, or negative?

   _____

   _____

Planning sheets, such as the example above, are helpful aids to planning and writing better business letters. They can be a first step toward developing writing skill. However, try eventually to employ the same process without the aid of the sheet. Once the question and answer formula becomes a mental habit, you will be able to attack your daily business correspondence with both skill and speed.

Types of Business Letters

An analysis of business correspondence indicates that most letters fall into three categories: response letters; follow-up letters; and original letters. Although the question and answer method of planning a letter functions well with all three of the types, there are differences between them. Let's look at how each type of business letter is unique.

Response Letters

Response letters are written in response to an original letter. Mr. Williams' letter to Mr. Lane was a response letter. It answered Lane's original letter announcing a change. Response letters are usually fairly simple to write. Read the original letter carefully. If questions are asked in the original letter, jot down answers in the margins. Make sure you understand the initial point of the letter. Check for additional points. Using the question and answer method, plan your response, employing the marginal notes to complete your answers. What is the tone of the original letter? What tone should you take in response?

The following letter of inquiry needs a response. As you read, notice the tone of the letter. Think about what tone can be applied in response that will best represent you, as the writer, and your company.

Gentlemen:

I've paid my electric bill regularly for years, and I've had no cause for complaint about your service, although I am dismayed, like everyone else, by the constantly rising price of electricity.

Now I find, however, that the cost to me of paying my bill goes up along with the unit price of electricity. When stamps went to 8 cents, you stopped enclosing a postage-paid envelope to use when paying. Now you have stopped enclosing the envelope itself. What is behind all this pushing of the cost of payment onto the customer? Your profits are guaranteed, yet you continue to nickel and dime us to death. Why?

Sincerely yours,

Angelina Smith

Angelina Smith

This customer of the electric company is unhappy about having to furnish her own envelope when paying her bill. However, the underlying cause of her unhappiness *may* be the continuingly higher price she pays for electricity. Let's use the question and answer method to plan the response.

- What is the purpose of your response to Ms. Smith's letter?

To inform her that enclosed envelopes, although a small thing, contribute to the escalating price of electricity.

■ What other points need or can be covered in this response?

That envelopes are, in themselves, cheap, but the labor to enclose an envelope within each bill is not cheap.

■ Will the reader benefit from the communication?

Ms. Smith will understand that, in the long run, it is cheaper for her to supply her own envelope than it is to receive one with her bill.

■ Who is the audience?

An irate customer, who, basically, is tired of constant increases in her electric bill.

■ What approach should be taken to best represent the company?

The letter should be understanding and patient.

The response letter to Ms. Smith's letter of complaint follows.

Dear Ms. Smith:

We agree that the cost of an envelope is a small thing, and we understand that you wonder why we are no longer able to supply return envelopes to our customers.

We mail over 3 million bills monthly. As the price of postage kept going up, we were forced to eliminate stamped envelopes in order to reduce our costs. The price of an envelope, of course, is not nearly so great— about one-half cent each. But the labor to stuff a return envelope into the billing envelope costs approximately five cents per bill. This figure was computed before recent increases in labor costs. Our total cost for monthly mailing of bills now comes to $165,000, which is nearly $2 million a year. Our rates reflect our operating costs, as well as other expenses. Reducing our outlay for mailing is only one aspect of our effort to avoid having to seek further rate increases.

We appreciate your taking the time to write to us, Ms. Smith, and we share your concern with rising living costs. If we can be of further service to you, please feel free to call upon us.

Sincerely yours,

The response to Ms. Smith's letter of complaint was patient, understanding, and informative. The electric company has discontinued sending envelopes to save itself and its customers money.

A more serious kind of letter of complaint follows. A mistake in billing has been made, and the customer asks that the mistake be corrected.

Gentlemen:

My account number with your store is 112–890–44. I have found mistakes on my account for three months running. In December you charged me for an item I did not buy. Last month you failed to credit my payment for the previous month's bill. This month, I was not credited for merchandise I returned to the store.

Enclosed are photocopies of documents related to my complaint. If you examine these against your own records, you will, I think, find that your bookkeepers are in error. I hope that these errors can be rectified as soon as possible. I have been a customer of the Block Department Store for thirty years and have never before encountered this kind of problem.

Sincerely yours,

Sylvia Revson

Sylvia Revson

After checking Ms. Revson's photocopies against store records, the manager of the billing department has found that the store has been in error.

■ What is the purpose of the response letter?

To apologize and to assure Ms. Revson that her account has been corrected.

■ What additional point can be made?

To explain that the billing department is being reorganized and to assure her that no further mistakes will be made.

■ Will Ms. Revson benefit from the letter?

Ms. Revson will be informed that her account is now correct.

■ Who is the audience?

A once loyal customer, who is now irate over her account.

■ What approach should be taken to improve relations with Ms. Revson?

Apologize and assure the customer that her account is now correct.

Dear Ms. Revson:

I have examined the documents enclosed with your letter of February 4 and have found that we are in error. I certainly apologize for the inconvenience this has caused you. Let me assure you that your account is now correct. A new bill is in the mail to document the correction.

Our only defense for this error is a reorganization within our accounting and billing department. Computers are wonderful, but getting the bugs out in the beginning can be trying. We handle approximately 100,000 charge customers each month. Although errors have been few, they have occurred. Your account, unfortunately, happened to be one of those few.

I have personally put your account in order, double checking a computer readout to ensure that the correct information has been entered. I am sure that you will not find further errors on your monthly statement. However, if you should have any further questions, please call upon me personally.

We value your continuing patronage and good will.

With kindest regards,

George W. Simpson

George W. Simpson

Give It a Try

The following letters of inquiry need responses. Read both letters and choose one to answer. How you answer the letter is unimportant. Invent responses to the questions. The form you use, however, is important. Check back over business letter formats. Make out a planning sheet and ask yourself the questions listed on page 165. Jot down the answers before beginning the response letter. As you read the following letters, think about the writer's tone. Remember your letter of response should include a tone that best represents you, the writer, and your company.

Gentlemen:

Your ad in Sunday's <u>Times</u> featuring dresses for tall women attracted me. I am 6'2". Try as I might, I could not find a store that handles your brand. So I have two questions. (1) Can you furnish me with the names and addresses of your outlets? (2) Can you send me to a catalog so I might see the variety of dresses you offer?

Sincerely yours,

Dear Mr. Thomas:

We spoke, as you may remember, last Thursday regarding the galley proofs for my book, The Cannibals of South America. As I told you over the telephone, I am leaving for Caracas to do research on the first of September. I must have those galley proofs before I leave the country.

You mentioned by phone that the manuscript has been with the typesetter for only two weeks and that it usually takes approximately six weeks to set the type on a book of this size. Can't anything be done to expedite this business?

I cannot emphasize strongly enough the importance of maintaining my current schedule. I should, instead of writing to you, be correcting the galleys. In four more weeks I will be out of the country and hardly in a position to correct proofs and mail them back to you.

I am sure you understand my position. What can be done to speed things up?

Sincerely,

Phil Measure

Phil Measure

Follow-up Letters

Follow-up letters are usually letters of inquiry or letters of complaint: "Last month I ordered the following items. . . Where are they?" or "Upon receiving your invoice #3307, I find that we have been charged for items we did not receive."

How Is an Effective Follow-up Letter Written?   As with any kind of business letter, you begin with the usual questions and answers. What is the purpose of this letter? However, a follow-up letter is somewhat different from a response letter in format. A follow-up letter asks that the reader either respond with information or respond with a solution to a problem. In either case, the letter must correctly state what information is needed or describe the problem in need of solution.

Research. Before beginning a planning sheet for a follow-up letter, research is usually necessary. The writer must fully understand what information is needed or what the nature of the problem is. So begin by checking the facts: review previous correspondence; compare invoices. If the letter requests information, first make a complete list of what information is needed. If the letter asks that a problem be solved, begin by describing the sequence of events that led to the problem.

Planning. Next make out the planning sheet. Ask yourself the usual series of questions (*see* page 165), answering them either mentally or on paper. While making out your list of answers, think carefully about the tone of the letter. A follow-up letter that asks for information is asking the reader for a favor. The tone should be courteous. A follow-up letter that asks the reader to correct a problem should be written in a tone that reflects the problem. If the problem is serious, the tone of the letter should be serious. If the problem is fairly unimportant, the tone should not be heavy handed. Avoid sarcasm or threats. Threats are usually empty, and sarcasm rarely achieves the desired end. The person to whom you are writing is probably not personally responsible for the problem. He or she may, however, be your only means to a solution. Avoid alienating the reader. It will accomplish little.

Writing the Follow-up Letter. An effective follow-up letter begins with a description of the problem.

> Dear Mr. Powell:
>
> While your salesman, Mr. Levin, did an excellent job giving us instructions on how to use our new word processing system, we have noticed that there are various aspects about the machine that we, as yet, do not understand.

It proceeds with a request for a possible solution.

> Could Mr. Levin either return for another training session or could we send a representative to your offices for individual instruction, which could be passed on?

Then proceed with any other points that can be made.

> We have also noticed that Mr. Levin did not leave
> an instruction booklet. If one is available, could a
> booklet be sent?

The structure of a follow-up letter is, thus, fairly simple. The problem is described at the beginning of the letter and various solutions put forward.

A letter requesting information is arranged in the same format: description of information needed and a request that the information be forwarded.

> Dear Mrs. Simpson:
>
> The personnel department at Worldwide Electronics
> is preparing a list of local doctors who participate
> in the Green Card Insurance Plan.
>
> We understand from our company physician that
> your office has a list of the doctors currently
> practicing in the city as well as their affiliations
> with various insurance programs. Is it possible to
> receive a copy of this list? We would, of course, pay
> for photocopying charges.
>
> Thank you for your cooperation in this matter.

The complexity of a follow-up letter, of course, depends upon the complexity of the problem and suggested solutions. The following letter was written by Mr. James, the purchasing agent for the Lemington Corporation. Some months before this letter was written, Mr. James purchased ten new typewriters from Mr. Hennings of the Standish Supply Company. They were to be delivered November 1, 1983. In anticipation of receiving the typewriters, Lemington Corp. hired ten clerk-typists to begin work on November 1. When the new machines were not delivered, Lemington was forced to rent temporary machines. Lemington Corp. expects Standish Supply to pay the rental charges on the temporary machines. Mr. Hennings, however, has just informed Mr. James that Standish Supply does not believe it should be responsible for paying these charges. Mr. James writes to Mr. Standish, president of the supply company, for a solution to his problem.

He begins by reviewing his file on the purchase of the typewriters. He then makes a list, in chronological order, of what has and has not happened in the matter of the missing typewriters.

- Oct. 12 Signed contract to buy 10 electric Wulitzer typewriters Model #3307B at $1,860.12 each. Deposited half of purchase price— $9,300.00—with Standish. Contract specified delivery date of November 1, 1983.
- Oct. 15 Personnel dept. hired ten clerk-typists to begin work Nov. 1, 1983.
- Nov. 1 Typewriters did not arrive. Clerk-typists did.
- Nov. 3 Spoke to Hennings. He suggests that we rent typewriters on a temporary basis. Standish will pay for them.
- Nov. 4 Rented typewriters at monthly rate of $105.50. Hennings OK's costs. Says "not to worry."
- Dec. 1 Typewriters have not yet arrived. Hennings says they are "en route."
- Jan. 4 Typewriters still "en route." Hennings says: "It is no longer company policy to pick up rental charges in this kind of situation."

Mr. James next makes out a planning sheet, jotting down answers as he goes.

- What is the purpose of the letter to Mr. Standish?

To ask if the shipment of typewriters can be speeded up.

- Are there additional points that can be made in the letter?

To ask the supply company to bear the responsibility for the rent on the temporary machines, as Hennings originally agreed.

- Will the reader benefit by the letter? (It is usual for the writer of a follow-up letter to benefit from the message.)

■ Who is the audience for the letter?

The president of the supply company.

■ What approach should be taken in the letter?

It should be noted that the delivery date is long past deadline. It should be noted that Lemington Corp. has, for a number of years, been an excellent customer of the supply company.

The LEMINGTON CORPORATION
100 East Hale Street
Winston, Wisconsin 54321

January 4, 1984

Mr. Miles Standish, President
The Standish Supply Company
33 North Main Street
Winston, Wisconsin 54321

Dear Mr. Standish:

The Lemington Corporation signed a contract with the Standish Supply Company on October 12, 1983, for ten electric Wulitzer typewriters, model #3307B. The delivery date, as specified in the contract, was November 1, 1983. The price per machine was $1,860.12. Lemington deposited one-half of the purchase price of each machine—$9,300.00 in total—with Standish Supply on October 12 of last year.

We have yet to receive the typewriters.

I have repeatedly questioned your salesman, Robert Hennings, about the delivery of the typewriters. I have, for the past two months, been assured weekly that the machines are on their way, are "en route."

In anticipation of November 1 delivery of the typewriters, Lemington Corporation hired ten new clerk-typists. Because the machines were not delivered, we then rented typewriters at a monthly rate of $105.50 per machine. Our total expenditure, for the two months since November 1, for rented equipment has now totaled $2,100.00.

Before renting the temporary typewriters, I informed Mr. Hennings that Lemington felt that the rental fees should be assumed by Standish Supply Company. Mr. Hennings agreed: "Yes, Standish will pay for renting temporary typewriters." This morning I presented Mr. Hennings with the invoices for the rental charges and he stated: "It is no longer company policy to pick up rental charges in this kind of situation."

Mr. Standish, the Lemington Corporation is hardly pleased with your company's inability to deliver the typewriters as promised and with the decision to reverse the policy on assuming rental charges when goods are not delivered on time. Lemington has been a customer of Standish Supply for 30 years. We have, until this incident, always been pleased with your service and manner of doing business. We are, however, most unhappy over this situation.

If Mr. Hennings was unable to supply us with machines on the specified date, he should have informed us of this problem before signing the contract. We would have readjusted our schedule.

If it is not your policy to supply temporary machines in this kind of situation, we should have been told of your policy from the beginning.

I suggest, Mr. Standish, that you and I meet before the end of the week to see if these differences can be ironed out. If there is any chance that we can receive the "missing" typewriters within the next week or two, we would prefer not to purchase the machines from another supply company. There is, of course, also the matter of the $9,300.00 deposit as well as the rent on the temporary machines. May I expect your call?

Sincerely,

Clark James

Mr. James's letter to Mr. Standish lists, in chronological order, the series of events that has led to the need for the current letter. The writer's research was, thus, put to good use. The letter covers all points listed on the planning sheet: Can delivery on the typewriters be speeded up? Will Standish assume the rental charges?

The tone of Mr. James's letter is forceful, but neither sarcastic nor threatening. After dealing with the salesman, Mr Hennings, James knows that if anything is to be done it will be through Mr. Standish. Alienating him with sarcasm or threats would be counterproductive.

Collection Letters.   Collection letters, letters that follow up on unpaid bills, are written after following the same procedure used for any other follow-up type of letter: research the problem and make out a planning sheet. The usual format is also employed within the body of the letter. Begin by describing the problem.

> Dear Mr. Smith:
>
> Our records indicate that your account of $98.76 is now overdue by four months. You received notification from us on September 1, October 1, November 3, and December 2. As we have received no response from you in regard to this bill, we must assume you do not intend to honor this debt.

Complete the letter of collection by describing a solution to the problem.

> We feel that we have no choice but to turn the matter over to our collection attorneys. We will, however, withhold action for five more days. We can offer you no further extension. If we do not hear from you within five days, we must proceed with collection by other means.
>
> Sincerely yours,

Give It a Try
Study the following descriptions of business situations that require follow-up letters. Choose one and write an ap-

propriate letter. Remember to write a brief chronology of the situation before beginning the letter. Also make out a list of answers to the usual questions (*see* page 165) as you plan the letter.

> You are the business manager of a law firm. Two legal secretaries are out on vacation for two weeks. To keep up with the work load, you have contracted with a secretarial service to supply help on a temporary basis. On Monday, August 15, two secretaries arrive at the agreed time and place. However, neither returns on Tuesday the 16th. On Wednesday, Thursday, and Friday only one secretary arrives for work. The week after, no one shows up from the service. You telephone the service daily, complaining of the situation. On September 3, an invoice arrives from the service, billing the law firm for the labor of two secretaries, working daily for two weeks.

> You are responsible for billing in a dentist's office. Mr. Wellington, an occasional patient, charged his last three visits with the dentist. Each visit costs $25.00. A bill was sent after each visit. Monthly bills were submitted, thereafter, for five months. Mr. Wellington has made no payment toward the $75.00 debt. A collection letter must be sent to Mr. Wellington.

Original Letters

Original letters are concerned with "new business": the ordering of goods, the announcement of new policy, the opening of a new store or outlet, or the sale of new merchandise or services. While original letters are not concerned with a problem, they are, like all kinds of business correspondence, carefully planned. An original letter, to be effective, must trigger a response—to fulfill an order, to comprehend a change in policy, to buy an item or use a new service. This kind of communication, while often a form letter, is written in a conversational style and with a personal tone. The writer tries to anticipate the reader's response and his or her questions.

Writing Order Letters

The purpose of an order letter is to request a shipment of goods. You should include the following information:

- An exact description of the goods—name, size, color, style, model number, series
- The catalog number, if there is one
- The quantity you want
- The price
- The address to which the goods are to be shipped
- How you want the order shipped—express, freight, parcel post
- The method of payment—company account, C.O.D., check, credit card, or money order.

An order letter should be brief, to the point, and courteous.

WILLIAMS & WILLIAMS
346 Oak Street
Minneapolis, MN
55106

April 22, 1984

Hollander Supply Company
1124 Hampton Road
Minneapolis, MN 55106

Dear Mr. Hollander:

Please send the following items to the above address:

1 gross of #2½ pencils, @ $15.00	$15.00
1 gross of #3 soft pencils, @ $18.00	18.00
1 gross of Favor felt-tip pens, @ $88.00	88.00
	$121.00

Please charge this order to our regular business account, #33701X, and deliver. If you have questions, contact me at 314–7790.

Sincerely,

Jane Paxton

Jane Paxton

Writing Sales Letters

A successful sales letter contains four elements:

- A beginning paragraph, designed to attract reader attention
- A statement that shows the advantages of buying your goods or services
- The development of further benefits, which offer proof to the original claim that buying the goods or services is an advantage
- A request that the reader place the order

The most important element is the first, a beginning paragraph that attracts the reader's attention. Great volumes of sales letters are mailed daily. The competition for reader attention is keen. If a sales letter is effective, it must attract the recipient's attention before the letter is thrown away.

A variety of opening paragraphs can be used with a sales letter.

- Startle the reader with a fact, a question, a statement, or an offer.

  Fact: Intensive care in a hospital can cost you $1,000 a day!

  Question: Do you know what one day in an intensive care unit in a hospital can cost?

  Statement: You can be free of financial worry should you need intensive care in a hospital.

  Offer: Here is your chance to shed financial worries should you need intensive care in a hospital.

- Tell the reader that he or she is "special."

  "You have an excellent credit rating."

  "Ideas stimulate you."

  "Your success in business has been outstanding!"

  "You are one of those people who insist upon quality."

- Offer a "free" gift.

  "Here is your free copy of . . ."

  "Simply mail the enclosed card for your free copy of . . ."

  "You've won a prize!"

- Ask a favor of the reader.

  "We know you are busy, but may we have a moment of your time?"

  "Please think about this for just one minute."

  "We would like to help you. . . May we?"

  "We want to do you a favor."

- Ask the reader a question.

  "What do you give the person who has everything?"
  "Would you like to make a million dollars without investing a cent?"
  "Do you really have enough insurance?"

- Suggest a negative thought.

  "Don't be dismayed. Everyone fails socially now and then."
  "Don't place your children's education at risk."
  "You are young, single, and healthy, so why do you need life insurance?"

An example of an effective sales letter follows. Note the first paragraph. It is designed to immediately catch the attention of the reader.

Dear Homeowner:

Who thinks about furnaces in the summertime?

The All-American Heating Company does, and we would like to get you into the habit as well. If your furnace acts up at the first drop in temperature, you will be sorry you did not give some thought to it during warm weather.

Furnaces are built to last. But for the most efficient and economical operation—and this means something when it comes to paying mid-winter heating bills—it pays to give a furnace a regular off-season check-up. Pipes and pressure gauges, combustion control and switch, thermostat and gas or oil line all need periodic checks. Parts showing excessive wear should be replaced.

Servicing at this time of year, when we are not busy with emergency calls, is cheaper and more efficient. It also means that you can enjoy peace of mind, knowing that your furnace will turn on and operate smoothly as cold weather sets in. It will save you the trouble of making an emergency call. It will also save you money.

Don't put it off. You may be sorry if you do. Like the ant in the fable, get ready now for winter's storms. Call us today—588–3100—and make an appointment. We will send a qualified mechanic at your convenience.

Sincerely yours,

The beginning of the letter attracts attention. Who *does* think about furnaces in the summer? The reader next learns why it is important to think about furnaces in the summer: it will assure one of a warm house on that first cold day. This, of course, is the advantage to the reader if he or she follows the letter's advice.

Further benefits are developed in subsequent paragraphs: economy of operation; cheaper service calls in the summer; avoiding a high-priced and inconvenient emergency service call during the busy season; first-rate mechanics; and peace of mind.

The letter closes by returning to the original advantage and asks for the sale.

Give It a Try
Write an original sales letter using the four elements listed on page 185. The letter may either deal with a product or a service. Remember to plan your letter before beginning to write. Make out a planning sheet. Pay particular attention to the first paragraph. A good sales letter must attract reader attention from the first sentence.

The Last Step—Checking Your Letter
Every business letter should be checked, reviewed for errors, before it is signed. As you check over a letter, keep the following point in mind.

- Is the letter concise? Do you get to the point with as few words as possible?
- Are all your points clear? Will the reader understand what you are trying to say?
- Does the letter progress in a logical fashion? Does each paragraph build upon information supplied in the previous paragraph?
- Is the letter grammatically correct?

- Are all words spelled correctly?
- Is the letter neatly typed?
- Does the letter positively represent the company for which you work?
- Will the reader benefit from the information you have supplied?

Writing Office Memorandums

Memorandums, or memos, are short communications, often a single page, circulated within a company or institution. They are usually informal and serve a single function—to inform. If the typical office memo is an indication, this single function, to inform, may be more difficult than it sounds.

Many memos suffer from trite phrases, cluttered sentences, and vocabulary known as "businessese." Consider the following example.

> Commensurate with overall plans to upgrade sales personnel and provide more viable opportunities for advancement, it is suggested that a revision of the existing compensatory plan be effectuated with a view toward tangible recognition of personal and individual performance. This is the thrust of the presentation which follows.

Now what does it mean? Where is the information, which is, after all, the sole function of a memo. The information is there. It's simply buried under a mound of muddled phrases and pompous vocabulary. A translation follows.

> If you want to boost sales and encourage advancement, pay salespeople commissions and bonuses as well as salaries. And here is why.

Now why did the author of the memo use 48 incomprehensible words instead of 24 understandable words? It is a good question without a good answer. Memo writers often think that big words are more impressive than small ones. They fill paragraphs with "upgrade," "viable," "effectuated," and "tangible recognitions commensurate with. . ." No one, of course, understands. Their memos are failures. They fail to inform.

Guidelines

Effective memos are written within the same guidelines as all effective writing.

Know What You Are Going to Say.   Before sitting at a typewriter, make a list of the points you intend to make. As you write, stick to those points.

Be Concise.   A memo is a short, informal piece of writing. Be concise. Say exactly what you mean in as few words as possible.

Choose Vocabulary Carefully.   If you want your memo to be understood, use words that the reader will understand. Avoid ten-dollar words when small ones function as well.

Be Precise.   Write exactly what you mean. Write it the way you would say it. Use conversational vocabulary and sentences. If you are trying to say, "Advance planning is the key to a well-managed office," write it that way; do not write, "A fundamental component of efficacious office management is a well-conceived plan for organization."

Stick to the Point.   A memo covers one subject. Stick to that subject. If you have two subjects you wish to cover, write two memos.

Develop Paragraphs in a Logical Progression.   Begin at the beginning and proceed to the end. A memo is the wrong place to get fancy. If there is a cause, list it first. If there are effects, list them in order, but after the cause.

Use Lists.   Memos are intended to convey information quickly and effectively. A list helps accomplish this end. If you can break the information down into a numbered list, do so. The reader will better understand and assimilate your points.

Review Your Writing.   After completing the memo, read it over. Check for grammar, punctuation, spelling, precision, and concise writing. If necessary, rewrite the memo. It is your job, as a writer, to make sure that you are understood.

An example of a typical office memorandum follows.

MEMORANDUM

To: Phyllis Bates

From: James Medfly

Subject: Office supplies

I came into the office on Saturday to catch up on some paperwork and found I was out of typing paper. I went to the supply closet and found the shelf empty. After searching through a few desks, I found some paper.

Midway through my work, the typewriter ribbon gave out. Again, I went to the supply closet and again the supply of ribbons was exhausted. (I did, however, find ribbons for typewriters that have not been used by this company for perhaps fifteen years.) Lacking a typewriter ribbon, I gave up.

It is my understanding that you are responsible for keeping the supply closet stocked. Let's keep it well stocked. It is a waste of company time and money for employees to spend time searching for such essentials as typing paper and ribbon.

If we are having delivery problems from the office supply company, let's change office suppliers.

Give It a Try

List the businessese words and phrases in the following sentences. Then rewrite the sentences into plain English.

- The basis for our rationale for recommending that we institute a company newsletter is that it will effectively stimulate a greater feeling of camaraderie among employees.
- It is imperative that before inventorying the department files, we implement a form in which can be entered the description, locale, and utilization of each record.
- Many of our offices report having experienced difficulty in hiring packers because the compensation level for this category of employee is relatively low

and the tasks required are not commensurate with the development of a positive self-image.

- Thinking maximally profitwise, I'm of the opinion that the company should computerize its records now instead of at some date in the future and I recommend that the decision to do so be definitized now.

Give It a Try

Write memorandums on each of the following subjects. Use plain English. Try to keep each memo under 50 words.

- You decide to call a meeting of sales managers. It will be held on January 18, 1985, in the conference room at 3:30 P.M. You want the managers to bring copies of their 1984 sales reports. The current sales training program will be evaluated in the light of the sales figures. The possibility of a new training program will be discussed.
- The parking lot will be closed Tuesday for resurfacing. This will inconvenience a large number of employees. Alternate parking space is not available.
- Your boss wants to know why your recent expense account shows an average daily expenditure of $55 when company policy clearly allows only $30 a day for meals. Your expense account covers 10 days in New York.
- The deadline on the project that the five people you supervise have been working on has been moved up by one week. You must ask them to work overtime, although company policy forbids overtime payments.
- Your boss asks you what you plan to do about the fact that three out of the ten people you supervise have been consistently late for work during the last month.

Writing Reports

A business report, like a memorandum, has a single function: *to present information in an orderly, objective manner.* A good report is based upon fact, not opinion. Opinion does, however, play an important role in many business reports. After the facts are presented, the writer of a report may explain or interpret that factual information. He or she may, even, analyze that information. But the information, the facts, are presented first and presented in an objective, orderly format.

There are two kinds of business reports: informal and formal. They differ, obviously, in their formality of structure. Formal reports are put together in a prescribed format, which includes an introduction, abstract, body, conclusions, recommendations, and appendix. Informal reports are arranged like lengthy memos, but include headings. The purpose of a report also determines the report's formality. Formal reports summarize major projects and the results of research investigations. Informal reports summarize the parts of such projects. A progress report is obviously an informal report as it summarizes how a major project is progressing.

Informal Reports

Most of the reports you will write as part of your job responsibilities are informal. Sales, status, progress, monthly, budget, and production reports are the usual range of informal report writing. Organizations often even have printed forms that are filled in to complete an informal report. While handy, printed forms do not teach very much about writing an effective informal report. Let's start from the beginning.

Content of an Informal Report

Base the content of your report on facts. Even an informal report is written after the researching of facts. The sources you use may vary according to the subject. You might gather information from personal observation, conversation, library research, correspondence, or from an experiment. Then decide which facts to emphasize and which to omit.

Develop a Central Idea. A good report centers on one specific problem or idea. All facts, results, conclusions, and recommendations must relate to this central idea or problem. Do not introduce irrelevant material into your report.

Develop a Logical Arrangement. The ideas around which a report are written should be arranged in a clear, orderly fashion. There are many different arrangements that you can use—chronological, spatial, simple to complex, or cause and effect.

Plan and Develop an Outline.   After deciding upon what arrangement is appropriate for your report, develop an outline. The outline will tell you where you are going, how the parts of the report fit together, and indicate gaps in your data. The outline may consist of only two main heads with subheads under each, or the outline may involve a detailed analysis of the final paper. But, however complete the outline, it is impossible to write a coherent, logical, and effective report without one.

You may use a topic outline, which consists of brief phrases.

    I. Factors in recommending Skylight Hotel
       A. Central location in city

Or, you may use a sentence outline, in which your headings and subheadings appear as complete sentences.

    I. The recommendation of the Skylight Hotel is based upon three factors.
       A. It has a central location within the city.

The type of outline you choose is unimportant. But develop an outline if you want the report to be logically arranged and consistent. After completing the outline, ask yourself the following questions.

- Does the outline reflect a single, clear purpose?
- Does the outline contain the report's essentials?
- Does the outline completely cover the subject?
- Is the outline clear? As you read it over, does it make sense? Does it progress logically?
- Is each heading sufficiently developed? Have you gone into enough detail?
- Do the headings reflect the emphasis you have chosen for the various sections?
- Are there at least two subordinate headings under each superior heading?

If your answers are positive to each of the above questions, you are ready to begin writing. If you have trouble with your outline, you may wish to reread pages 120–121 on preparing a complete outline.

Writing an Informal Report

Use your outline. It is the foundation upon which the report will be written. It will also supply you with headings. The headings in a report are rather like lead sentences. They introduce the next topic of discussion and are road markers for the reader, as well as for the writer as he or she works.

Headings.   Headings are usually numbered or lettered to identify their sequential place in the development of the narrative. We will use letters to show the breakdown. An "A" heading is centered and typed in capital letters. It is used to introduce a major subject, the equivalent of a Roman numeral (I., II., III.) in the outline.

SHIPS OF THE LINE

A "B" heading is subordinate to an "A" head and is also centered, but set in capital and lower case letters. A "B" head is equivalent to a capital B on the outline.

The Pacific Fleet

A "C" heading is subordinate to a "B" and is equivalent to an Arabic number on the outline. It is typed in capital and lower case letters and placed against the left margin.

Aircraft Carriers

A "D" heading is subordinate to a "C" head and is equivalent to a lower case letter on the outline. "D" headings are typed in capital and lower case letters and run in to the first sentence of the paragraph. A "D" heading is punctuated with either a period or a colon.

The Bridge on an Aircraft Carrier.

Audience.   As you write the report, consider the audience and their expectations. Do not assume that the reader has as much background in the subject as you have. You are the expert; you have done the research. Write the report so that the readers can share, understand, and use the information you have gathered.

Find out to whom the report will be sent—your immediate supervisor, the president of the company, all managers, the stockholders, or the plant's supervisors. When you know who your readers will be, you can choose appropriate language and reading level for the report. In general, the vocabulary should be kept simple. Sentences should be relatively short. The length of most paragraphs should be less than 200 words. You are writing to communicate information, not to impress the reader with your vocabulary or grasp of the language.

Vocabulary.   Do not use technical jargon when it is not necessary. Avoid "businessese" language. If you cannot explain in simple and clear language how a system or method works, *you* may not understand how it works.

Voice.   Write the report in the active voice, with concrete nouns and specific examples.

Final Check.   Proofread the report and ask an objective person to read and criticize it before you submit it. After you are satisfied that the report is as good as it can be, have it typed in the format customary within your organization.

An example of an informal report follows. Notice the headings and structure.

Date: January 3, 1985
To: Mary Overhold, President
From: George Summers
Subject: RECOMMENDATION FOR SITE OF 1985 NATIONAL
            MEETING

Recommendation of the Skylight Hotel

My research into a site for our annual meeting in August leads me to recommend the Skylight Hotel. This decision is based upon these factors:

1. The Skylight has a central location, which is an important consideration for the people attending the meeting and for their spouses.
2. There is no significant difference in accommodations between the Skylight and Hopewell.
3. The Skylight offers rooms costing 30 percent less than the Hopewell, although the charge at the Skylight for providing conference rooms is a total of $250 higher than at the Hopewell.

From the standpoint of cost and location, the Skylight is the better choice.

Origin of Assignment and Procedure

You asked me to look into both hotels at our meeting on December 21. I visited both and gathered data on the basis of three criteria I believe most important in deciding on a site. Location is first; accommodation adequacy is second; cost is third. Findings and evaluations based upon these criteria follow.

Central Location. The central business district surrounds the Skylight. This makes it convenient to shopping and entertainment for those attending the meeting. The Hopewell is located six blocks from the business area. This location makes it less desirable as a meeting site, although there are ground-level shops that could fulfill all essential needs of those attending the meeting.

Accommodations. Both hotels will hold available the 450 rooms we require. Room sizes at the Skylight are slightly smaller than at the Hopewell, but they are more modern.

We need nine rooms for small-group meetings and a ballroom for general meetings and the final-day banquet. Both hotels provide appropriate public spaces. The general meeting space at the Skylight appears smaller than that at the Hopewell, although the manager has assured me that it will hold all who will attend. On the accommodations criterion, the sites are equal.

The Cost Factor. The cost of the meeting rooms at the Skylight is $250.00 higher than at the Hopewell. Both hotels offer complimentary accommodations for the company president and secretary.

Rooms at the Skylight range from $40 to $50 a day for singles and $45 to $55 a day for doubles. At the Hopewell rooms rent for $55 to $65 for singles, $60 to $70 a day for doubles. The difference in cost is approximately 30 percent. The banquet dinner will cost $12.50 per person at the Hopewell and $12.75 per person at the Skylight. Considering other factors favoring the Skylight, these differences are insignificant.

Mr. Summers's report was written to satisfy the company president's request for a study and recommendation on a possible location for the annual national meeting. The president asked for a recommendation. The report, therefore, begins with Mr. Summers's opinion on the best site. Does this break the rule that facts should be presented first? No. The purpose of the report was to recommend. He wasted no time fulfilling the purpose.

The recommendation is immediately followed by a list of criteria that he used to make his decision. The criteria are backed with facts.

Mr. Summers has, thus, offered his recommendation and given all of the facts upon which it is based. He supplied Ms. Overhold, the company president, with enough information to make a decision. As she asked for Mr. Summers's advice, she will probably follow it.

Notice that Mr. Summers used only "B," "C," and "D" headings. Because the report was short and informal, he lowered the range of headings to prevent them from overpowering the actual writing. This is perfectly legitimate. He maintained a logical progression of ideas; each heading reflected the importance of information that followed.

Give It a Try

Reconstruct Mr. Summers's outline based upon the finished report. Remember that the writer dropped the size of headings as he wrote the report.

A Formal Report

A long, formal report follows an established format, consisting of eight parts:

- Covering letter
- Title page
- Table of contents
- Abstract
- Body of the report, including introduction and conclusions
- Appendix or appendices
- Bibliography
- Index

Many companies have their own established structure for formal business reports. Some structures place the conclusions or recommendations before the body of the report; others put the abstract before the introduction. There are, however, specific kinds of information that make up each part of a long, formal report.

Covering Letter

The covering letter formally presents the report to the person or group requesting it. The letter relates the report's authorization to the report's purpose. An example follows.

July 28, 1985

Mr. Tomás Sánchez, President
THE APPEX CORPORATION
Pinola, New Mexico 54321

Dear Mr. Sanchez:

I hereby present the report on four makes of cars, which you requested that I analyze as a preliminary step to purchasing a fleet of automobiles for the company's sales force.

Data has been gathered from reports by consumer research engineers and from other written sources, from auto agencies, and from the experience of fleet managers in other companies.

I trust that my analysis will help you to make a decision. Should you need assistance interpreting the data, please call on me.

Sincerely yours,

Juan Hernandez

Juan Hernandez

Title Page

The title page contains the report's title; the person or group to whom it is submitted; the name of the person who prepared the report; and the date of submission. An example follows.

FINDINGS AND RECOMMENDATIONS
CONCERNING THE PURCHASE OF AUTOMOBILES FOR
THE APEX CORPORATION SALES PERSONNEL

Based Upon
A Comparison of Four Types of Automobiles

Prepared for
Tomás Sánchez,
President, The Apex Corporation

Prepared by
Juan Hernandez,
Comptroller, The Apex Corporation

July 28, 1985

Table of Contents

The table of contents lists the page numbers on which the various sections of the report are found. The contents should list "A" and, perhaps, "B" and "C" headings from the body of the report. The sections, if any, that appear before the contents page are not listed. An example follows:

The table of contents continues, supplying page numbers for various headings from the body of the text as well as for the conclusions, appendices, bibliography, and index.

Notice that the preliminary pages of the report, that is, the pages preliminary to the actual text, are numbered with Roman, rather than Arabic, numbers. Arabic numeration begins with the actual text—the body of the report.

The Abstract

An abstract summarizes the report. It gives, within the first sentence or two, the report's conclusions and recommendations. It then relates the origin of the report, the basis on which the problem or question was investigated, and finally provides the reader with a brief description of the evidence that supports the conclusions and recommendations. An example follows:

It is our recommendation that the Ford Coupe is the best buy for the Apex Corporation as the basis for a fleet of cars for the sales force.

The study was authorized in a memorandum, dated May 1, 1985, by Mr. Tomás Sánchez, President of Apex Corporation.

The recommendation is submitted July 28, 1985, to aid in the selection of the most suitable type of car. Factors in this analysis include cost, safety, and performance of four makes of cars—the Ford Coupe, the Studebaker Avante, the Packard Clipper, and the DeSoto X15.

The difference in ownership costs between the four vehicles is insignificant, considering the initial outlay per car, minus trade-in value at the end of two years. Significant differences appear in operating costs, however. A summary of all costs involved shows the Ford Coupe to be the least costly at $150,000.00 for 60 cars. The Packard Clipper is the most expensive, at a cost of $175,000.00. Ford Coupe also ranks first in safety consideration as well as in riding comfort.

The Body of the Report

The body of the report takes the reader, step-by-step, through the details of the investigation: how the problem was attacked; how the research was carried out; what information was gathered; how the information was analyzed; and how the analyzed information was used to reach a conclusion.

The exact purpose of a formal report should be kept in mind as the report is planned, outlined, and written. While a recommendation may be requested, the actual decision regarding a course of action is the responsibility of the person or group that authorized the study. That person or group will reach a decision that is based upon the findings of the author of the report. The decision may, or may not, reflect the author's recommendations, but it will most certainly reflect the information, the facts, presented in the report. The writer, in effect, takes his or her audience on the same journey he or she took in the process of writing the report. If the report's reader or readers are to make a valid decision, they must fully understand the problem; they must know how the research behind the report was carried out; they must be presented with an objective survey of the writer's findings, that is, the facts; they must understand how the facts were analyzed before the writer reached his or her recommendations. If the facts are presented objectively and completely and if the writer's analysis is logical, the reader's decision will coincide with the author's recommendations. The report will, therefore, be successful.

The body of the report, thus, must include the following information:

- A description of the problem
- Who authorized the study
- The date the study was authorized
- How the research was carried out
- The findings of the research, that is, all of the information gathered during the study
- The criteria used to analyze the information
- A comparison of data based upon the criteria given
- The writer's recommendations based upon the analysis of information

The most important item on this list is the presentation of the facts gathered during the investigation. It will be the largest single section of the report. It *must* be presented *objectively* and *thoroughly* if the reader is to make an informed and effective decision.

Understanding one's audience is an important ingredient for
a successful business report. The effective writer does not
assume knowledge or background that readers may lack. He
or she supplies sufficient information for the audience to
make informed, logical decisions.

Structure of the Body.   The structure of the body of the report is based upon the outline (*see* pages 120–121 on preparing an outline). All effective writing is based upon a plan, and writing of any complexity is based upon a formal outline. It will provide you with both structure and headings for the text (*see* page 194 on headings). The outline for a formal report should be fairly complete. Time and work put into the outline will pay off as the actual text is written.

Appendices

The writer of a report may wish to include additional information related, but not essential, to the data given in the body of the report. This might include similar reports, statistical data, tables, charts, or graphs. Information of this type is included in an appendix, which follows the conclusions at the end of the body of the text.

Data are usually given in an appendix without introduction or explanation. It is referred to in the body of the text and cross-referenced—(for further information *see U.S. Statistical Reports, 1968, 1969, and 1970.* Appendix A).

The Bibliography

If the writer uses another writer's work, either published or unpublished, in the writing of the text, the source should be acknowledged with a notation in the text and a listing in a bibliography. The use of another writer's work may involve either direct quotation or paraphrase of original ideas or thought.

A bibliography is placed between the end of the text and an index. If an appendix is included, the bibliography follows the appendix. (*See* pages 123–124 in Chapter 4, "Writing for School," on how to prepare a bibliography.)

Steps in Preparing a Report

Now that you know something about the format and content of a formal report, let's look at the steps involved in the actual writing.

Know the Purpose.   Know the problem with which your report will deal. Find out what has already been suggested or done to attempt to solve the problem. Why are you writing this report?

Although a request for a formal report might define purpose, this is not always the case. You may be asked to turn in a complete analysis of the company's advertising activities for the past six months. That seems clear—but is it? All activities? Or only certain activities? Do not take the assignment and run until you have found out exactly what is wanted. If you do not nail down the purpose, you may have to go back and ask. If you go into the project blind, you may turn in a report that no one really wanted.

Know Your Audience.   A requested report springs from someone's desire or need to know something. This seems obvious, yet it is surprising how often a report writer will go about gathering data and putting them together without giving sufficient thought to the person or group for whom the report is intended. Such a report will read as though it were addressed "To Whom It May Concern." The report might not be entirely worthless, but a report without audience focus falls short of achieving its purpose. Audience will determine:

- The formality of the wording you use. Usually when you report to a subordinate or to an equal, you adopt an informal tone and language. When you report to an immediate supervisor, the same may hold true. But certainly when a report is intended for higher levels of management, formal writing and language are more the rule than the exception.
- The use of charts and graphs. In some cases your audience may want only a "quick picture." You may then present much of your data in chart or graph form, with a minimum of written language.
- The facts you emphasize. Your reader may be more interested in what a piece of new machinery costs than in how it might simplify an operator's work. In this situation you would emphasize increased productivity in relation to the cost of the machine and the possibility of increased profits.
- The inclusion of background information. How familiar is the reader with the subject or the problem? Is his or her knowledge extensive or sketchy? Perhaps high officers in your company lack detailed knowledge of individual operations. If your report deals with these operations, more background information would need to be included.
- Whether you use everyday English, technical language, or jargon peculiar to your business. If your audience is familiar with personnel terms, you might write in "personnel" vocabulary. If they are en-

gineers, you might write in "engineering" vocabulary. The company's annual report, on the other
hand, is read by a variety of people. If you were writing or contributing to that report, you would use
plain, everyday English. Audience and purpose define how a report is written.

Set Boundaries.   When you define the purpose of your report, you are not only setting a course for your investigation, but establishing boundaries as well. This is imperative. You must know the limits in which you are working.

A good report is confined to one major subject. Stick to
it. If you are comparing word processors, do not question
whether the company needs word processors. If you are
dealing with the subject of furnishing cars to sales people,
do not edge into a discussion of brands of cars. Set boundaries and keep within them.

Research the Project.   After you know the problem you
are dealing with and what the boundaries of that problem
are, begin gathering the facts. Use company files, correspondence, the library, personal interviews, experiments,
and tests.

As you research the problem, keep records of your findings. Use index cards for a record of sources. Photocopy
material, writing relevant information about the source on
the margins. If your company has computer facilities, use
them.

Prepare an Outline.   Make an outline that organizes your
facts into logical groups of ideas. Review the section on
outlines, pages 120–121, in Chapter 4, "Writing for
School."

Dealing with Figures.   It is a rare report that does not
contain figures of some kind. Hourly wages, price quotations, units of cost of production, and similar matters
usually call for precision. When you deal with such items
as sales figures, you might round off to the nearest 50 or
100. You might do the same with earnings from sales, as
well as with percentages.

As a rule it is best to use figures sparingly. Keep them to
a minimum in the narrative itself; a string of sentences
containing figures taxes the reader's comprehension and
patience. Place figures in tables and refer to the tables in
the text. You may, for example, show sales figures from
each of your company's six regions in a table. An example
follows.

SALES BY REGION

Region	Sales	Percentage of Total
1	10,000	20
2	8,000	15
3	7,000	14
4	9,000	18
5	6,000	12
6	11,000	21
Totals	51,000	100

Note that the percentages have been rounded off. You can assume sales figures have also been rounded.

Figures may also be presented in graphs. The data listed above could be presented in a circle graph, also called a pie graph. The wedges represent percentages. The number of sales is placed in each wedge.

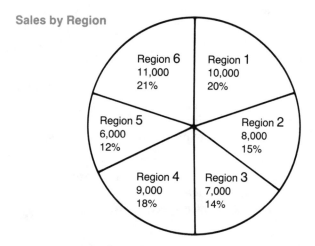

Bar graphs are particularly useful for comparisons. Assume the previously listed sales figures represent 1984; you want to compare 1983 with 1984 figures. Sales for 1983, by region, were:

1	8,000
2	8,000
3	9,000
4	7,000
5	4,000
6	13,000

A bar graph comparing the data could be constructed either vertically or horizontally. The following example is in vertical form:

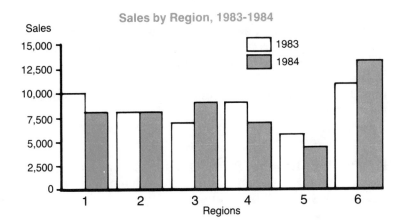

Sales by Region, 1983-1984

You might use a line graph to show total sales or a single region's sales over a five-year period. Let's take total sales as an example:

1984	51,000	1981	38,000
1983	49,000	1980	55,000
1982	32,000		

A line graph illustrating this data is pictured below.

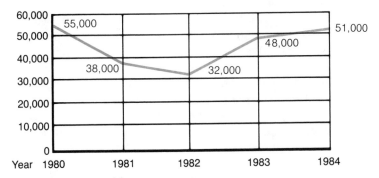

Total Sales

Two or even three items can be compared on a line graph by using solid lines, dots, and dashes to distinguish each.

Writing the Report.   Use the outline! An outline is like a Christmas tree. As you write, you simply decorate it with words, sentences, and paragraphs. Without an outline, paragraphs, like decorations randomly scattered across the floor, end up disordered, confusing the reader.

As you write, remember the fundamentals. Eliminate unnecessary words. Use familiar words, unless technical language is appropriate. Use short, direct sentences. Use the active voice. The passive voice is dull.

Carry the logic and order of your outline into your writing. Give paragraphs unity and connect them with smooth transitions.

The purpose of a report is to inform. Do it economically and effectively. Review Chapter 2 on effective writing.

Proofread the Report. Before submitting the report, check it carefully. Review the structure, logic, and analysis. Review the spelling, grammar, and punctuation. Ask an objective person to read and critique your writing.

An Exercise in Writing Formal Reports

Your company, the EmEx Corporation, employs about 5,000 people. The administrative committee has become concerned with the problem of effective management-employee communication with respect to decisions affecting employees, policy and procedural changes, and communication about company aims, growth, and progress. Issuing occasional announcements and bulletins, as when the company was smaller, no longer seems an effective way to communicate. With rapid company and branch expansion, communication lines have lengthened. Perhaps a regular company publication of some kind is the answer.

In a memo to you on June 9, John Dawkins, chairman of the administrative committee, outlines the communication problem and asks you to investigate the publication question and report with recommendations and supporting data. The purpose of your report seems clear, and there is no question about the audience.

Where will you get the information you need? It occurs to you that there probably are books and articles on the subject. Other company publications and the people who produce them will also be sources of information. Printing companies can furnish data on production costs. You might also get an idea of how EmEx people feel about a company publication by talking with some.

You then set about pulling the pieces together and making decisions on what to include and what to leave out of your report. The results of your research are listed below, in no particular order of importance.

1. Except for publications large corporations circulate regularly among the public, company periodicals are printed in one color.

2. You decide to call the publication a newspaper. *House organ* carries public relations connotations. *Magazine* suggests slick paper and perhaps color illustrations. *Newsletter* seems too weak, casual, and management oriented.

3. In 1970, 40 percent of companies with fewer than 1,000 employees had newspapers. The figure for those with from 1,000 to 5,000 was 80 percent, and for those with more than 5,000 employees, 89 percent. In 1980, the percentages were, respectively, 47, 86, and 92.

4. Employees prefer that their papers resemble in design and format similar publications they read frequently. Pleasing appearance seems to count with them.

5. At present, there are approximately 6,700 company papers with a total readership of around 190 million people, published at a total cost of $375 million.

6. Employees also seem to favor articles written in a personal, simple, and conversational style.

7. Editors of company papers agree that the publications should not be vehicles for company directives or indoctrination or propaganda. One editor told you: "We learned the hard way that an employee newspaper cannot be the voice of management and have any real impact on employees."

8. They further agree that writing, design, and graphics are directly related to reader interest and should not be left to amateurs or volunteers.

9. You decide that the administrative committee does not want a cost-effective study, which in this case would be difficult to develop.

10. Among company papers, 80 percent appear monthly, 17 percent biweekly, and 3 percent on a weekly basis.

11. Conversation with 27 EmEx supervisors, managers, and lower-echelon people in both the home and branch offices indicated favorable attitudes toward establishing a company newspaper.

12. A successful company publication requires a full-time staff of reporters, editors, photographers, designers, and production people. Some of these tasks can be combined—reporter/photographer, for example. The usual staff includes from three to six people, depending on the paper's size.

13. You decide that details on a paper's shape, size, length, and so on are not needed at this point. Those

items would be addressed after a decision to publish has been made.

14. Readers of company papers like to see such personal items as news of promotions, births, and marriages, and appropriate photographs. They also like news about company athletic teams and social groups. And they like opportunities to voice opinions in print.

15. There seems general agreement that the presence of a company paper has a favorable influence on employee morale and productivity; that it affords an effective means of employer-employee communication; that it promotes a feeling of belonging among employees; and that it enhances outside as well as inside public relations.

16. A company paper should be based on readers' interests, which can be determined through a study of employees on the basis of education, ethnic background, sex, position in the company, and so on.

17. The annual cost of an eight-page paper would come to approximately $100,000. This figure includes a three-person, full-time staff, production/printing, distribution, and general overhead costs. Assuming a run of 5,000 copies, the cost breaks down to $2 a copy.

18. Most company papers are the responsibility of the public relations department; this department is most accustomed to producing printed material.

19. You talked with four editors of company papers and examined issues of 17 different company papers from various parts of the country representing several types of businesses. You have the samples on file.

20. You read five books and eight articles on company publications in general and on employee publications especially. You can furnish a bibliography.

21. You think that if a paper is to be established, the company should first hire an editor. The editor should be authorized to hire two staff members to decide on the paper's size and format following consultation with printers in the area.

22. You conclude that management should appoint a publications committee representing divisions of the company to assist the editor with respect to content, style, and so forth.

Give It a Try

Use this information to perform the following tasks:
- Make an outline for a report. All the data listed is pertinent, but arrange it in logical order.

- Write headings and subheadings for the report.
- Write an abstract.
- Indicate what information you will show in tables and graphs.
- Write conclusions and recommend actions.
- Make a table of contents.
- Write a covering letter for the report.

Writing Proposals

Proposals are similar to sales letters. They seek to persuade the reader to a particular course of action. A proposal, however, never relies on emotional appeals. It deals with facts in a restrained and formal manner. A proposal is, essentially, a plan designed to solve a problem.

Government agencies often advertise their needs and solicit proposals from companies to fulfill those needs. Examples include the Department of Defense dealing with various parts of a weapon system or the Department of Agriculture concerned with the development of a new grain seed. A company may wish to change its accounting procedure and asks accounting firms to submit proposals for studying the question. An executive within a company might propose a study of accidents in a factory, seeking ways to prevent them. Or any company employee might have an idea he or she thinks would benefit the company and proposes that the idea be studied or tested.

In some companies—for example, those dealing frequently with government agencies—proposal writing is vital to the business. This is also true of consulting firms and companies dealing with research and development. Such proposal writing demands fully as much skill as writing sales letters, often considerably more time, and usually a great deal of technical knowledge. The many companies that develop persuasive proposals have stimulated the establishment of new firms that specialize in the professional writing of proposals.

A proposal, like a report, is addressed to some person or group, is accompanied by a covering letter, and usually begins with a statement of the problem. If the justification of need for the study is not readily apparent with the presentation of the problem, a separate section, "justification of need," follows the introduction.

The proposal might then relate the aspects of the problem that have been studied and discuss various sources of published material. The problem, of course, may never before have been under study or may be peculiar to a particular organization. In that case there will be no literature to survey.

With these elements out of the way, the proposal continues with the "sales pitch," which states advantages. Benefits are listed next. Benefits conclude with an additional statement listing the writer's qualifications to carry out the proposal.

> Our company has established a sound reputation for conducting cost analysis studies. We have pioneered in developing and testing numerous procedures that have enabled companies to increase efficiency and reduce costs. All that experience will be brought to bear to implement this proposal.

The procedure the writer plans to follow is described next. The readers of the proposal will pay particular attention to this section. The description of procedure should be specific on methods, tests to be performed, and equipment to be used.

An estimate of costs follows the description of procedures. This section is listed under "Requirements" and concludes the proposal. Requirements include personnel, equipment, time needed, and a list of expenditures necessary for each item. Cost breakdowns should then be totaled.

Writing Want Ads

The writing and placing of help wanted ads is, in large companies, performed by the personnel department. However, in smaller companies, individual department heads are usually responsible for writing and placing newspaper notices advertising for help.

Want ads listing employment opportunities are found in magazines and newspapers. Sunday editions often carry page after page of job opportunities. Ads may be column-wide or display-size. Display ads run two or more columns in width and are usually deeper than column-width ads. They are also surrounded by a border.

Many of the help wanted ads you find in newspapers are blind ads. That is, they do not list the name of a company,

Wanted: A Secretary, Should be able to write, type, process, staple, duplicate, cover for, coddle, and charm while leaping tall buildings in a single bound. Equal opportunity employer; however, multiple-appended, Hindu goddesses favorably considered. Send résumé. . . .

but instead direct that résumés and applications be addressed to a box number in care of the newspaper. The paper gathers the letters that come in and forwards them to the advertiser.

Firms advertising job openings rely on blind ads for two reasons: they may be replacing people; and/or they do not want to be bothered with the phone calls that result from listing an organization's name in the paper.

Want ads are paid for by the line. A column-wide ad appearing one time only might cost $10 a line. A discount is given if the ad appears on three or seven consecutive days. Display ads cost a little more per line, and there often is a minimum number of lines; sometimes 100.

Space is limited, information needs to be compacted. It is possible, however, to be too brief:

> **DRAFTSMAN 2–3 years residential experience. Near north office. Send résumé to: ABC 901 Pinola Gazette, Pinola Ark 34619**

This ad tells what is wanted, minimum experience required, and it gives a general idea of location. But it tells too little. It says nothing about the duties of the job nor about salary. The ad might attract applicants who are out of work; but it would probably not appeal to anyone with a job who might wish to change.

> **GOVERNMENT JOBS $16,559- $50,553/year. Now Hiring. Your Area. Write EFG 20, Randy Gazette, Randy, Mont 78645**

This ad does not mention what kinds of jobs. Although salary is mentioned, the range is so great as to give no clues as to how much experience or what skills a person needs to fit anywhere within it.

The following ad is well-written, contains a great deal of information, and will attract qualified candidates.

DRAFTSPERSON

Leading electrical manufacturer, located on the north side of Salt Lake City, seeks an experienced individual. Will be responsible for detailed mechanical component and assembly drawings of electrical boxes and fittings along with drawing changes and bill of materials entry. Knowledge of sand castings, die castings, stamping and screw machine processes necessary. Some layout drafting and lab testing will be required.

Good starting salary and liberal benefits package. For immediate consideration, please submit résumé to:

Dept. 00
P.O. Box 129
Salt Lake City, Utah
equal opportunity employer m/f

Display ads can run across an entire newspaper page
and run a page in depth. Two- and three-column displays,
at varying depths, are the most common. An example of a
two-column display ad follows.

---

word processing

OFFICE
INFORMATION
SYSTEMS
ADMINISTRATORS

Prominent health care association seeking experienced
Wang Office Information Systems (OIS–140) Administrators. Duties involve OIS software; telecommunications; on-
line/off-line information storage and retrieval; hardware
maintenance and systems documentation.

Positions demand flexible personality and good written and
oral skills to enable effective interaction with approximately
100 users including managerial, professional and support
staffs. Two years OIS administration experience required;
two years college preferred.

We offer a salary in the mid- to high teens and generous
benefits. Please send résumé to:

OWX 698, Courier-Express 69801
Affirmative Action/Equal
Opportunity Employer M/F/H

This ad indicates the kind of company seeking applicants. It describes the job in some detail, adding details

concerning working conditions and skills needed. It spells out the experience required and education preferred. The ad is specific regarding salary range.

An effective help wanted ad, whether column-wide or display, contains the following information:

- Name of position
- Kind of company
- General location
- Job description or duties
- Skills, experience, and education required
- Salary range and benefits offered
- Travel requirements, if any
- Address for résumé and letter of application

Most of the examples given have been blind ads. If company policy permits, you are free to write open ads, giving the name of the company, address, and phone number, and the person or department to address a résumé. Many companies run this kind of ad, although the blind ad remains common, especially in larger cities.

Give It a Try

Read and criticize the following ads. Edit and rewrite until you are satisfied that the ad lists sufficient information, but remains compact enough to fit within typical newspaper space requirements.

WAREHOUSE MANAGER
We are a leading home health care equipment supplier. We seek an individual with minimum 5 years exrience in dispatching, inventory control, driver and warehouse supervision. Excellent starting salary with benefits. Send résumé to XCB Pineridge Bugle, Pineridge, NC 47651

Sales/Marketing
Leading N.V.O. seeking sales marketing person for new branch office opening in Tulsa area. Send résumé to GHI 112, Tulsa Northwestern 92806

am th

nt for my

eautiful drapea

my sofa, and the color is

all the time an

*P*ersonal Correspondence

In this age of inexpensive communication, when one can even telephone a friend in Europe for just a few dollars, does anyone still correspond? *Yes.* Although fewer personal letters per capita are written today than a hundred years ago, tremendous volumes of personal correspondence still are written and posted daily. For one thing, personal correspondence covers more than the personal letter. Whenever you reply to a wedding invitation, you are corresponding. A thank-you note for a Christmas gift is correspondence. A letter to an appliance company complaining about your washing machine is personal business correspondence. Letters to the editor or a letter to your precinct committeeman, asking that the alley be cleaned, is personal correspondence. Even filling out your IRS income tax form can be considered a type of personal correspondence. So we all correspond fairly regularly, even if we *never* write a letter, that is, a personal letter.

Many people, of course, do still write personal letters, which is the first category of correspondence covered in this chapter.

Personal Letters

Like writing short stories or painting, writing letters can be a unique form of self-expression. When you telephone a relative or even speak to a friend face-to-face, you express yourself in one way. A letter, however, is a very different medium. It allows time for thought. It allows time for positioning words in a sequence designed to trigger a specific kind of response. A telephone call is spontaneous; a letter is reflective.

People often say that they are too busy to write personal letters. This is, in most cases, simply an excuse. Extremely busy people, for example, Thomas Jefferson, Benjamin Franklin, and Robert Louis Stevenson, kept up extraordinary correspondences, which have since been published and used as the basis for biographies and histories. The Adams family—John Adams, Abigail Adams, John Quincy Adams, and Henry Adams—were all great letter writers and diarists. Their voluminous records of the first 150 years of this country's history give us a vivid picture of the founding of the nation, the writing of the Constitution, the Civil War era, and the early years of the twentieth century.

Your letters may not help write the history of the present era, but they will help you sit back and assess your life and the times in which you live. Give it a try. You may be missing a very interesting opportunity every time you dial long distance.

Writing personal letters need not be a complicated or time-consuming process. With practice, it can become almost as easy and natural as talking to someone in person. As with most forms of writing, the personal letter is made up of various parts. Let's begin with these.

Parts of a Personal Letter

A personal letter has five parts: the heading, the salutation, the body, the complimentary close, and the signature. Refer to the sample letter on page 222 as each of these parts is discussed.

Heading.   The heading, which is placed in the upper right-hand corner of the letter, consists of your street address; your city, state, and *ZIP* code; and the date. You may wish to omit your address in letters to people with whom you correspond frequently. Use either the block form shown in the sample letter on page 222 or the indented form shown on the following page.

1105 Birch Avenue
Kokomo, IN 47905
July 25, 1984

Do not use abbreviations in the heading except for the state abbreviation used with the *ZIP* code. Remember that there is no period after the state abbreviation.

Salutation.   The salutation, or greeting, is placed about four lines below the heading, at the left-hand margin of the letter. It usually begins with *Dear* and is always followed by a comma.

Dear Janet, *or*
Dear Father, *or*
Dear Mrs. Lawson,

Body.   The body, which contains the message of the letter, is placed two lines below the salutation. In the sample letter on page 222, the paragraphs in the body are aligned with the left-hand margin of the letter. Note that extra space is left between paragraphs. You may also indent the first line of each paragraph in a personal letter. If you do so, do not leave extra space between paragraphs.

Complimentary Close.   The complimentary close is placed two lines below the body and is aligned with the heading. It is always followed by a comma.

Your friend, *or*
Sincerely, *or*
Love,

Signature.   The signature may be aligned with the first letter of the complimentary close, as in the sample letter on page 222. It also may be aligned with the last letter of the complimentary close, or it may be centered below it.

Your friend,

Sid

or   Sincerely,

Paul

or   Love,

Jane

Include your return address on the envelope, either in the upper left-hand corner or on the back flap. Center the address of the person to whom the letter is written slightly below the middle of the envelope. Note that the sample envelope on page 223 uses the block style that was used in the heading of the sample letter below. If you use the indented style in the heading of a letter, use that style on the envelope as well.

Friendly letters such as the ones discussed in this section may be either typed or handwritten. Although many people consider handwritten letters more personal, feel free to type your letters, especially if your handwriting is difficult to read.

Personal Letter Format

1105 Birch Avenue
Kokomo, IN   47905
July 25, 1984

Dear Leslie,

I received your letter last week. I am glad to hear that you are feeling better and are back at work.

Dave and I plan to visit my parents in Chicago over the Labor Day weekend. Will you and Phil be in town? If so, perhaps we can get together for dinner and a movie.

Please write soon and let us know your plans for that weekend. We would enjoy seeing both of you again.

Sincerely yours,
Kathleen

Envelope for a Personal Letter

K. Mooney
1105 Birch Avenue
Kokomo, IN   47905

Ms. Leslie Ames
9816 Landis Street
Chicago, IL   60643

Content of Personal Letters

The *content* of a personal letter consists of the topic or
topics discussed in the body of the letter. When planning
the content of a personal letter, consider both the purpose
and the audience.

Purpose

People write personal letters for a variety of purposes.
These include sharing news about personal experiences or
plans, inquiring about a person's health or an important
event in his or her life, and sharing information about individual or family activities and achievements. The main
purpose of the personal letter on page 222 is, for example,
to share information about plans for the Labor Day weekend and to try to arrange a meeting between the two couples.

Specific kinds of personal letters are referred to as *social
correspondence.* These include invitations and replies; announcements; thank-you notes; and letters of congratulations, condolence, and apology. Social correspondence is
discussed on pages 227-245 of this chapter.

Audience

Once you have decided on the purpose or purposes of your
letter, you must consider the audience—the person or persons to whom you are writing. Your personal letters will
not be effective if you write only to please yourself. Always
keep the audience's feelings and interests in mind as you
plan your letter.

Suppose you are writing to a friend who loves jazz music, but is bored by politics. This person obviously would
enjoy reading about a jazz festival you attended. Thus, you

would focus on that topic and probably not mention the political debate you recently watched on television.

Considering your audience also means not allowing your personal letters to become too self-centered. You should show interest in the other person's feelings, concerns, and activities. Ask yourself these questions as you plan your letter: What noteworthy events have occurred recently in this person's life? Has this person or someone in the family been ill? If we were to meet face to face, what would we talk about? Asking these questions will help you avoid writing letters that focus only on you and your concerns.

Tone

The tone of a personal letter depends to a large extent on its purpose. For example, a serious and concerned tone

---

June 1, 1984

Dear Aunt Betty and Uncle Tom,

I wanted to let you know that I was graduated from Central High School last week. The graduation ceremony was quite nice. Mother, Dad, and Grandma Phillips all attended and seemed quite proud of me.

As I mentioned in my last letter, I had some trouble in chemistry class this year. Fortunately, I was able to improve my performance and earned a final grade of C for the course.

Mother and Dad tell me that Joyce may be valedictorian of her graduating class. You must be very proud of her.

I'm looking forward to seeing all of you at the lake this summer. I'm sure we will have a wonderful time, as usual.

Love,
Susan

would be appropriate in a letter inquiring about a friend's health. A light or humorous tone might be used when describing a series of minor mishaps around the house. When writing a letter of condolence, a sympathetic tone would be used (*see* pages 241-243).

The audience also influences the tone of a letter. You might use a light or joking tone when writing to a close friend or relative your own age. However, such a tone would be inappropriate in a letter to an older friend or relative. Always consider the person's age, background, and relationship to you when deciding on an appropriate tone for your letter.

Note the differences in tone and emphasis in the letters listed below. Both were written by the same person; one was written to an aunt and uncle; the other to a cousin.

June 1, 1984

Dear Joyce,

Believe it or not, I made it. I am now officially a high school graduate. Hooray!

As I told you in my last letter, I didn't think I would make it through chemistry class. Things looked really grim at midterm. So I buried my head in my chemistry text practically every night and just hoped for the best. You will be surprised to hear that my final grade for the course was a <u>C</u>.

Mother and Dad tell me that you may be class valedictorian. What an honor that would be! I'll certainly keep my fingers crossed for you.

When I see you at the lake in a few weeks, you'll have to give me some tips on good study habits. You obviously know a lot more about the subject than I do.

Love,
Susan

Organization

Personal letters, like any other type of writing, should be clearly written and well organized. Each paragraph should deal with a single topic. Be sure to give enough details about each topic so that the reader understands what you are describing.

Group all your ideas about a topic in one paragraph or group of paragraphs. Keep in mind that jumping from one topic to another can confuse and annoy the reader. If possible, include transitions between paragraphs. Remember that transitions will make your letter easier to read.

Before writing the letter, you might list the main points you want to cover. Next, group related details under each main point. Finally, decide what order to use in presenting these points. Refer to Chapter 2, "Writing Clearly," for further help in organizing and writing your letter.

Things to Avoid

Personal letters are one of the least restrictive forms of writing. You use your own judgment to determine the purpose, audience, tone, and organization of a personal letter. Although few hard and fast rules apply to writing personal letters, there are certain things you should avoid.

Avoid careless and thoughtless remarks or remarks that may be misunderstood. These can be quickly amended in conversation, but not in a posted letter. What you may have intended as a joke may be misinterpreted by your reader. Think before you write; always reread your letter before mailing it.

You may feel like writing a letter when you are under emotional stress. If you are feeling hurt, angry, resentful, fearful, or envious, you may want to vent your emotions in a letter. This is perfectly acceptable. *However, do not mail the letter.* A few hours later, or the next day, you will be happy you waited. People who send such letters usually feel foolish and regretful after they have calmed down.

People generally do not like to be around those who never have anything positive to say. Similarly, people do not enjoy receiving letters that are gloomy, pessimistic, and full of complaints. Try to include something positive in every letter you write. Be sure to show an interest in the other person's activities and concerns. It is fine to seek the advice and comfort of friends in personal letters. But avoid writing letters that do nothing more than pour out your troubles or recite a list of complaints.

Avoid using stilted and highly formal language in personal letters. Write in a way that is natural and sincere. Use correct English and choose words that express your ideas clearly. Always avoid using a fancy word when a simpler word will do. Remember, the purpose of the letter is to communicate with your reader, not to impress him or her with the size of your vocabulary.

Social Correspondence

Social correspondence consists of invitations and replies; announcements; thank-you notes; and letters of congratulation, condolence, and apology.

Formal Invitations

Written invitations to events such as weddings, anniversary celebrations, parties, and dinners may be either formal or informal. Formal invitations follow a rigid format and should always be engraved, printed, or handwritten (never typed). An example of a formal invitation for a wedding and reception follows.

Formal Wedding Invitation

> Mr. and Mrs. John Dawkins
> request the honor of your presence
> at the marriage of their daughter
> Pamela Jane
> to
> Theodore Gray
> on Saturday, the fifteenth of September
> nineteen hundred and eighty-four
> at four o'clock in the afternoon
> Calvary Baptist Church
> Golden, Colorado
>
> and afterward at
> The Regency Hotel
> R.S.V.P.

Note that the invitation contains the following information: the names of the people extending the invitation; the type of occasion; the date, time, and place of the event; and a request to respond. (*R.S.V.P.* stands for the French phrase *Répondez s'il vous plaît,* which means "please respond.") All formal invitations should include this information.

An example of a formal dinner invitation follows. Notice the similarity in wording between the two types of formal invitations. A formal invitation for dinner is also either engraved, printed, or written by hand.

Formal Dinner Invitation

> *Mrs. Dorothy Reece*
> *requests the pleasure of your company*
> *at dinner*
> *on Tuesday, the fifth of May*
> *at seven o'clock*
> *295 Sunset*
> *Mount Pleasant, Michigan*
>
>
> *R.S.V.P.*

Replies to Formal Invitations

Formal invitations require formal replies. A formal reply includes your name(s), whether or not you accept the invitation, the name or names of those who extended the invitation, and the occasion and date. The form is dictated by the form used for the invitation.

Formal Reply (Acceptance)

> Mr. James Young
> accepts with pleasure
> the kind invitation of Mrs. Dorothy Reece
> to dinner
> on Tuesday, the fifth of May

Formal Reply (Regrets)

> Mr. James Young
> regrets
> that he will be unable to accept
> Mrs. Dorothy Reece's
> kind invitation to dinner
> for Tuesday, the fifth of May

Informal Invitations

Informal invitations are sent for events such as luncheons, dinners, parties, and overnight and weekend visits. Such invitations are handwritten and follow the same format as personal letters (*see* pages 222–223).

An informal invitation should include the same information as a formal invitation: the occasion, date, time, and place. There is, however, no set form when presenting this information. An example of an informal invitation follows.

Informal Invitation

> 955 Mountain Road
> Hot Springs, AR 71913
> May 15, 1984
>
> Dear Phil,
>
> As you may know, my brother Bob will be graduated from medical school on Friday, June 1. I am giving a party in his honor at 8:00 o'clock that evening at my apartment. Will you be able to attend?
>
> Bob mentioned that he would enjoy seeing you again. I hope that you will be able to join the celebration.
>
> Sincerely,
> Mike

Replies to Informal Invitations

You should reply promptly to an informal invitation. Although your reply does not have to follow a set form, you should always express your appreciation for the invitation. If you cannot accept the invitation, you may wish to explain why. Sample informal responses follow. One accepts the invitation on page 230; the other declines it. Note that both replies follow the format for a personal letter (*see* pages 222–223).

Informal Reply (Acceptance)

356 Main Street
Little Rock, AR 72212
May 18, 1984

Dear Mike,

The graduation party for Bob on June 1 sounds like fun. I look forward to seeing both of you again—it's been a long time.

Thanks so much for thinking of me. I'll see you on the first.

Sincerely,
Phil

Informal Reply (Regrets)

356 Main Street
Little Rock, AR 72212
May 18, 1984

Dear Mike,

Thanks for the invitation to Bob's graduation party on June 1. I'm sorry that I will be unable to attend. My company's annual dinner dance is being held that evening.

Please give my congratulations to Bob, and tell him that I'll be in touch with him soon. I hope the three of us can get together sometime over the summer.

Sincerely,
Phil

Formal Announcements

Announcements are sometimes sent to inform family and friends about weddings, births, graduations, and adoptions. Like invitations, announcements may be either formal or informal.

Formal announcements should be engraved, printed, or handwritten. They usually follow a specific format, as in the following examples.

Formal Wedding Announcement

Mr. and Mrs. Paul Levine
have the honor of announcing
the marriage of their daughter
Barbara Louise
to
Mr. Howard Goldfarb
on Sunday, the nineteenth of August
nineteen hundred and eighty-four
Atlanta, Georgia

Formal Adoption Announcement

Martin and Carol Goodson
joyfully announce
the adoption of
Elizabeth Anne
born January 25, 1984

Informal Announcements

Informal announcements, like informal invitations, are handwritten and follow the format used in a personal letter (*see* pages 222–223). An example of an informal birth announcement follows.

Informal Birth Announcement

116 Berry Avenue
Defiance, OH 43512
June 20, 1984

Dear Aunt June and Uncle Henry,

Patrick Joseph arrived early on the morning of June 5. He is a happy baby with a healthy set of lungs, as we discovered as soon as he came home from the hospital.

Felicia keeps asking when you are coming to see her new little brother. We all hope you can visit us soon.

Love,
Jean and Bill

Thank-you Notes

The writing of thank-you notes causes a good deal of consternation, especially for young people. Why are thank-you notes so hard to write? When should one be sent? How soon "after" should a note be sent? What can be said after "thank you for the . . ."?

Thank-you notes are not really hard to write if you keep a few rules-of-thumb in mind. Four occasions generally require a thank-you note: when a gift is sent by mail, the giver normally expects an acknowledgment—a thank-you note—so he or she will know that the gift has arrived safely; the givers of wedding, shower, and baby gifts, regardless of how the package was delivered, expect a thank-you note; the guest of honor at a party thanks his host or hostess with a formal, written note; and it is common courtesy to thank a host or hostess with whom one has stayed overnight.

Writing a thank-you note for other types of social situations is entirely up to you. You may, for example, wish to write a note thanking a hostess for a dinner party. While you undoubtedly thanked her before you left the party, a note is a nice gesture, which tells the hostess that you appreciated her efforts. Similarly, children can be encouraged to write thank-you notes for gifts they receive for their birthdays or for other occasions, even if they expressed their thanks in person. This will help them to develop the habit and skill of writing thank-you notes. It is never wrong to send a note of thanks, which expresses your appreciation and reflects your good manners.

How Soon After One Receives a Gift or Attends a Function Should a Note Be Written? This is simple—as soon as possible. If you cannot write a note the day after, then write before the week is out. Only brides are excused for tardy thank-you notes, and brides are only excused for two or three weeks.

What Can Be Said After "Thank you For The . . ."? Actually, a good deal can be written besides the obvious "thank you." Again, there are few handy rules-of-thumb concerning what the body of a thank-you can include. Do not, initially, thank the giver for "a gift." Express how you feel about the "blue sweater," or the "beautiful garnet ring," or the "place setting of china." Name and describe the object. Let the giver know that you know exactly what he or she gave to you.

> *Dear Aunt Kate and Uncle Jim,*
>   *Tom and I were thrilled with the antique silver butter spreaders.*

Continue your thank-you with a description of how you plan to use the gift or how the gift reflects the giver's personality or why the gift is unique.

> *The pattern on the blade goes beautifully with our new flatware. Mother told me after the wedding that the knives originally belonged to Grandma Moore. Whenever I use them, I'll think of her and of you. I expect that she would have been pleased to know her things are being used by yet another generation.*

You might additionally note how pleased you were to see the giver when he or she delivered the gift (or how sorry you were that he or she was unable to attend).

> *Tom and I were so pleased that you were able to be with us for the wedding.*

Close the note by repeating your appreciation for the gift.

> *Again, thank you for your thoughtfulness and for the very special wedding gift.*
> *Love,*
> *Helen*

This formula can be used to write notes for any type of gift, regardless of the occasion. Although based upon a formula, each note sounds personal and original. Another example of how the system can be adapted to a different situation follows.

Thank-you Note for Gift

> Dear Elaise,
>
> I just opened your Christmas package and found the tin of divinity. You do know me, don't you! Sarah and I both love divinity. The holidays wouldn't be the same without it.
>
> Do you plan to be in the city during the holidays? If so, please call and plan to spend an evening with us.
>
> Thank you again for remembering us. (Sarah has already put the candy under lock and key. She says I can't have any more until Christmas Eve. Drat!)
>
> Your cousin,
> Bill

Can This Formula for Writing Thank-you Notes Be Used For Notes Covering Other Types of Occasions? Yes. The basics are the same for a gift thank-you as well as for a bread-and-butter, or dinner, thank-you. Simply change the descriptions. Instead of describing a gift and how it can be used, describe the highlights of the evening, or the dinner, or the weekend. As with a thank-you for a gift, begin the note with your appreciation for the occasion.

> Dear Jane,
> I had such a good time on Saturday night.

Continue with what you remember were the highlights of the evening. This could be the food, party games, the decorations, or even the company. If you found one of the guests particularly interesting, mention him or her.

> *While the dinner was, of course, delicious, the conversation was even better. You have a knack for bringing together the most delightful people. Bill and Jan Billingsly are fascinating; imagine traveling to all of those places. I certainly enjoyed meeting them.*

As with a thank-you for a gift, close your bread-and-butter note with another statement of your appreciation.

> *Again, thank you for the invitation. Being your guest is always a treat.*
> *Your friend,*
> *Eve*

A note thanking a host or hostess for an overnight stay or for a weekend follows the same format. Note the occasion, describe the highlights, and repeat your appreciation.

A thank-you note is always handwritten. Write on either a standard-size sheet of stationery or use an "informal," which is a smaller than standard-size sheet folded in half.

Thank-you Note to Host or Hostess

955 Montain Road
Hot Springs, AR 71913
August 30, 1984

Dear Lu and Dick,

Last weekend was terrific. It was wonderful to just lie on the beach and soak up the sun. It's something I rarely have time to do at home.

I also enjoyed the clambake on Saturday night.

Your new boat, by the way, is really something. I don't think I've water-skied since we were kids.

Thank you again for everything. I'm looking forward to your visit in October; don't disappoint me!

Your brother,
Mike

A Final Note on Thank-you's. If you are a smart job-hunter, you will always send a thank-you note to prospective employers with whom you have interviewed. The note will make you stand out from the other applicants, as few people still observe this courtesy. It will also give you a chance to restate your qualifications for the job and to emphasize any points not covered during the interview.

Letters of Congratulation

Letters of congratulation are used to acknowledge note-worthy events in the lives of friends, relatives, and acquaintances. Such events include a new job or job promotion, an engagement or marriage, the birth or adoption of a child, a graduation, and the award of an honor or other distinction.

Follow the format for personal letters (*see* pages 222–223) when writing letters of congratulation. Such letters should always be handwritten. Be sincere as you extend best wishes or give someone credit for a job well done. In the first sample letter of congratulation that follows, note that the address has been omitted, since the person writing the letter and the person receiving it correspond frequently.

Letter of Congratulation

May 29, 1984

Dear Ted,

Congratulations on your recent election to the National Honor Society. Your parents tell me that you are one of only twelve students in the junior class to be elected this year. That's quite an honor.

Your grandfather and I are very proud of you. Of course, we knew all along that you could do it.

Love,
Grandmother

Letter of Congratulation

> 1101 Maple Avenue
> Hanover Park, IL 60103
> March 5, 1984
>
> Dear Eileen,
>
> I read about your promotion to vice - president in charge of public relations in Sunday's paper. Congratulations! I know you'll do a superb job.
>
> Please give my best to Herb and the children. I am sure they are all quite proud of you.
>
> > Sincerely,
> > George

Letters of Condolence

The purpose of a letter of condolence is to give comfort. A successful condolence letter avoids, at all costs, false sentiment. Write with sincerity. If this is not possible, do not write at all.

What you say in a letter of condolence depends on your relationship with the person who has died and with the person to whom you are writing. If you knew well the person who has died, you may wish to mention a special memory you have of that person.

I will never forget how your father always included me in your family outings—the Saturday football games and weekend camping trips. It meant a great deal to me.

Or you may wish to describe one of his or her unique characteristics.

Lucy's sense of humor was such a joy. How she could make us all laugh and forget our troubles!

It is sometimes necessary to write a letter of condolence to a close friend or relative about a person you did not actually know. This kind of letter can be difficult. The only real choice you have is to mention that you were not acquainted with the person, but nevertheless, share your friend's grief.

As you know, Ralph, I never actually met your father. However, you spoke of him often and with such warmth that I share your sense of loss. He must have been a remarkable man.

When writing letters of condolence, avoid dwelling on your own sorrow. Always keep in mind the feelings of the person to whom you are writing. You may wish to close a condolence letter with an offer of help, if that offer is sincere and realistic. An example of a full letter of condolence follows.

Letter of Condolence

> 3001 Church Avenue
> Urbana, IL 61801
> February 3, 1984
>
> Dear Carole,
>
> I was saddened to hear of your father's death. I know how close you were to him and how deeply you must feel his loss.
>
> The whole team enjoyed having your father cheer for us at our softball games last summer. As I recall he didn't miss a single game.
>
> Please let me know if I can do anything for you or your mother. I would be happy to help with shopping, housework, or anything else that needs to be done.
>
> Sincerely,
> Judy

Letters of Apology

A letter of apology may be written for a variety of reasons: failing to keep an appointment or a promise; offending someone by an inappropriate or misunderstood remark or deed; or damaging another person's property. The letter should explain what happened and how you plan to remedy or make amends for the situation.

A letter of apology is identical in form to any personal letter. The tone or level of formality used depends, of course, upon the audience—the intended reader. It can also depend upon the seriousness of the situation. You would certainly employ a lesser degree of formality in a letter to a good friend than to a mere acquaintance. Two letters of apology follow. Notice that the different tone used in each of the letters is based upon both the level of acquaintance and the seriousness of the offense.

Letters of Apology

Route 2, Box 356
Plymouth, IN 46563
September 4, 1984

Dear Marcia,

I'm so sorry that I was unable to help you move into your new apartment as I promised. As I mentioned on the telephone, my sister and her husband came into town unexpectedly and stayed with me the entire weekend.

I hope the move went smoothly. Could you use some help settling in your new place? I'm good at such things as unpacking boxes, hanging curtains, and organizing closets. I'd be happy to help in any way possible. And I promise to show up this time.

Sincerely,
Roberta

415 Aldine
Chicago, IL 60313
October 12, 1984

Dear Mrs. Elliot,

Upon returning home from a business trip, I learned of the unfortunate situation over your garden. I regard this as more than a harmless prank. It is difficult to comprehend why a boy would purposely damage someone's flower beds. I want to assure you that Mark has been punished. I believe he now understands the sanctity of other people's property.

This, of course, does not remedy the damage to your flowers. Please let me know the extent of the problem, and I will replace any plants you think necessary.

Mrs. Arthur and I apologize for this vandalism and ask that you please allow us to make amends. I understand that Mark has already apologized in person. However, if he can be of any service in the cleaning up of your garden, please call us.

With kindest regards,
James Arthur

Business Correspondence

Although a great deal of personal business is now conducted on the telephone, you may still have occasion to write various kinds of business letters. These include letters requesting information, letters of inquiry, letters of complaint, and letters ordering merchandise. In addition, you may be required to fill in a variety of forms related to personal business: social security forms, credit card or loan applications, school or college admission forms, and order forms. (*See* Chapter 5, "Writing for Work," for information on writing business letters on the job.)

Parts of a Business Letter

The six parts of a business letter include the heading, the inside address, the salutation, the body, the complimentary close, and the signature. Refer to the sample letter on page 248 as each of these parts is discussed.

Heading.   The heading consists of your street address; your city, state, and *ZIP* codes; and the date. Arrange the heading in block form, and place it in the upper right-hand corner of the letter. Note that abbreviations are not used in the heading, except for the state abbreviation used with the *ZIP* code. If you are using letterhead stationery, the date should be placed two or three lines below the letterhead, flush with either the right-hand margin or the left-hand margin.

Inside Address.   The inside address includes the recipient's name and title; the name of the office or department, if any; the name of the company or institution; and the street address, city, state, and *ZIP* code. Use the block form for the inside address. Place it flush with the left-hand margin, four lines below the heading.

Always include the proper title before a recipient's name. Examples include *Mr., Ms., Dr.,* or *Professor.* If the recipient has a job title, place it after the person's name. Use a separate line if the job title is long.

> Dr. Felicia Patterson
> Vice President of Research
> ABC Chemical Corporation
> 3356 W. Prairie Avenue
> Oshkosh, WI 54901

Salutation.   The salutation, also called the greeting, is placed two lines below the inside address. Use a colon, rather than a comma, after the salutation in a business letter. Address the recipient using the appropriate title and last name—for example, *Dear Dr. Patterson.* If you are not writing to a specific person in a company, you may use *Ladies and Gentlemen* as a salutation, since most companies have both male and female employees.

Body.   The body, which contains the message of the letter, begins two lines below the salutation. A block style for the body of the letter is appropriate for a business letter. Do not indent the first word of each paragraph, but leave extra space between paragraphs.

Complimentary Close.   The complimentary close is placed two lines below the body of the letter. It can be aligned with the heading or with the left-hand margin. The following complimentary closes are appropriate for business letters: *Sincerely yours, Yours very sincerely, Respectfully yours, Yours truly, Yours very truly,* and *Cordially yours,.*

Signature.   The signature is written in ink below the complimentary close. The name is typed below the signature, about four lines below the complimentary close.

Enclosures.   If you are enclosing something in a letter, indicate this by placing the word *Enclosure* or *Enclosures* flush with the left-hand margin, two lines below your typed name. Examples of enclosures include checks, money orders, and copies of a bill.

Carbon Copies.   You may sometimes send a carbon copy or a photocopy of a letter to another person. Indicate this by writing *cc:,* which stands for carbon copy, followed by that person's name. Place this notation flush with the left-hand margin, two lines below your typed name. If an Enclosure notation was used, place the *cc:* notation two lines below it.

The sample envelope on page 248 shows the proper format to use when addressing an envelope for a business letter. Your full name and address should be placed in the upper left-hand corner of the envelope. The recipient's name and address should match the information given in the letter's inside address. Center this information slightly below the middle of the envelope.

Business Letter Format

Heading —————————————————— 9816 Landis Street
Chicago, IL 60643
July 30, 1984

Mr. Eli Grant, Director
Customer Service Department
Acme Seed Company
Inside ——————— 350 Poplar Lane
Address Des Moines, IA 50336

Salutation ——————— Dear Mr. Grant:

On May 28, 1984, I received five rosebushes that I
had ordered from your current catalog. I planted
the bushes promptly and cared for them according
Body ——————— to the instructions that were inclosed. Within a
month, however, four of the bushes had died. The
fifth one died last week.

I feel that a full refund in the amount of $35.50 is
due me. I am enclosing a copy of my canceled
check for that amount.

Complimentary
Close —————————————————— Sincerely yours,

Leslie Ames

Signature ———————

Typed Name ——————— Leslie Ames

Notation ——————— Enclosure

Envelope For a Business Letter

Leslie Ames
9816 Landis Street
Chicago, IL 60643

Mr. Eli Grant, Director
Customer Service Department
Acme Seed Company
350 Poplar Lane
Des Moines, IA 50336

Note that the sample business letter and envelope were both typed. Business letters that are typed usually make a better impression than handwritten letters. If you cannot type your business correspondence, write legibly and follow the proper format.

Kinds of Business Letters

Letters Requesting Information

Writing a letter requesting information is usually very simple. Begin by identifying yourself. Then describe the information you need, being as specific as possible. In some cases, you may give the reason why you need the information and how you plan to use it. Finally, express your appreciation. A sample letter requesting information follows.

> 516 Chelten Avenue
> Elmhurst, IL 60126
> June 6, 1984
>
> Ms. Dorothy Hubbell
> Sales Manager
> Worldwide Tours
> 1505 Walnut Avenue
> St. Louis, MO 63114
>
> Dear Ms. Hubbell
>
> I am a member of the National Motor Club. Please send me brochures and other information about the European tour that was advertised in the May issue of National Motor Club News. The tour will take place the first two weeks in September.
>
> Thank you for your help.
>
> Yours truly,
>
> *Candace Haig*
> Candace Haig

Letters of Inquiry

Letters of inquiry request detailed information. To respond to such a letter, the recipient may have to gather information or do research. When writing a letter of inquiry, begin by identifying yourself. Explain why you are asking for the information and how you plan to use it. Then request the information you need. Make your questions as specific as possible. Number the questions and arrange them in a list if there are more than two or three. Let the recipient know if you must have the information by a certain date. However, be sure to write early so that there is enough time for your letter to be answered. Finally, express your appreciation.

356 Elm Street
Chicago Heights, IL 60411
February 9, 1984

Mr. Michael Avery
Public Information Officer
Cartography Association of America
105 Canal Street
Chicago, IL 60606

Dear Mr. Avery:

I am a high school sophomore who is taking a minicourse on careers. One of my assignments is to do research and write a report on a career that interests me. I have chosen cartography, since I am fascinated by maps and mapmaking.

I would appreciate it if you would answer the following questions:

1. What kind of education or training does a cartographer need?
2. What colleges or universities have programs in cartography?
3. How can computers be useful to cartographers?
4. What kinds of jobs are available to cartographers?

My report is due on March 9. I would appreciate having the information I am requesting by February 24.

Thank you for your help.

Yours truly,

Cynthia Foster

Cynthia Foster

Letters of Complaint

Customers write letters of complaint about such things as defective merchandise, missing parts, wrong or delayed deliveries, erroneous billings, and unsatisfactory service. The purpose of a letter of complaint is to ask that a problem be remedied.

When writing a letter of complaint, use the standard business letter format. In the body of the letter give a detailed description of the product or service, including the date the product was purchased or the service was performed. Include copies of any purchase receipts or receipts for service work completed. Then describe the problem. Be as brief as possible, but include all the necessary details. Conclude by stating the action you would like the company to take.

People are sometimes angry and frustrated when they write complaint letters. They may vent their feelings by writing letters that are rude, sarcastic, or threatening. Resist this temptation. Keep in mind that the person who reads the letter is probably not responsible for the problem, but may be able to help you. He or she is much more likely to be helpful if your letter is calm, courteous, and reasonable. A sample letter of complaint follows.

17905 Garden Avenue
Homewood, IL 60430
August 23, 1984

Ms. Sarah Abrams, Director
Customer Relations Department
Videotronics Corporation
1515 Downing Road
Rochester, NY 14608

Dear Ms. Abrams:

On August 15, 1983, I purchased a model 5561 Videotronics color television set from Anderson Electronics in Homewood, Illinois. The set worked fine until August 5, 1984, when a thick band of white "snow" appeared across the top of the picture. Because the set was still under the one-year warranty, Anderson Electronics repaired it free of charge.

The picture was fine until August 20, when the band of "snow" began to reappear. Because the warranty has now run out, Anderson refuses to repair the set without charge. I feel that the set was not fixed properly the first time, when it was still under warranty.

Can you help me resolve this problem? I have always been pleased with Videotronics products and would like to get my set back in working order.

I am enclosing copies of the purchase receipt and the receipt for the service performed on August 5.

Sincerely yours,

Edward Harper

Enclosures
cc: Anderson Electronics   Edward Harper

Letters Ordering Merchandise

A letter that is written to order mechandise is "all business." Get to the point immediately: "Please send the following items. . ." Your aim is clarity. You want the reader to understand exactly what you want, how many you want, and what you expect to pay. Use the standard business letter format and always include the following information:

- A description of the items—
  name, color, size, style, model
  number, and catalog number
  (if there is one)
- The quantity you want of each item
- The price
- The address to which
  the order should be sent
- How the order should be shipped
- The method of payment—
  check, money order,
  C.O.D., or credit card

Again, make sure your letter is to the point and clearly written. The person who reads it is interested only in filling your order; extraneous information will slow him or her down. If possible, type your order. It will be easier to read, and the transaction will, therefore, be more likely to be completed without error. A sample order letter follows.

950 Holden Court
Cambridge, MA 02138
April 21, 1984

Mr. Jeffrey Wallace
Jazz Records Unlimited
P.O. Box 999
Drexel Hill, PA 19026

Dear Mr. Wallace:

Please send the following record albums to the above address:

#97	*Percussion Discussion*	$ 5.00
#65	*Marchin' On!*	6.00
#84	*After the Morning*	4.50
#39	*In Tandem*	5.00
	Postage and Handling	2.50
	Total	$23.00

Send this order by fourth class mail. Enclosed is a check for $23.00.

Sincerely yours,

Francis Istad

Francis Istad

Enclosure

Letters to the Editor

All of us, at various times, read something in a newspaper or magazine or hear something over the television or radio with which we strongly agree or disagree. Our immediate impulse is to sit down and write a letter, voicing our feeling. Most of us, however, never go any further: "It's too much trouble" or "I don't write well enough to have a letter published in the paper." Voicing one's opinion in a public forum—and newspapers and television editorials are, to some extent, public forums—is participating in the democratic process. Elected officials *do* study the editorial pages to get a feel for what the public is thinking.

A letter to the editor of a newspaper or magazine may express agreement or disagreement with statements made in the publication. Such a letter may also express an opinion on an issue of public interest, or it may point out factual errors made in the publication.

When writing a letter to the editor, make sure you have all of the facts. In some cases, you may wish to name your sources of information. This is especially important when pointing out a factual error. If you are writing about a statement that appeared in the publication, you may quote the statement directly. (You may wish to review the "Argument" section in Chapter 4, "Writing for School.")

A letter of this type should be written in the format of a standard business letter (*see* pages 246–248). Keep the letter brief. Short, well-written letters are more likely to be published than long, rambling ones. Use a calm, courteous, and reasonable tone. A logical, step-by-step progression of ideas is more seriously considered than an angry attack. Avoid sarcasm and insults, and offer any criticisms in a constructive manner. If you express emotions, be sure to back them with facts or reasons.

After you finish your letter, wait a day or so before mailing it. Reread it with a fresh eye. If necessary, revise or rewrite it.

Always sign your letter. Most editors will not publish unsigned letters. Many editors will, however, honor a request to omit your name if the letter is published.

Type the letter. A busy editor is more likely to read a neatly typed letter than a handwritten one. A sample letter to an editor is given on page 255.

Letter to an Editor.

17905 Garden Avenue
Homewood, IL 60430
May 9, 1984

Ms. Nancy Garcia, Editor
<u>South</u> <u>Suburban</u> <u>Star</u>
P.O. Box 11505
Homewood, IL 60430

Dear Ms. Garcia:

I am shocked and dismayed by the school board's
decision to close Prairie View School in June, 1985.
Why was the community not consulted about this
decision? As a parent and a taxpayer, I feel I should
have a voice in such decisions.

Students who now attend Prairie View School will be
bused to Washington School. Many of these studens
will have to wait for the bus on busy streets and
highways. Did the school board consider safety
factors when making this decision?

I think that an open school board meeting should
be held to allow community residents to voice their
opinions on this issue. In my opinion, the school
board should reconsider its decision.

Sincerely yours,

Edward Harper

Edward Harper

Letters to Elected Officials

Writing to an elected official, such as the President, your
United States senator or representative, or to the governor
of your state, is both a right and, at times, even a duty.
They are elected to represent you. If you have an opinion
or simply a question on an issue, write a letter (or send a
telegram). During the Watergate scandal of the early
1970's, the extraordinary volume of mail sent to members

of Congress greatly influenced their positions on the issue. Although a painful time for the country, the Watergate episode was a wonderful example of democracy in action. The American people clearly expressed their wishes in the form of millions of letters to Congress.

Letters to elected officials can, of course, deal with any issue, regardless of the scope. You may write to ask for information or to seek help with a particular problem. Letters may deal with such topics as laws and regulations, foreign or domestic policy, taxes, or even potholes in city streets.

A letter to an elected official should be written in the standard business format (*see* pages 246–248). The heading is particularly important, as the official may want to respond to your letter. The inside address and the address on the envelope for a United States senator should be written as in the following example:

> The Honorable Jane Fenmore
> United States Senate
> Washington, D.C. 20510

A letter to a United States representative is written in the following manner:

> The Honorable Philip Morgan
> House of Representatives
> Washington, D.C. 20515

The salutation for a United States senator should be *Dear Senator* or *Dear Senator Fenmore.* For a United States representative, any of the following may be used:

> Dear Mr., Miss, Mrs., *or* Ms. Morgan:
> *or* Dear Representative Morgan:
> *or* Dear Congressman *or* Congresswoman Morgan:

State senators and representatives are addressed in the following manner:

> Dear Senator Morgan:
> Dear Representative Morgan:
> *or* Dear Mr., Miss, Mrs., *or* Ms. Morgan:

When writing the body of the letter to an elected official, keep in mind the following points:

- Be as specific as possible. If you are writing about a particular piece of legislation, for example, give its number. If you are writing to obtain information, describe exactly what you need.
- When expressing an opinion or arguing for a course

of action, give facts or reasons to support your position.

- Avoid threats, sarcasm, and rude remarks. State your message in a calm, courteous, and direct manner.
- State clearly what action, if any, you would like the official to take.
- Keep your letter brief and to the point. Avoid discussing topics unrelated to the purpose of the letter.

After completing the first draft of your letter, reread it to make sure you have expressed your ideas clearly. Revise and, if necessary, rewrite the first draft. Type the final copy or write it neatly and legibly. A sample letter to an elected official follows.

Letter to an Elected Official

955 Mountain Road
Hot Springs, AR 71913
August 26, 1984

The Honable John Layton
United States Senate
Washington, D.C. 20510

Dear Senator Layton:

I am writing to express my opposition to the proposed increase in the social security tax. Last year, I paid more than $2,500 in social security taxes. Surely I cannot be expected to pay more into a system whose future remains somewhat uncertain.

Wage earners are already overburdened with taxes of all kinds. Raising the social security tax would add to this burden.

I strongly urge you to oppose any increase in the social security tax.

Sincerely yours,

Michael J. Grimes

Michael J. Grimes

Completing Forms

The completion of various types of forms is now a part of everyday life. When you apply for a driver's license, a credit card, a social security card, or even a library card, you fill out a form. When you apply for a loan, admission to school, or file your income taxes or an insurance claim form or respond to questionnaires and surveys, you fill out a form. Is this personal correspondence? In a sense, it is. You are giving vital information about yourself to someone or something, that is, to a school board or government agency. You most certainly want that information to be correct. It can be a shock to find that you have paid social security tax into someone else's acount for 20 years; and it can easily happen when a form is incorrectly filled out.

Keep these points in mind when you complete a form:

- Read the directions carefully. If you do not understand what to do, ask for help.
- Answer the questions honestly and completely. If you feel a question is inappropriate, write "Does not apply" in the space provided for the answer. (Forms, by nature, look official. You do not *have* to fill in all of the spaces. Your income, for example, is no one's business except the IRS.)
- Write neatly and legibly. You may wish to print or type if your handwriting is difficult to read.
- Reread your answers before handing in or mailing the form.
- If possible, keep a copy of the completed form for your records.

Most forms include little space for answers. For these types of forms, keep your answers brief and to the point. Choose words and phrases carefully.

Some forms, such as school or college admission forms, leave space for lengthy answers. In many cases, the person reading the form will judge you on the way you expressed yourself as well as the answers themselves. He or she will consider the way you organized your thoughts and will also evaluate your spelling, grammar, and vocabulary. Your answers will usually make a better impression if you write and revise a first draft of each answer on a separate sheet of paper. Then, neatly type or write the answers on the application form.

Samples of various kinds of forms follow.

REQUEST FOR STATEMENT OF EARNINGS
(PLEASE PRINT IN INK OR USE TYPEWRITER)

FOR SSA USE ONLY

AX

SP

I REQUEST A SUMMARY STATEMENT OF EARNINGS FROM MY SOCIAL SECURITY RECORD

NH | Full name you use in work or business
First | Middle Initial | Last

SN | Social security number shown on your card

DB | Your date of birth
Month | Day | Year | A

MA | Other Social Security number(s) you have used

SX | Your Sex
☐ Male | ☐ Female

AK | Other name(s) you have used (Include your maiden name)

PRIVACY STATEMENT

The Social Security Administration (SSA) is authorized to collect information asked on this form under section 205 of the Social Security Act. It is needed so SSA can quickly identify your record and prepare the earnings statement you requested. While you are not required to furnish the information, failure to do so may prevent your request from being processed. The information will be used primarily for issuing your earnings statement.

I am the individual to whom the record pertains. I understand that if I knowingly and willingly request or receive a record about an individual under false pretenses I would be guilty of a Federal crime and could be fined up to $5000.

Sign your name here: (Do not print) | Date

I AUTHORIZE YOU TO SEND THE STATEMENT TO THE NAME AND ADDRESS BELOW: *(To be completed in all cases)*

PN | Name of the addressee

AD | Street number and name

City and state | ZP | Zip Code

Form **SSA-7004 PC** OP 1   (9-82) Previous Editions are Obsolete

---

Quick Charge Card Application

Type or print all answers legibly

Name ————————————————————————————

Street Address ————————————————————————

City, State, Zip Code ———————————————————————

Telephone Number ————————————————————————

Name of Employer ————————————————————————

Employer's Telephone Number —————————————————————

Length of Employment ————————————————————————

Name of Bank ——————————————————————————

Account Number ——————————————————————————

I affirm that the above information given on this application is correct to the best of my knowledge.

Applicant's Signature ————————————————————————

Date ————————————————————————————————

STATE UNIVERSITY

Application for Admission

Print or type all answers.

When do you plan to enroll in State University? _____
                                                                    Semester/Year

Social Security Number _____

Name _____
        Last   First   Middle

Address _____
              Number and Street   City, State, Zip

Date of Birth _____ Telephone Number _____

Are you a U.S. citizen? Yes _____ No _____

If not, indicate type of visa. _____

Names of schools previously attended, including colleges, universities, and high schools. Begin with the most recent.

Name of Institution	Location	Dates Attended	Degree Diploma

What field or fields of study do you plan to pursue at State University?

Why do you want to enroll in State University?

What are your career plans?

Forms are often used to order merchandise by mail from catalogs and from newspaper and magazine advertisements. A sample order form follows.

ACME SEED COMPANY
350 Poplar Lane
Des Moines, IA 50336

(Please print or type.)

SHIP TO: Name _____

Address _____

City _____

PAGE NUMBER	QUANTITY	ITEM NUMBER	NAME OF ITEM	TOTAL PRICE

*Sales Tax: We must collect state sales tax from residents of Florida, Iowa, Michigan, New Mexico, and Wisconsin.

Sales Tax*	
Shipping and Handling	
TOTAL	

Credit card number _____

Expires _____

ACME GUARANTEE: Your money will be refunded if you are not completely satisfied.

Before completing such a form, read it carefully. Pay particular attention to column headings and to information about sales tax and shipping and handling charges. Neatly print or type the requested information on the form. Check that all information is complete and correct; delays often result from missing or incorrect information.

Writing for the Community

Americans are joiners. They belong to an endless variety of clubs, fraternities and sororities, lodges, societies, auxiliaries, orders, councils, coteries, boards, unions, and organizations affiliated and nonaffiliated, formal and informal. There are, coast to coast, tens of thousands of groups, each with a purpose; each seeking its share of the public's attention.

As members of these various organizations, we all take our turn pushing the cause: volunteering our time, experience, and talents. We help coordinate efforts, publicize events, and raise funds. Chapter 7, "Writing for the Community," examines how our efforts and skills can be sharpened in the various roles we assume as members of a community group: how we can most effectively help our organization gain attention in the local newspaper or over the local television or radio station; how an organizational newsletter is written, printed, and distributed; how posters and fliers are most effectively produced and exhibited for maximum exposure; and how other types of publications are successfully organized, written, edited, typeset, and printed for the benefit of an organization, as well as the community at large.

Newspapers

Newspapers, especially community and local weeklies, publish stories covering the activities of various organizations. Many of these stories are, in fact, based upon news releases that organization members write and submit. The steps involved in writing a news release include choosing a topic, gathering the facts, writing the lead, writing the body, revising and rewriting, and preparing the final copy.

Choosing a Topic

Choosing a topic that will interest the newspapers' readers is the first step in writing a news release. Routine meetings, for example, are usually not newsworthy. However, a meeting that features a prominent speaker, a debate, or a demonstration may have news value. Other events or topics that may be of interest to readers include organization elections; news of members' activities and accomplishments; craft, hobby, and fashion shows; awards presented and received; civic events involving organization members; fund-raising drives; and positions taken on matters of community interest.

Keep in mind that the definition of a newsworthy event usually depends on the type of newspaper. For example, newspapers in large metropolitan areas generally give little coverage to community organizations. Of course, if a prominent person speaks to an organization, or if it is involved in an activity of general interest, a large metropolitan newspaper may cover the event. In general, however, stories about community organizations in large cities appear in neighborhood or community newspapers. Newspapers in smaller cities, suburbs, and towns often specialize in news about community groups.

Many newspapers, whether large or small, employ a staff editor in charge of local news coverage. If you frequently write stories about your organization, you should become acquainted with this editor. He or she can tell you what kinds of stories the newspaper is likely to publish and what format to follow when submitting news releases.

In addition, you should carefully read a variety of news stories about community organizations. This will guide you in choosing newsworthy topics and will increase the chances of getting your story published.

Once you have chosen a topic, the next step is to gather the facts.

Gathering the Facts

Assume you are writing a news release about a benefit auction your club plans to hold. Begin by listing the facts you have:

- The auction will be held from 10:00 A.M. until 2:00 P.M. on October 20 at the Greeley Center.
- Admission is free.
- All proceeds will go to the Lake City Youth Foundation.

Next, talk to the club member in charge of the auction to gather any additional facts:

- Local merchants have donated more than $3,000 worth of merchandise for the auction.
- Logan's department store has donated a $500 gift certificate.
- Foundation director Janet Phillips plans to use the money raised at the auction to award college scholarships to needy high school seniors.
- Food will be sold during the auction.

Gathering the facts for a newspaper story on your organization can include interviews and photographs shot specifically for the news release.

- The goal for the auction is $2,500. Last year's auction netted $2,000.
- Anyone wishing to donate merchandise should call 777–1234.

After gathering the facts for the story, write the lead.

Writing the Lead

The first paragraph of a news story is called the *lead*. A good lead briefly summarizes the important information in the story. It should be able to stand alone; when space is a problem, the editor may cut everything except the lead.

The lead should include the 5 W's: *who, what, when, where,* and *why.* It may also tell *how:*

> The Civic Club will hold a benefit auction on October 20 at the Greeley Center. All proceeds will be donated to the Lake City Youth Foundation.

Note that the lead answers the following questions:

> *Who?* The Civic Club
> *What?* A benefit auction
> *When?* October 20
> *Where?* Greeley Center
> *Why?* To raise money for the Lake City Youth Foundation.

Although the sample lead summarizes the important facts of the story, it lacks interest. The following lead might create more interest in the event.

> A $500 gift certificate for Logan's department store is just one of the many items to be auctioned October 20 at the Greeley Center. The Civic Club, sponsor of the auction, will donate all proceeds to the Lake City Youth Foundation.

Keep in mind that a good lead not only presents the important facts, but also creates interest in the story. This is especially important in news releases that provide publicity for upcoming events.

Always avoid expressing an opinion in the lead or any other part of a news release. A busy newspaper editor will not edit out the opinion, but simply drop the entire story. The writer of the following lead did not follow this rule.

> The Conservation Club has filed a lawsuit seeking to stop XYZ Chemical Corporation from dumping waste products into Lake Shabbona. Club members have appealed to local politicians to help stop this shameful and immoral practice.

Note that the writer expresses an opinion in the second sentence by calling the practice "shameful and immoral." The sentence can easily be rewritten: "Club members have appealed to local politicians to help stop this practice." Remember, always avoid including an opinion. Newspapers only publish the opinions of the owners and top editors and only on the editorial page.

Give It a Try

Use the information given in each item to write a lead for a news release. Remember to place the most important or most interesting information at the beginning.

- *When?* March 5 at 2:00 P.M.
  Who?   State Senator Joseph Daly
  Where? Applewood Senior Center
  What? Will speak on issues affecting the elderly
  Why?   Monthly meeting of Applewood Senior Citizens Club

- *What?* Will sponsor an art fair
  When? April 7–8 from 10:00 A.M. until 5:00 P.M.
  Who?   The Fine Arts Club
  Where? Oak Ridge Mall
  Why?   To raise money for the new Village Artists Center

- *Where?* Sweeney's Restaurant on Route 30
  Who?   Cambridge Canoe Club
  What? Annual dinner meeting
  When? September 22 at 7:30 P.M.
  Why?   Elect officers for next year

- *Who?*   John Rogers, author of *How to Get Rich Buying Stocks*
  Where? Ambassador South Hotel
  What? Conduct seminars for Investors Club members on investing in the stock market
  When? July 24 and 26 from 7:00–9:30 P.M.

Writing the Body

Although the lead is the most important part of a news story, the body paragraphs deserve careful attention; they give additional information about the facts presented in the lead. This information helps the reader better understand the story.

When writing the body of a news release, begin by reviewing the lead. Refer to the lead on page 266 concerning the story about the benefit auction. Note the important facts: (1) a $500 gift certificate and many other items will be auctioned; (2) all proceeds will go to the Lake City Youth Foundation. The body of the news release should give additional information about these facts. Refer to the notes you took when gathering the facts as you write the body.

The body of the story on the benefit auction might be written as follows:

> Local merchants have donated more than $3,000 worth of merchandise for the auction, which will be held from 10:00 A.M. until 2:00 P.M. Admission is free.
>
> A variety of homemade foods will be sold during the auction.
>
> The money raised at the auction will be used to award college scholarships to needy high school seniors, according to Janet Phillips, Lake City Youth Foundation director.

Other body paragraphs can give additional information about the facts of the story, even if these facts are not mentioned in the lead. The following paragraphs could, for example, be added to the news release on the benefit auction:

> Auction chairperson Andrew Frank says that the Civic Club hopes to raise at least $2,500 from the auction. Last year's auction netted $2,000.
>
> Anyone wishing to donate merchandise for the auction may contact Mr. Frank at 777–1234.

Note that the paragraphs are arranged in order of decreasing importance. This allows the editor to cut the news release from the bottom up. Also, the most important information is given first in each paragraph.

When writing the body, make sure that all the sentences in each paragraph *cohere,* or stick together. In addition, check for coherence in the news release as a whole. Make sure that all the body paragraphs relate to the main idea or ideas expressed in the lead.

The body pragraphs in the news release on the benefit auction cohere because they are all related to the ideas expressed in the lead. In addition, certain key words and phrases are repeated, including *auction, Civic Club, Lake City Youth Foundation,* and *merchandise.* The repetition of key words gives the news release coherence and the paragraphs a smooth, flowing narrative.

Transition words and phrases can also help a news release flow smoothly. Such words and phrases include *now, meanwhile, soon, at the same time, finally*, and *later.*

Avoid expressing opinions in the body of a news release. You may, however, quote opinions that others give, as in the following example:

> "City government should provide greater financial support for the arts," said Dorothy Hanson, president of the Fine Arts Council.

Consider the following points when writing the body of a news release. Many of these points also apply to writing the lead.

- Use familiar words, words that the reader is likely to know. Do not try to make an impression by using big, fancy words.
- Keep your sentences fairly short, but not choppy. Long, involved sentences are usually more difficult to read than shorter ones.
- Limit most of your paragraphs to one or two sentences. At most, include three or four sentences. Remember that newspaper columns are narrow. Long paragraphs result in large blocks of type that readers may avoid.
- Include all the important facts, but be as brief as possible. Eliminate unnecessary words and words that say the same thing twice.
- Check and double-check all the facts. Do not assume that something is true; check it out.
- Stick to the facts. For example, do not say that Professor Brown gave "an interesting speech." Some people may have found the speech dull. Also avoid statements such as "The audience received Professor Brown's speech enthusiastically." Instead stick to the facts: "The audience applauded spontaneously throughout Professor Brown's speech." Let the reader conclude that the audience was enthusiastic.
- Spell names correctly. Anyone who has ever had his or her name misspelled in print knows how annoying this can be.
- Check the accuracy of all quotes. When in doubt, contact the person you are quoting. If this is impossible, do not use a direct quotation. Rather, paraphrase, or put into your own words, what the person said.

Give It a Try

Write a news release using the information given in one of the following items. Remember to give the most important facts in the lead. Give more information about these facts in the body paragraphs. Arrange the body paragraphs in order of decreasing importance.

- Margaret Lindsey will be the guest speaker. Monthly meeting of World Travelers Club. April 10 at 2:00 P.M. Ms. Lindsey has traveled throughout the world during the past 20 years. She is the owner of the Vagabond Travel Agency and the author of five travel books. Meeting to be held at Skylark Hotel. Subject of speech will be "Preparing for an Ocean Voyage." Newly elected officers will be installed after the speech. Refreshments will be served after the meeting.

- Annual competition for the Power-Driven Model Airplane Club. June 16 at 9:00 A.M. Central High School athletic field. Last year's winners were Jane Towley, Centerville; Tim Thomkins, Eastwood; and Tom Smith, Rankin. The club has 31 members from 9 communities. Competition includes loops, snaprolls, slow rolls, Immelmann turns, lazy eights, and buzzing. Admission is free; the public is invited. Three classes of competition: ages 8 to 10; 11 to 15; and 16 and up.

Revising and Rewriting

After completing the first draft of your news release, you may wish to revise and, if necessary, rewrite it. Ask yourself the following questions as you reread the story:

- Does the lead briefly summarize the important information in the story?
- Is the most important or most interesting information given first?
- Would the lead be able to stand alone if all the body paragraphs were cut?
- Does the news release stick to the facts and avoid expressing the writer's opinions?
- Do the body paragraphs give more information about the facts presented in the lead?
- Are the body paragraphs arranged in order of decreasing importance?
- Is the most important information given first in each body paragraph?

- Do all the sentences in each paragraph cohere, or stick together?
- Do all the body paragraphs relate to the main idea or ideas expressed in the lead?
- Are key words and transition words and phrases sometimes used to make the story flow smoothly?
- Are there errors in spelling, grammar, word usage, capitalization, or punctuation?

Give It a Try

Following the guidelines just discussed revise and rewrite the news story you wrote for the Give It a Try exercise on page 267.

Preparing the Final Copy

Now that you have revised and rewritten your news release, prepare the final copy. The newspaper to which you are submitting the release may have specific guidelines for you to follow regarding style and format. Always check with the editor before submitting your news release. These guidelines will probably be similar to the ones described below.

Type double spaced on 8½- by 11-inch bond paper of good quality. Anything less than 16-pound bond paper may be too flimsy. Avoid erasable paper; ink on such paper smears, making it difficult to work with. This is also true of carbon copies. If you are sending the story to more than one newspaper, photocopies may be acceptable. Check, however, with individual editors.

In the upper left-hand corner, six lines from the top of the first page, type your name, the name of the organization, the address, and the telephone number. This information may be single spaced. If the story should run in the newspaper's next issue, type the words "Immediate Release" in the upper right-hand corner. If the story should run in a later issue, indicate this by giving the appropriate release date: "Release on January 14." Below the release date, indicate the other newspapers, if any, to which you are sending the news release.

Do not write a headline for your story. Headlines are the editor's responsibility. But do include a *slug*, a phrase that identifies the story, three lines below the telephone number. Examples of slugs include *Benefit auction*, *Model airplane competition*, or *Ms. Lindsey to speak*.

```
Your name                    Release date
Name of the organization     Other papers to
Address                      which the release
Telephone number             is being sent

Annual awards dinner


        Charles Smith and Susan Jones received
certificates of merit at the Wednesday Club's
annual awards dinner on January 8 at the Wilshire
Hotel. The awards recognized their contributions
to the organization during the past year.
        Smith's award read: ''For outstanding
achievement in conducting the anual membership
                    (MORE)
```

Begin typing the news story approximately one-third of the way down the page. This allows room for the editor to write the headline and typesetting directions. Double space all copy, and indent the first line of each paragraph five spaces. If the story continues on the next page, type (*MORE*) after the last line. Repeat the slug and the name of the organization six lines from the top of the second page and any succeeding pages. At the end of the story, type *END* or *###*.

After typing the news release, proofread it carefully. Most editors do not mind if a few corrections are written in by hand. However, if the page is even slightly difficult to read, retype it. Getting information about your organization into the newspaper is your responsibility, not the edi-

```
Annual awards dinner/Wednesday Club    2



drive.'' Jones won her certificate for

organizing the club's tour of Old Fort Morgan

last September.

        John Black, Wednesday Club president,

presented the awards.

        The dinner was attended by 150 people.

        At its next meeting, February 10,

the Wednesday Club will hear Ira Kane speak

on ''Clubs and Community Relations.''


                        END
```

tor's. Make sure that he or she can read and understand your copy.

Photographs.   If you are submitting photographs with a news release, make sure they are of good enough quality to reproduce in the paper. Submit an 8½- × 11-inch halftone original. Do not send in a snapshot or a color print. (Quality is lost when color is reproduced in black and white.)

All photographs *must* include a caption, identifying the picture. Type the caption on standard typing paper. Trim this to the width of the photograph, leaving two or three inches of space above the caption copy. The editor will use this space to write typesetting instructions. Place the caption, with the extra two or three inches of space, at the bottom of the photograph. Fold the extra paper under the

All photographs are examined by a photo editor before they appear in a newspaper. Before submitting an illustration, make sure it is of good quality and properly identified with a caption attached to the bottom.

photograph and either tape or glue, with rubber cement, this fold to the back. Do not tape or glue the caption to the front; this might spoil the illustration. Also, do not write on the illustration, front or back. The reverse imprint of writing on the back will show on the front and diminish the quality for reproduction. If people appear in the photograph, identify them in the caption, giving full names, correctly spelled.

Submission and Deadline. Now you are ready to submit the news release. Be sure it is in the editor's hands before the deadline. If the newspaper is a weekly, check with the editor for the day and hour of deadline. Remember that no editor will hold the press for your story.

Radio and Television

Many organizations use radio and television as well as newspapers to publicize their activities. Most radio and television publicity for organizations consists of brief news and public service announcements. However, radio and television stations sometimes feature longer news stories about an organization's activities or broadcast interviews with organization members. Occasionally, an entire program focuses on an organization.

Try to get to know those in charge of community news and public service broadcasting at local radio and television stations. These people will offer suggestions on how to prepare copy and what type of material the station is most likely to broadcast. They will also give you deadlines for submitting material that must be aired at a particular time.

News Announcements

News releases should be sent on a regular basis to radio and television stations as well as to newspapers. Address the news release to the news director or the person in charge of community news.

Write the news release following the same procedure used for writing news releases sent to newspapers (*see* pages 264–274), unless the station has different requirements. Be sure to include all the important facts in the lead and to arrange the body paragraphs in order of decreasing importance. In many cases, the story will be shortened because of time limitations, or it will be rewritten to conform with a particular station's broadcasting style. However, if you have written a good lead and have arranged the body paragraphs in the proper order, it is not likely that important copy will be dropped.

Public Service Announcement

Although radio and television stations are not required by law to give air time to community organizations, they are required to operate in the public interest. Evidence of air time devoted to public service announcements and programming helps a station when the Federal Communications Commission reviews its application for license renewal. Organizations, thus, have a good chance of getting public service announcements on the air. Keep in mind, however, that stations will not provide free advertising for organizations unless such advertising is clearly in the public interest.

Check with the public affairs director to learn the station's policy on public service announcements. Some stations, for example, refuse to air appeals for funds. Anything involving gambling, including bingo and lotteries, will not be publicized.

Check with the station regarding the format to use when submitting public service announcements. You will also need to know the deadlines for submitting announcements and any time limits involved. A radio announcement that runs for 10 seconds will include about 25 words. Twenty seconds allows 50 words; 30 seconds allows 75 words; and 60 seconds allows 150 words. The pace on television is a little slower: 10 seconds equals approximately 20 words; 20 seconds allows 40 words; 30 seconds allows 60 words; and 60 seconds allows approximately 120 words.

Keep these time limits in mind as you write your announcement. Get as close as possible to the required time. If your announcement runs too long, it may be shortened by the station, and important information may be deleted.

Public service announcements are written in a style that is much less formal than news release style. Such announcements are more conversational, both in tone and in speech patterns.

Getting air time for an announcement of your organization's activities requires an understanding of how television stations work. Make the acquaintance of the public affairs director at your local station and ask him or her about format and procedures.

After writing an announcement, read it aloud, listening for words or phrases that may cause the announcer to stumble. Substitute different words or phrases, if possible. Give the pronunciation of any difficult or confusing names in parentheses.

You may wish to supply visual aids, such as slides and photographs, to accompany television announcements. Some stations will accept only slides (color transparencies); always check in advance. If you submit photographs, avoid glossy prints, as they reflect studio lights.

The following shows the format and content of a typical radio announcement.

Phyllis Sanderson   For use October 1–12
Claireville PTA
145 School Street
Claireville, IL 61844
Telephone: 335–1256

Time: 20 seconds

Well-educated young people are America's greatest asset for the future. During National Education Week, October 15–19, Claireville teachers and the Claireville PTA urge you to visit your schools to see education in action. See for yourself how our schools are preparing students for the challenges of the future.

END

The same announcement could be adapted for use on television:

Phyllis Sanderson   For use October 1–12
Claireville PTA
145 School Street
Claireville, IL 61844
Telephone: 335–1256

Time: 20 seconds

VIDEO	AUDIO
Slide No. 1 (Students carrying books with school building in background)	Well-educated young people are America's greatest asset for the future.

Slide No. 2
(Close-up of school entrance, showing name of the school and students entering)

These are *our* schools educating *our* children. During National Education Week, October 15–19, Claireville teachers and the Claireville PTA urge you to visit your schools to see education in action. See for yourself how our schools are preparing students for the challenges of the future.

END

Radio and Television Programs

Radio and television stations sometimes feature community organizations on regularly scheduled programs or on specials. Contact the public affairs director at the station to find out how your organization can become involved in such programs or call the producers of programs that focus on community news.

In most cases, you will not be expected to write the script for a program about your organization. The station will usually be responsible for planning and writing the program. However, your cooperation will be needed in supplying information, arranging interviews, and coordinating member participation in the actual program.

Newsletters

Many organizations produce newsletters. In many cases, the primary purpose of a newsletter is to inform readers about the activities of the organization. A newsletter may also inform readers about new ideas, events in the news, and publications that may interest them. It might be used to promote membership, attendance at meetings, participation in organization activities, or the organization's positions on various issues. A newsletter with a humor or "personalities" column may also entertain readers.

The audience for a newsletter is not always limited to members of the organization. It may also include prospective members or members of similar organizations. Re-

Newsletters inform members of activities, both within the organization and about the membership. They provide new ideas, information on recent publications, and news of other organizations with similar goals and interests.

porters for the various media may read the newsletter if the organization's activities are in the news.

If your organization does not have a newsletter but is thinking of starting one, it might be wise to first explore whether some other means of communication might fulfill your purposes. A brief calendar of events that is distributed to members may be enough to keep them informed of activities. Word of mouth may be sufficient to attract new members. Do not assume that every organization needs a newsletter. Keep in mind that producing a newsletter involves a substantial investment of time and effort. It also costs money.

Content

Assume that your organization already has a newsletter or has plans to start one. What topics might the newsletter cover? The following is a list of possible topics that may be covered in the newsletter:

- Recent or upcoming meetings, programs, projects, or special events
- Election of new officers
- Installation of newly elected officers
- Membership drives
- Interviews or feature stories about organization members or other interesting or prominent people
- Fund-raising drives
- The financial status of the organization
- Activities of similar organizations in the community or elsewhere
- The history and purpose of the organization

Some newsletters include regular features, such as a calendar of events; a president's column; or news from state, national, or international affiliates. Others include a news column on members in each issue, which reports marriages, births, deaths, job promotions, and special activities and accomplishments of members.

Deciding which topics to cover in each issue of the newsletter is the editor's job. However, most newsletter editors welcome story suggestions from organization members. After deciding which topics to cover in a particular issue, the editor usually assigns reporters to research and write the stories. However, many newsletter editors do not have reporters to gather news and must write all the stories themselves.

The following sections deal with writing news, feature, and interview stories for your newsletter.

News Stories

Assume your newsletter editor has given you a news story assignment. The first step in writing such a story is to gather the facts.

Gathering the Facts

Gathering the facts for a newsletter story is very similar to gathering the facts for a news release (*see* pages 265–266). Begin by listing the facts you have. Then gather additional information by talking to appropriate people in person or on the telephone. In some cases you may look at past issues of the newsletter for stories on the same topic or similar topics. These stories may include information that you can use in your own news story.

A member of an arts and crafts club for senior citizens gathered these facts for a news story:

- Arts and Crafts Club members will begin a new project next week.
- Will use coat hangers and yarn to make poodles.
- The poodles make perfect gifts for grandchildren and other young relatives.
- A sample is now on display in the crafts room.
- Members are asked to bring their own materials.

Once you have gathered the facts, you are ready to write, revise, and rewrite the news story.

Writing, Revising, and Rewriting

The process of writing, revising, and rewriting a news story for a newsletter is similar to that used when writing a news release (*see* pages 266–271). The following story about the Arts and Crafts Club closely follows newspaper style, except that the lead is less formal and is written to get the reader's attention.

"How much is that doggie in the window?" That may be the new theme song for Arts and Crafts Club members as they begin their new project next week.

Club members will make poodles using coat hangers and yarn. A sample is now on display in the crafts room.

Members are asked to bring their own materials for the project.

> The poodles make perfect gifts for grandchildren and other young relatives.

Although newsletter stories are often written in newspaper style, avoid simply reprinting news releases in the newsletter. Members will not be interested in reading the same story that they just read in the newspaper. The following story illustrates how a news release can be rewritten in a fresh, interesting way.

> What happens when, after miles and miles of riding your bicycle in solitude, you suddenly find yourself in a "metropolis" of 15,000 people?
>
> What happens when you get to a place that can only be reached by a helicopter flying across a rushing river?
>
> What happens when you and your equipment are soaked through and through, it's 40 degrees, and you're miles from nowhere?
>
> Get answers to these questions and more as Carol Manning shows her slides and tells fascinating and sometimes hair-raising stories about her bicycle trip across Canada.

Feature Stories

Newsletters sometimes include feature stories—human interest stories, stories about personal experiences or achievements, and personality sketches. Such stories usually deal with current or former members of the organization or with organization activities. Feature stories may entertain, motivate, or teach by example. An example of a human interest story follows.

> A life may have been saved as a result of a fire safety program sponsored by the Parent-Teacher Association at Crosby School.
>
> Jill Winter, a fifth-grade student at the school, was awakened by a smoke detector in her home about midnight last Thursday.
>
> Remembering what she had learned at the fire safety program, she felt her bedroom door and discovered that it was hot. She left the door closed and stuffed a blanket under the crack in the door.
>
> Jill then opened a window and sat by it, breathing the fresh air. Within ten minutes she was rescued by fire

fighters. The other members of her family also escaped
without injury.

The PTA plans to repeat the fire safety program before
the end of the school year.

Note that a feature story lead, unlike a news story lead,
does not have to give all the important facts. Rather, it
should stimulate the reader's curiosity or get the reader's
attention.

The important facts must be included somewhere in the
story. However, the reporter can choose how to present
these facts and the order in which to present them. Since
feature stories are usually not shortened, the paragraphs
need not be arranged in order of decreasing importance.

Interviews

Newsletters sometimes include interviews with interesting
or prominent people. These people are often members of
the organization, although they need not be. Interviews
can inform, entertain, and motivate. In addition, most
readers like interviews because they enjoy learning about
other people.

If you plan to profile an individual in the newsletter,
schedule the interview well in advance of the copy deadline. Agree on a location for the interview, preferably one
that is comfortable and free from outside distractions. Tell
the subject of the profile the kinds of information you
need. Ask about time limits and topics that cannot be discussed. You may wish to ask for a biography or résumé,
which you can review before the interview. This will eliminate the need to ask routine questions about the subject's
background. It may also suggest additional avenues for
questioning.

Plan the interview questions carefully, keeping the readers' interests in mind. Doing background reading on the
topics you plan to discuss may help you write better questions. List the questions in order of importance in case
you do not have time to cover all of them. In general, avoid
questions that can be answered with a flat *yes* or *no*. Plan
questions that provoke thoughtful and interesting responses.

Arrive early for the interview. This will allow time for a
final review of the questions.

Begin the interview by briefly discussing the topics you
plan to cover. Then ask the prepared questions, taking

careful notes on the subject's answers. Ask for the correct spelling of any names you write down. If you plan to use direct quotes, ask permission to do so. Make sure that any quotes you write down are accurate. If the subject refuses to be quoted directly, you will need to paraphrase his or her words.

Some interviewers use a tape recorder, thus eliminating the need to take notes. However, some people object to having an interview recorded; always ask permission in advance.

Keep in mind that a successful interviewer lets the subject do most of the talking. However, if the subject strays too far from the topic, the interviewer must get the discussion back on the track by asking appropriate questions.

At the end of the interview, remember to express your appreciation. You might also ask permission to contact the person if you need additional information.

Organize your notes and write the story as soon as possible after the interview. Keep in mind that writing an interview story is similar in many ways to writing a feature story. The first paragraph is designed to grab attention or stimulate curiosity. The rest of the story, which for the most part consists of direct quotations or paraphrases, can be organized in whatever way the reporter considers most effective. Paragraphs need not be arranged in order of decreasing importance, as interview stories are usually not shortened. A sample interview story follows.

"Selling is not just taking orders," says Henry Reiss, Reliable Life Insurance's salesperson of the year for the past five years. "You can't stand around waiting for someone to come into the office. You have to be aggressive and go after the sale."

Like many insurance salespeople, Reiss started out in a different line of work.

"I was an accountant for six years, but eventually I got tired of spending most of the day dealing with numbers. I needed to be with people more. So I decided to get into sales," Reiss says.

A chance meeting with an old friend who had achieved success selling life insurance led to his current job.

What's the most difficult part of the job? Reiss says without hesitation, "Hearing *no* more often than any other word. You can contact 100 people and make only 3 appointments. Out of those three appointments you may make only one sale. That's a lot of rejections. But you get used to it."

What about the rewards? Reiss cheerfully admits that money is one of the big rewards of his work. But he says there is more to the job than just making money.

"I enjoy helping my customers. I get satisfaction from showing people the best and most economical way to provide for the future. I really believe that you can't be a success in sales unless you like people."

What about his own future—will he be number one again next year?

Reiss laughs: "Who knows? I'll certainly give it my best shot."

Producing the Newsletter

Newsletters may be reproduced using a variety of methods, including photocopying, mimeographing, and offset printing. Before a newsletter can be reproduced, however, its contents must be typed, typeset, or entered into a word processor and then printed out.

Typing

If you decide to type your newsletter, it is best to use an electric or electronic typewriter. Manual typewriters often produce uneven lines of type. Also, some letters may appear darker than others because typists often exert uneven pressure when striking the keys.

Clean the typewriter thoroughly before you begin. Always use a film or carbon ribbon, rather than a cloth ribbon, if you plan to photocopy the newsletter or use offset printing. Use white bond paper of high quality or a good stencil.

Decide how many columns there will be on a page and the maximum column width. In addition, decide whether the right-hand margin in each column will be ragged (uneven) or justified (even). If you choose justification, you can use a typewriter with a proportional spacing mechanism to achieve this result. Or you can follow the procedure described below using any standard typewriter.

Set margins at the established column width. Then type the copy to full column width. If any spaces remain at the end of a line, type as many slash marks as are needed to fill the spaces. Next, go back over the copy, adding check marks where you will insert an extra space between words to fill out each line evenly. Add one space for each slash mark at the end of a line. Avoid lining up check marks one below the other. This creates "rivers" of white space that

A ✓$500 ✓gift ✓certificate for ✓Logan's////
department ✓store is just one of the many/
items ✓to be auctioned ✓October 20 at the//
Greeley Center. ✓The Civic Club, sponsor/
of ✓the event, will donate ✓all ✓proceeds///
to the Lake City Youth Foundation.

A $500 gift certificate for Logan's
department store is just one of the many
items to be auctioned October 20 at the
Greeley Center.   The Civic Club, sponsor
of the event, will donate all proceeds
to the Lake City Youth Foundation.

distract the reader. Finally, retype the copy, adding space where the check marks fall. An example of this technique is produced above.

Typesetting

Some organizations typeset their newsletters. Although having a newsletter set in type is much more expensive than having it typewritten, the result is a more professional appearance. Typeset copy is also easier to read than typewritten copy.

A typesetter can offer a large variety of type styles and sizes. Typeset letters are sharper and clearer than those produced by even the highest quality typewriter. In addition, typesetters do a good job keeping lines straight and the spaces between letters and words uniform.

When deciding whether or not to have your newsletter typeset, consider not only the cost, but also the time involved. In general, using a typesetter will add several days to your production schedule, that is, the length of time between submitting copy to a typesetter and the publication of that copy.

Word Processing

It is becoming more and more common to use word processors with attached printers to edit and prepare newsletter copy for reproduction. If your organization owns or has access to such equipment, you should strongly consider using it for your newsletter.

Word processing can greatly speed up the writing and editing process. The machine makes it possible to add, delete, or correct copy without retyping the entire document. Margins can be set and justified automatically or left ragged. At any point during the typing on a word processor, a paper copy of the text can be produced via the attached printer.

The expense of a word processor, however, limits its use to major editorial projects. A monthly newsletter may not warrant the costs involved.

Proofreading

Proofread your newsletter carefully, whether it is typed, typeset, or produced by a printer attached to a word processor. Typeset copy *must* be proofread both before and after it is sent to the typesetter. Keep in mind that typesetters are not paid to catch your errors. They set what they see, errors and all. If there is an error in your copy, it will probably show up in the proof. Your organization will be financially responsible for correcting it. (Review Appendix B for proofreader marks and procedures.)

Proofreading is an important step in the process of publishing a newsletter. Carefully proof all copy before it is mimeographed, photocopied, or printed. Appendix B, at the end of this volume, provides instructions and examples of professional proofreading.

Careful proofreading will spare you and your organization the embarrasssment that often results from errors in print. Use the following checklist as you proofread.

- Are there typographical errors?
- Are all words and proper names spelled correctly?
- Are there errors in grammar, punctuation, or capitalization?
- Has any copy—words, lines, or paragraphs—been dropped or been incorrectly placed?
- If the copy was typeset, are there any characters from a different type face?
- Does each sentence make sense?

Reproducing the Newsletter

Photocopying, mimeographing, and offset printing are the most common methods of reproducing newsletters. Each has both advantages and disadvantages.

Photocopying can be used with newsletters that are typed, typeset, or produced on a computer printer. If you do not have immediate access to a photocopier, copies can be made, at fairly reasonable cost, by a commercial copier. Most newer photocopy machines can produce good quality copies on a wide variety of paper stocks. In addition, many machines can reduce the copy in size. In quantities beyond 200 to 300 copies, offset printing may be more economical than photocopying.

Mimeographing is less expensive than either photocopying or offset printing; this is especially true if your organization owns a mimeograph machine. It is also much faster than the various steps involved in offset printing. If you find the process of typing and proofreading stencils tedious, electronic stencils can be commercially made, at reasonable cost, from either typed, typeset, or computer printout copy. The greatest drawback to mimeograph reproduction is quality, which is inferior to both photocopying and offset printing.

Offset printing is usually the most expensive of the three methods. As mentioned earlier, however, the cost of offset printing is dependent upon quantity; as the number of copies printed increases, the cost per copy decreases. If the print order, that is, the number of copies you need printed, of your newsletter is several hundred or even thousand, definitely investigate offset production. The quality is far superior to either photocopying or mimeo-graphing. Offset printing can reproduce either typed, type-set, or computer printout copy. The process, however, is substantially more complicated than the other two and may add from a day to a week to the production schedule. The result, however, is highly professional.

Most newspapers, magazines, and books published in the U.S. are printed by offset. Differences in the printing quality usually reflect the differences in paper stock used by the different mediums. Print and photographs repro-duce less well on inexpensive newsprint, used by newspa-pers, than on the much heavier paper specified by book publishers. Better magazines are printed on paper coated with enamel, which is designed to faithfully reproduce black-and-white and color illustrations. If your organiza-tion is contemplating printing a publication by offset, ask the printer about various paper stocks. The most expen-sive paper is not always the best choice for a particular job. Most papers are manufactured for fairly specific kinds of printing jobs. Ask what stock is appropriate, both in terms of quality and cost, for your publication. Paper stocks are graded by both weight and color. The paper stock used in this book is 55 pound, which means that a thousand sheets (not pages) weighs 55 pounds. A newslet-ter, which is not designed to be permanent, might appro-priately be printed on 20- to 30-pound paper, white or cream in color.

Correspondence

Members of organizations write letters for a variety of pur-poses: raising funds, requesting speakers, soliciting new members, and enlisting volunteers for a particular project. In addition, an organization may state its position on var-ious issues in letters to the editor. Letters to elected offi-cials may state a position or encourage officials to follow a particular course of action. Chapter 6, "Personal Writing and Correspondence," contains information on writing business letters, letters to the editor, and letters to elected officials (*see* pages 246–257). A sample fund-raising letter follows. Note that it is written on the organization's letter-head.

CITY YOUTH COUNCIL
1056 Maple Avenue
River City, IL 60021

February 1, 1984

Ms. Andrea Martin, President
ABC Engineering Corporation
3303 W. Prairie Avenue
River City, IL 60021

Dear Ms. Martin:

If you have recently been downtown on any weekday afternoon, you may have noticed the large number of high school students ''hanging around'' on street corners. You've probably wondered if these young people might not use their time more productively.

The City Youth Council believes that the answer is yes. Our organization is developing a new program that will provide after-school training for high school students. Courses in such areas as typing, computer operation and programming, cooking, and auto mechanics will be offered. As you know, recent budget cuts have eliminated many of these courses from the regular high school curriculum.

In addition to training students, our organization will attempt to place them in part-time jobs in the community. We are sure that you will agree that our project will benefit the community as a whole as well as the students who participate in it.

Can we count on your support?

Please send your tax-deductible contribution in the enclosed envelope.

Sincerely yours,

Philip Parsons
President

Enclosure

The following letter requests a speaker for an organization meeting.

THE GIFFORD PINCHOT SOCIETY
11 Conservation Place
River City, IL 60021

April 2, 1984

Mr. Ambrose Dikeman, President
The Conservation League of America
3112 Cody Drive
Springfield, IL 62701

Dear Mr. Dikeman:

Members of our organization have read about your innovative program for the restoration of native prairies. Mr. Laurence Sabine, who recently lectured in this area on the destruction of natural habitat, has recommended both your ideas and qualifications as a speaker. Would you be able to speak at the regular meeting of our society on either Thursday, July 26 or Thursday, August 30, 1984?

We are all greatly interested in your success with the restoration of native flora and how your methods can be adapted in our area.

The meeting will be held in the Central City Room, Hotel Florence in River City, at 8:00 P.M. We would appreciate it if you would be willing to answer questions after making your presentation.

The Gifford Pinchot Society pays an honorarium of $100 for speakers and, of course, covers all travel and accommodation expenses.

If you are able to speak on either of these dates, please let us know at your earliest convenience.

Sincerely yours,

Oscar Maxwell

Oscar Maxwell
President

Posters and Fliers

Posters and fliers are an effective method of advertising an organization's special event or calendar of events. They can also be used to state a position or promote a cause. Both posters and fliers can be produced fairly quickly and inexpensively.

Posters

Effective posters are simple in content and design. They have a dual function: to catch people's attention and to communicate a message, quickly and dramatically. Posters must also include all important facts. A poster advertising an event, for example, must give the date, the time, the location, and, if relevant, the price of admission.

Effective posters are easy to read and visually appealing. Avoid crowding too many words, pictures, or designs onto a poster. Examples of two posters, announcing the same event, are given below. Which do you think is more effective?

When making a poster that states a position or promotes a cause, choose the words and visual images carefully. Think about how the poster will attract attention
and get its message across. Note in the following examples
how visual images and the messages are inseparable.

When making posters by hand, you will need some or all
of the following materials: poster board; pencils and erasers; a T-square for making horizontal lines; triangles for
making vertical and diagonal lines; a ruler; lettering
brushes and pens; and poster paints. These materials can
be purchased at an art supply store. If you plan to attach
pictures or design elements to the poster, you will need
rubber cement.

Letters in various colors and type faces that are attached
to thin plastic sheets can be purchased from art supply or
stationery shops. The letters, called transfer type, can be
individually removed from the sheets and transferred to
the poster board. Using letters of this kind eliminates the
need for hand lettering.

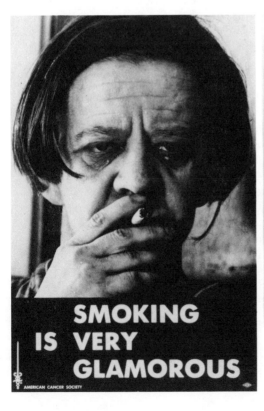

If your organization has people skilled in poster making, by all means enlist their help in designing and laying out the poster. Keep the design simple if volunteers are to copy the poster by hand. If your budget permits, you may wish to have the poster printed. Also, some sign shops and print shops offer design and layout services as well as printing services.

Fliers

Like posters, fliers are a form of advertising. Their greatest advantage is their portability; the reader picks up the flier and carries it with him or her. An effective poster attracts attention and transfers a message that can be remembered. An effective flier attracts enough attention to be picked up and carried away.

The information on a flier is often the same as that given on a poster; an event and the date, time, place, and admission fee, if any, are announced. A flier has the additional advantage of allowing the space for additional information, for example, telling the reader the rationale for the event or describing the event in full detail. A flier announcing a political rally might, for example, outline the ideas around which the rally is being promoted—"why nuclear arms proliferation is dangerous." A flier advertising a musical event might describe the music to be performed and the eminence of the performers—"Mr. Lizt has performed with the Paris Opera and La Scala."

An effective flier should be simple. Artwork is generally kept to a minimum. Like the front page of a newspaper, the copy on a good flier attracts attention with headlines—"Ban the Bomb" or "Lizt to Perform Tonight." The front page of a newspaper is designed to attract enough attention that a reader will pick it up and carry it home. A flier should do exactly the same.

Fliers can be either a single sheet or a large sheet of paper folded in half or in quarters. The first arrangement—the single sheet—is ideal for announcing an event, a musical performance, for example. The second arrangement—the large sheet folded—allows space for extra copy and is typically used for fliers where the message, rather than an event, is of greater importance. If your organization is holding a bake sale, opt for the single sheet. If you are trying to combat industrial wastes or stop local pollution, you will need the space provided by a folded flier to explain your message.

A flier can be typewritten, typeset, or even handwritten. It can be reproduced by photocopying, mimeographing, or offset printing (*see* the section on newsletters in this chapter). However, remember that the more professional the appearance of your flier, the greater the chance that it will be picked up, taken home, and read.

The success of a flier is often dependent upon how the sheet is distributed. Fliers left in a pile by a door are often left in a pile by a door by the public. If you want your message in the hands of the public, put it there. Station volunteers on busy street corners when foot traffic is heaviest—in the morning when people are going to work, at noon, and in the evening when people are leaving from work. Shopping districts or suburban shopping malls are usually the best locations if a flier is to be distributed on a weekend.

The success of a flier is dependent upon how the sheet is distributed. If you want your message in the hands of the public, put it there.

Cookbooks

Organizations often publish cookbooks consisting of recipes contributed by members. Sold to both members and nonmembers, an organization cookbook provides a way to share recipes as well as raise funds.

Some organizations publish general-purpose cookbooks containing a wide variety of recipes. Other organization cookbooks may specialize in recipes for main dishes, desserts, salads, or some other part of a meal. Still other cookbooks focus on a particular kind of cooking: Mexican, Chinese, Italian, or French.

Once an organization has decided what kind of cookbook to publish, it should appoint an editor. Although the editor will need assistance from various members, he or she will take responsibility for directing the project.

The editor's first task is to inform members of the cookbook's theme, if any, and to ask them to contribute appropriate recipes. Members should be given these guidelines to follow when submitting recipes:

- Type the recipe double spaced on 8½- by 11-inch bond paper, not on an index card. If you cannot type, print legibly on lined paper.
- Include your name and telephone number on each recipe.
- List the ingredients in the order in which they are used.
- To avoid confusion, do not use abbreviations.
- Proofread the recipe against the original to make sure it is complete and correct.
- Reword any instructions that might confuse the reader.

In addition, ask members to *only* submit recipes that they themselves have *tested.* Emphasize that the reader should not play the role of "guinea pig." *Establish a deadline* for submitting recipes. Give frequent reminders as the deadline approaches.

Decide, as soon as possible, how the book is to be organized. Many general-purpose cookbooks are divided into sections: appetizers, soups, main dishes, salads, and desserts. Within each section, recipes may be arranged alphabetically or grouped with similar recipes. Look at a variety of other cookbooks before deciding how yours will be organized.

Next, begin sorting recipes into appropriate categories. This will help you determine if you need more recipes in a particular category, or if you have any duplicate recipes.

The next step is to edit the recipes. If you decide to use abbreviations, make sure you use them *consistently* throughout the cookbook. You should also include a list of abbreviations at the front of the book.

Check each recipe for errors in spelling, grammar, and punctuation. Directions should be given in complete sentences and should be easy to understand and follow. If anything in the recipe is unclear, check with the person who submitted it.

Decide whether to list ingredients in a one- or two-column format. Using a two-column format, as shown below, saves space and will result in lower paper and printing costs.

1 c. white sugar	1/4 tsp. salt
1 c. brown sugar	2 eggs
3 c. sifted flour	1 c. buttermilk
1 c. butter	1 c. chopped walnuts
1 tsp. baking soda	(optional)

Plan to include a table of contents and an index in the cookbook. Also include a table of weights and measures and a table of substitutions and equivalents in the front of the book. Divider pages in front of each section will make the cookbook easier to use.

Keep in mind that producing the cookbook will involve a substantial investment of time, effort, and money. Once the copy has been edited, it can be typewritten, typeset, or entered into a word processor and printed out. The cookbook can be reproduced by photocopying, mimeographing, or offset printing. The steps involved in producing a cookbook are similar to those for producing a newsletter. Refer to pages 285–289 for more detailed information on the production process.

The Professional Writer

The previous chapters of *How to Write Effectively* dealt with learning writing skills and applying those skills to school, work, and one's personal and community life. The final chapter, "The Professional Writer," examines how the mastery of writing skills can form the basis of a career.

Professional writers, whether newspaper reporters, magazine writers and editors, scriptwriters, book authors, or advertising copywriters, all share a common passion—a passion for words. They love to write. They may complain about guidelines, limitations, and deadlines, but they love the challenge of piling words into sentences and sentences into paragraphs; of juxtaposing thought against thought and idea against idea.

Writing, if you think about it, is an extraordinary thing. It is the process by which thought is transformed into speech—human sounds recognized as specific things, persons, places, and ideas—and speech is transformed into visual symbols—words that represent the same specific things, persons, places, and ideas.

This process may be humanity's most fundamental accomplishment. We take it all for granted. It has been around for so long. But, for just one minute, contemplate the magnitude of it all. Until one human being was able, without speaking, to transfer his or her thoughts into the brain of another human being, what was life like? What could be accomplished? Remembered? Planned? With the advent of writing, we could not only communicate with each other, we could communicate with the past and with the future. Whenever we pull a work by Voltaire off the shelf, he still speaks, two hundred years after his death. And two hundred years from now, our ideas, our thoughts, will also be read and contemplated by yet unborn generations.

To be a writer, to be part of that process by which all that we are and all that we know is transferred from one generation to the next, is to belong to an important profession. It is taking a part in something that stretches back as far as we know and looks forward even further than we can imagine.

Newspaper Reporters

Newspapers play a vital role in a free society. They inform, entertain, and help shape public opinion as they present and interpret the news. They serve the public interest by monitoring the activities of government agencies and public officials. They sometimes expose various kinds of corruption, wrongdoing, and unfair practices. In addition, newspapers may investigate and inform readers about dangers to public health and safety.

The United States has about 1,800 daily, 7,000 weekly, and 550 semiweekly newspapers. Circulation of daily newspapers totals about 60 million. Some daily newspapers have a circulation of more than one million. Clearly, newspapers are an important and influential means of communication.

Kinds of Writing

Newspapers could not exist without reporters to gather and report the news. In addition to news stories, reporters may also write feature stories, columns, editorials, news analyses, sports stories, and reviews. Let's begin by discussing news stories.

News Stories

Reporters may cover news at the local, state, national, or international level. Such news may involve politics, government, business, medicine, science, education, enter-

tainment, or the arts. Reporters also cover such news as crimes, fires, natural disasters, and wars.

Writing a News Story.   The first step in writing a news story is to gather the facts. Reporters use a variety of methods: interviewing, observing, examining public records, checking past issues of the newspaper, and doing library research. Some reporters take notes as they gather information; others use a tape recorder, especially when conducting interviews.

Once a reporter has gathered the facts, he or she may go back to the newspaper office to write the story. If this is impossible because of the newspaper's deadline, or because the reporter has other stories to cover, the story may be telephoned to a rewriter. The *rewriter* takes down the facts supplied by the reporter, gathers additional information if necessary, and then writes the story. In some cases, the reporter may actually write the story and then dictate it over the telephone.

Regardless of who actually writes them, news stories usually follow a set format. The first paragraph of the story, called the *lead*, briefly summarizes the important

The average person no longer chases after clanging fire trucks. This has become the speciality of the newspaper and television reporter, who keeps the public abreast with what is happening around the corner as well as around the world.

information in the story. The lead focuses on the 5W's: *who, what, when, where,* and *why.* It may also explain *how* the event happened. The most important information is usually given at the beginning of the lead.

The *body* of the news story gives more information about the facts presented in the lead. Body paragraphs are arranged in order of decreasing importance. This allows the editor to cut the story from the bottom up if space is a problem. The structure of a news story is often represented using a pyramid, as shown in the diagram below.

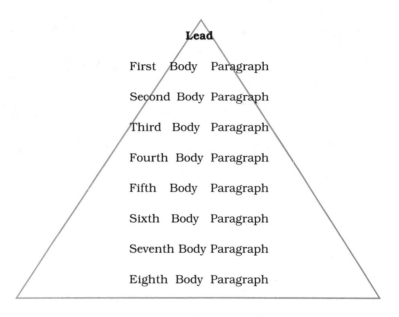

After the story is written, it is given to a copy editor, who corrects any errors in spelling, grammar, and punctuation. He or she may also reword certain parts of the story to make it clearer or easier to understand. The copy editor then writes a headline and shortens the story if necessary.

Kinds of News Reporters.   Many newspapers have several categories of reporters. *Beat reporters* may cover a particular building, such as police headquarters, city hall, or the courts. Or they may cover a particular subject, such as education, business and finance, consumer affairs, or science. Reporters who cover a particular subject often have a background in the field or a special interest in it.

General assignment reporters do not cover a beat; they cover stories assigned by the editor or find their own stories. *Investigative reporters* interview, observe, and do extensive research to uncover evidence of wrongdoing, such as political corruption. The newspaper then prints stories reporting these findings.

Reporters who are sent to other locations to gather and report the news are called *correspondents.* As a rule, only larger newspapers have correspondents in various cities throughout the United States and in foreign countries. Most newspapers rely on *wire services* for news from other locations.

Wire services, also called *news services,* supply about 90 percent of the foreign news and about 75 percent of the national news to newspapers throughout the United States. The Associated Press (AP) and United Press International (UPI) are the major wire services in the United States. Each employs hundreds of reporters to gather and report the news in various domestic and foreign locations. These wire services transmit news stories and photographs to newspapers across the country.

Reporters on smaller newspapers may be required to cover all kinds of stories, since there may be too few reporters to assign to specific categories. In addition to gathering the news and writing stories, these reporters may also take photographs, edit stories, write headlines, lay out pages, and write columns and editorials. For more information on news *see* pages 130–137.

Feature Stories

Reporters write feature stories as well as news stories. Most feature stories entertain the reader, explain how to do something, or communicate other useful information. Examples of feature stories include interviews with famous or interesting people; human interest stories; and articles on such topics as gardening, home maintenance and repair, life styles, and interesting places to visit.

Unlike news stories, feature stories do not follow a set format. Feature story leads are written to capture the reader's attention. They need not summarize the important facts of the story as in a news story lead. Also, feature stories are usually not shortened. Therefore, the paragraphs of a feature story do not have to be arranged in order of decreasing importance. The reporter is free to present the facts in the order that he or she considers most effective.

Feature stories, like news stories, are based on fact. However, reporters sometimes use the techniques of fiction in feature stories. Such techniques include narration, description, suspense, and dialogue.

Columns

Many newspapers print the work of columnists who write about a variety of topics. Types of columns include general information, political and social commentary, humor, advice, and how-to columns. Editors of particular sections of the newspaper, such as sports, business, or fashion, may write regular columns.

Syndicated columnists have their writing printed in more than one newspaper. Such columnists receive a fee from every newspaper that prints the column.

Other Kinds of Writing

Newspaper reporters may do other kinds of writing, including editorials, news analyses, obituaries, and sports stories. (For more information on writing sports stories, *see* pages 138–139.) Some reporters write reviews of movies, plays, books, musical performances, or restaurants.

Careers

We have seen that newspaper reporters play a vital role in gathering and reporting the news. This section will discuss careers in newspaper reporting, including nature of the work, education and preparation, and employment opportunities.

Nature of the Work

Newspaper reporting is a challenging field that offers many rewards. Reporters have the satisfaction of seeing their stories in print and knowing that these stories may influence readers or serve to protect the public interest. They have the opportunity to meet and talk with a great many people. They are sometimes able to travel throughout the United States and foreign countries as they gather and report the news.

The work of a newspaper reporter is seldom routine. Each story may be different and offer a new challenge to the reporter.

Despite the many rewards, the job of newspaper reporter has its drawbacks. Working conditions are sometimes difficult. Reporters constantly work under the pressure of deadlines. Although they must work quickly, reporters must also be fair and accurate. Statements that are untrue or libelous can result in costly lawsuits.

Newspaper reporters may be required to work nights, weekends, and holidays. The work may also be dangerous. Reporters are sometimes injured or even killed while performing their duties. Assignments may take them to the scenes of fires, floods, earthquakes, demonstrations, riots, and wars. Reporters are sometimes harassed by people who disagree with their stories.

Successful newspaper reporters are dedicated to their work. They have a "nose for the news," which helps them uncover news stories. They also have sound news judgment. Such judgment helps them decide which news is important and will be of interest to readers.

Good reporters have almost endless curiosity about people and events. They try to find out not only *what* happened but also *why* it happened. They are persistent, since getting the story may involve long hours of tedious research.

A love of language is another trait of most newspaper reporters. Good reporters have a keen ear for the sounds words make on paper. In addition, they are able to write clearly and directly.

Education and Preparation

A large number of colleges and universities in the United States offer four-year programs leading to a bachelor's degree in journalism. Such programs usually consist of about 25 percent journalism courses and 75 percent liberal arts courses. Journalism courses teach students how to gather news and write and edit stories. These courses also deal with laws governing the press, journalistic ethics, and the history of journalism.

Some junior or community colleges offer journalism courses. Credits earned in such courses can sometimes be transferred to four-year programs at colleges and universities.

Although some editors will hire reporters with liberal arts or other college degrees, an increasing number of editors prefer graduates with a bachelor's degree in journalism. At some newspapers, a master's degree in journalism is preferred.

Some newspaper reporters do not have a college degree. Many of these reporters entered the profession some years ago when a college degree was less important. Today, how-

A college course in journalism may include an internship program. Students receive on-the-job training by working part-time for newspapers, magazines, or television news departments.

ever, many editors will not consider applicants without a bachelor's degree.

People who wish to become newspaper reporters should learn how to type and should take courses in English, speech, history, political science, business, economics, foreign languages, and sociology. Those who want to specialize in a particular field, such as science or finance, should take courses in that area. A knowledge of shorthand and photography can also be very helpful.

High school students interested in becoming reporters should work on their school newspapers and yearbooks. They should also enroll in a journalism class if one is offered at their high school. Summer internship programs at local newspapers may be open to high school students. A number of internships for college journalism students are available at various newspapers.

Working as a stringer is another way to get reporting experience. *Stringers* are part-time reporters who write stories on assignment or develop and submit their own stories. Stringers are often responsible for covering news in one part of a town or community.

Employment Opportunities

Most large-city newspapers look for reporters with several years of experience, although a few outstanding journalism school graduates may be hired each year. Reporting experience can be gained at community newspapers or newspapers in smaller towns and cities.

Reporters may begin as general assignment reporters. Later, they may be assigned to a beat or may cover a particular subject for the newspaper. Some reporters eventually become columnists or write columns in addition to their regular reporting duties. At smaller newspapers, reporters may cover a wide variety of stories, write columns and editorials, edit copy, and lay out pages.

In general, competition for reporting jobs on larger newspapers is keen. More opportunities exist on newspapers in smaller cities and towns and with local and community newspapers.

Participation in summer internship programs may lead to a job offer after college. Experience as a stringer may also be helpful in getting a full-time reporting job. Applicants with bachelor's or master's degree in journalism sometimes have an advantage over those with other college degrees.

Reporters generally are required to work 35 to 40 hours a week. Most get fringe benefits such as health insurance, paid vacations and sick days, and pension plans.

Salaries vary depending on the size of the newspaper, its location, and the reporter's length of service and merit. Salaries also vary depending on whether or not the newspaper has a contract with the Newspaper Guild, an employee union.

Magazine Staff Writers

More than 16,500 magazines are published each year in the United States. Magazines usually are classified by the audience they serve. These classifications include trade and business magazines, men's magazines, women's magazines, hobby magazines, children's magazines, and intellectual magazines. Other types of magazines include newsmagazines, digests, guide magazines, and scholarly journals.

Magazines inform, entertain, and instruct readers. Although magazine articles may cover a wide range of topics, most fall into one of four categories: human interest, how-to, personality profile, and news.

In addition to nonfiction, some magazines publish short stories, poems, and excerpts from novels. Since the majority of magazines publish little or no fiction, this section will discuss nonfiction writing only.

The editor has the job of planning each issue of the

Planning issues
several months in
advance, magazine
editors decide the
subject matter and
illustrations for
articles. Writing and
art assignments are
then given to either
staff or free-lancers.

magazine. Such planning usually begins several months
in advance. The editor decides which articles will appear
in the magazine and usually assigns these articles to staff
writers or free-lance writers. Assignments are sometimes
made based on ideas suggested by writers.

Some magazines, such as *Time* and *Newsweek*, are
written by staff members. Other magazines, such as *National Geographic*, contain articles written by free-lancers
as well as staff members. Still other magazines rely almost
exclusively on free-lancers to write articles; such magazines usually do not employ staff writers. (For a discussion
of free-lance writing for magazines, *see* pages 312–317.)
At some magazines, editors may write articles and regular
columns in addition to performing editorial duties.

Researching and Writing the Article

Although there are certain similarities between newspaper
and magazine journalism, there are important differences
as well. As a rule, magazines cover topics in much greater

depth than do newspapers. This is because magazine writers generally have more time to do in-depth interviews and research. Their deadlines may be weeks or even months apart. Newspaper reporters may have one or more deadlines every day.

In addition, magazines usually have more space to devote to individual articles than do newspapers. Also, newspaper articles usually focus on the news value of the story. Although news value may be important in magazine articles, more emphasis is usually placed on exploring a topic in depth.

Because of the emphasis on in-depth coverage, magazine writers usually spend a considerable amount of time interviewing, observing, and doing library and other kinds of research. Gathering the facts for a major article may take from a few weeks to more than a year.

Once the research is complete, the actual writing can begin. Some writers spend a day or more developing the lead—the first paragraph of the article. A magazine article lead, unlike a newspaper story lead, does not have to give the important facts of the story. Instead, the lead uses a variety of techniques to "hook," that is, capture, readers' attention or arouse curiosity. Unless the lead does this, most readers will not finish reading the article.

Some writers write the lead first. Others write it last, after they have finished the rest of the article. After the first draft of the article has been completed, most writers spend considerable time revising and rewriting. They make sure that they have presented the topic clearly and in a manner that is appropriate to the audience. They review the article to make sure it covers everything promised in the lead. Careful writers also double-check all facts for accuracy.

In addition, writers must carefully check the article's length, which the editor usually specifies in advance. Although the editor may shorten the article somewhat, it should be very close to the specified length.

Careers

The following section discusses careers in magazine staff writing, including nature of the work, education and preparation, and employment opportunities.

Nature of the Work

Working as a magazine staff writer offers many rewards, including the opportunity to see one's words in print, influence readers, learn new things, and meet a variety of interesting people. Some magazine writers are also able to travel extensively while gathering material for articles.

Some magazine writers get satisfaction from writing articles that help individual readers or that serve the public interest. In addition, magazine writing, more so than newspaper writing, allows writers to explore topics in depth. Magazine staff writers, unlike free-lancers who write magazine articles, have the security of regular employment and a regular paycheck.

Despite its many advantages, being a magazine staff writer has its drawbacks. Writers may work long hours and be under a great deal of pressure to meet deadlines. Editors expect writers to produce articles that are accurate, thoroughly researched, well written, and appropriate for the magazine's audience. This is sometimes difficult because of time pressures. Writers may also have to spend long hours doing research, some of it tedious.

Like newspaper reporters, magazine staff writers must be curious about people and events. They must be persistent—willing to keep searching until they find all the information they need for an article.

Magazine writers must also be able to write well. They must be able to present ideas so that the reader can understand them. Good writers are also able to get and keep the reader's attention. In addition, magazine writers must be willing to spend considerable time revising and rewriting their work.

Some magazine staff writers are general-assignment writers, working on articles the editor assigns or developing their own articles. Others are specialists, writing about such topics as politics, music, religion, business, economics, finance, and social issues.

Education and Preparation

Some people prepare for careers in magazine writing by attending journalism schools. Some of these schools offer courses or even majors in magazine journalism. (For more information on journalism schools, *see* pages 305–306.)

While some magazine editors prefer to hire journalism school graduates, others look for people with a liberal arts background or training in a particular subject area. Although magazine staff writers are not required to have a college degree, it may be difficult to get such jobs without a degree. Because the field is highly competitive, those without a college degree may be at a disadvantage.

Working as a newspaper reporter usually provides good training for magazine writing. Writers for news magazines, for example, often have previous experience as reporters for the wire services and for newspapers in larger cities. Experience in book publishing may also be helpful when applying for a job as a magazine writer.

Some magazine editors suggest writing articles on a free-lance basis as a way to get noticed and possibly hired as a staff writer. (For more information on free-lance writing for magazines *see* pages 312–317.)

High school and college students can get valuable experience by working on school newspapers, magazines, and yearbooks. Working as a stringer—a part-time reporter—for magazines and newspapers is also helpful. Internships at magazines and newspapers also provide good training for magazine staff writing.

Employment Opportunities

Many magazines do not employ staff writers, relying instead on free-lancers. Staff editors may also occasionally write articles. Other magazines use free-lance material in addition to writing done by the staff. Relatively few magazines are entirely staff written. Thus, job opportunities for magazine staff writers are limited, and competition for these jobs is keen, especially on larger magazines.

Opportunities may be better at smaller magazines, especially trade, professional, industrial, and special-interest magazines. Staff members of such magazines may be required to perform a variety of tasks, including writing, editing, and some design and production work. Keep in mind, however, that many smaller magazines also rely heavily on free-lancers and may have as few as one or two staff members.

News magazines such as *Time* and *Newsweek* are staff-written. Competition for writing positions on such magazines is intense. Many news magazine writers (and editors) have experience as wire service reporters or reporters for large-city newspapers. These writers may work on a variety of assignments or may specialize in a particular subject.

News magazine writers may work at the magazine's headquarters. Many, however, work at bureaus across the United States and in foreign countries. These writers are known as correspondents and function in much the same way as newspaper correspondents.

Many magazines, both large and small, employ stringers. In some cases, talented stringers may be offered staff positions.

Salaries for magazine staff writers vary widely, depending on the type of publication, its size, and the writer's experience and ability. Most magazine staff writers receive fringe benefits, such as paid vacations and sick days, health insurance, and pension plans.

Free-Lance Writing

Some free-lance writers earn money by selling articles to magazines. Others write books for a variety of publishers, including trade, educational, business and professional, and scientific and technical publishers. In addition, various organizations may engage free-lancers to write reports, brochures, newsletters, and other materials.

Working full-time as a free-lance writer can involve a considerable degree of financial risk. Free-lancers are paid only when someone buys their work or engages their services. Because of the risks involved, many free-lance writers also hold salaried jobs. Also, some free-lancers view writing only as a sideline and have no desire to pursue it on a full-time basis.

People who take the financial risks associated with full-time free lancing range from those who can barely make ends meet to writers who earn a comfortable, or even handsome, living. But few free-lancers choose the profession based on money alone. The opportunity to communicate one's thoughts, ideas, and feelings is also important to most writers. In addition to the personal satisfaction that comes from writing, most free-lancers also value the freedom to choose when, how, and for whom they will work.

Free-lance writing is a demanding and challenging field with almost unlimited opportunities. Let's begin by looking at writing for magazines.

Magazines

We learned earlier that more than 16,500 magazines are published each year in the United States. Free-lancers write many of the articles that appear in these publications. A discussion of the steps involved in writing and submitting a nonfiction article for publication follows.

Getting Published

Study the Markets. Smart free-lance writers study the possible markets for their articles before they invest a substantial amount of time in researching and writing. A book called *Writer's Market* is published annually and lists the names, addresses, and editorial policies and needs of a large number of literary markets, including magazines.

Studying the listings in *Writer's Market* helps free-lancers learn what individual magazine editors want and do not want. Free-lancers often get article ideas from these listings or use them to identify possible markets for ideas they would like to develop. If a particular magazine is not listed in *Writer's Market* or another reference source, free-lancers can usually get information by writing directly to the editor of the publication.

In addition to studying market listings, free-lancers also study current and back issues of the magazines themselves. They look at the types of articles published, including subject matter, tone, writing style, and length. They try to understand the magazine's "personality"—the way it approaches its audience and what makes it different from other magazines of the same type. They learn whether certain types of articles are usually written by staff members rather than free-lancers. This can be done by comparing the by-lines on the articles with the names of staff members listed at the front of the magazine.

Choose a Topic. Once a writer has studied the markets, it is time to choose a topic for the article. Where do ideas for articles come from?

As mentioned earlier, some writers get article ideas from listings in *Writer's Market* or from studying the magazines themselves. Some writers also keep "idea files" as another source of possible topics for articles. An idea file consists of index cards or separate sheets of paper, each containing a single idea. These ideas are filed alphabetically or in some other logical order. Writers often review their idea files when looking for possible topics for articles.

In some cases, topics for magazine articles come from editors. Once a free-lance writer establishes a good track record with a magazine, the editor may contact the free-lancer to write particular articles on assignment.

Most free-lancers, however, must choose their own topics and try to interest an editor in these topics. The most common way to do this is to write a query letter to the editor.

Change in magazines over the last 100 years reflects change in American lifestyle and technology. Mass literacy in the late nineteenth century created a vast market for poetry, short stories, and serial novels. Movies, radio, and television forced magazines to specialize in news, non-fiction articles, and even gossip. *The New Yorker* is one of the few mass-market periodicals that still publishes first-rate fiction.

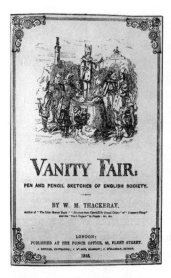

Query the Editor.   Once a free-lance writer has chosen a topic for an article, he or she may write the article and submit it to one or more magazines. This is called a *blind submission.* With luck, the writer will send it to an editor who can use the article now or sometime in the future. However, the chances of an editor accepting a blind sub-

mission are usually slim. This is why it is generally best to query the editor before actually writing the article. The only exception to this rule is when the magazine will accept only complete articles.

Most editors prefer to receive queries by mail rather than by telephone. A good query letter follows the format for a business letter and addresses the editor by name. It briefly explains the writer's article idea and tells why the magazine's readers would be interested in such an article. It gives the free-lancer's qualifications for writing the article and lists publications (if any) in which the writer's work has appeared. Most editors want an estimate of the article's length and also want to know whether photographs or illustrations will be provided.

Writing a good query letter does not guarantee an assignment from the editor. Editors receive queries about more articles than they can possibly use. Even good ideas can be rejected for a variety of reasons.

Successful free-lancers understand this and do not take such rejections personally. Instead, based on their study of possible markets, they submit the idea to editors at other magazines. In each query letter, they tailor the idea to the interests and needs of the magazine's readers. Such persistence usually pays off, since most good ideas for articles are eventually accepted.

An effective query letter can result in an assignment to write the article. A sample query letter follows.

1215 Oak Avenue
Flossmoor, IL 60422
January 29, 1984

Ms. Elizabeth Hopper, Editor
Family Living
126 Sunset Lane
Des Moines, IA 50350

Dear Ms. Hopper:

What comes to mind when you think of summer camp? Hiking through the woods? Canoe races on a sparkling lake? Sitting around a campfire telling ghost stories?

Although the youngsters who attend summer music camps may participate in such activities, most of their time is spent practicing their instruments, taking lessons, and performing.

I am sure that an article about summer music camps would interest subscribers to Family Living, since the majority are parents of school-age children. Such an article would be of particular interest to working parents who need to plan their children's summer activities. Your readers may be surprised by the high quality of instruction offered at these camps.

The article would run approximately 1,500 words. In addition, I will provide photographs and a list of summer music camps in the Midwest.

I have worked as a music teacher and camp counselor at music camps in four Midwestern states. In addition, I recently helped organize a music camp in Illinois and am currently the assistant director. My articles on music education have appeared in Music Teacher and in local newspapers.

Can I expect to hear from you about my proposed article? Thank you for your consideration.

Sincerely yours,

Roger Trimble

Roger Trimble

Research and Write the Article. Most magazine articles, except those based purely on personal experience, require research. Successful writers understand the importance of careful research. Nothing can turn off an editor faster than an article full of factual errors or an article that has not been adequately researched.

The writer usually does some research during the process of formulating story ideas and writing query letters. Once an editor approves a story idea, the writer may need to do in-depth research before writing the article. Research can take many forms, including personal observation, library research, talking to people informally, and formal interviews. Many writers read what other authors have written about the topic as part of their research.

Once the writer finishes researching the article, the next step is to write a first draft. Although each writer's style is unique, writers may vary their styles to suit the subject matter, the audience, and the magazine for which they are writing. Writers who do this successfully can save the editor a great deal of time, thus increasing their chances for publication.

After writing the first draft, the writer usually spends considerable time revising and rewriting. The article is compared with the query letter to make sure the article contains all the material that was promised. The writer rereads the article to make sure it is clear, interesting, and will hold the reader's attention. Finally, the writer prepares the final copy and submits the article to the magazine editor. (For more information on researching and writing magazine articles, *see* pages 208–209.)

Books

About 1.75 billion books are sold each year in the United States, costing buyers a total of about $8.25 billion. Each year, more than 30,000 new books are published. Most books, both fiction and nonfiction, are written by free-lance writers.

Many people, especially free-lance writers, dream of becoming successful authors, writing books that bring them fame and fortune. Although some authors become rich and famous, most do not. To understand why, let's consider a few facts about the business of writing books and getting them published.

To begin with, writing a book requires a substantial amount of time and effort. An author must write about 60,000 words to produce a 125-page book. A 300-page book requires about 144,000 words; an 800-page book requires 384,000 words.

Most authors also spend a considerable amount of time revising and rewriting. Some may write as many as six or seven drafts of a particular section or chapter. In addition, most books require research. An author may spend months or even years doing research before writing a single word.

How much money can an author expect to earn from all this effort, assuming that a publisher agrees to publish the book? Authors' incomes vary widely. Best-selling authors can become millionaires. Most books, however, sell less than 5,000 copies and earn less than $8,000 for their authors.

Despite the odds against striking it rich, large number of authors and would-be authors continue to write and submit manuscripts to book publishers. These publishers generally deal with one or more of the following categories of books: trade books, textbooks, business and professional books, and scientific and technical books.

Trade Books

Trade books are books of a general nature that are sold mostly through bookstores and the book departments of other stores. About 390 million trade books are sold each year, costing buyers a total of about $2 billion.

Trade books may be fiction or nonfiction. Fiction books include novels, short story collections, and dramas. Books on history, biography, travel, cooking, religion, current events, and "how-to" books are examples of nonfiction trade books. Many books for children and young people also are classified as trade books.

The steps involved in writing a trade book and getting it published are discussed below. Much of this discussion also applies to the writing and publication of other types of books.

Choose and Test an Idea.   Book ideas come from a variety of sources. Some authors keep an idea file similar to the one described on pages 313–314. Authors may also get ideas by browsing in bookstores to see what types of books are being published or by reading publications such as *Writer's Market* and *Publishers Weekly*. Some authors are experts in a particular field and write about a topic in their area of expertise. Writers who have published one or more articles about a topic may decide to write a book about it. Authors often write books about a particular hobby or other interest. Many authors share skill or knowledge by writing "how-to" books.

One and three quarter billion books are sold each year in the United States, costing buyers $8.25 billion. Most of the 30,000 new titles published each year are written by free-lance writers.

Although book ideas can come from almost any source, such ideas must be carefully tested to determine their suitability. Authors should always test ideas before proposing them to editors. Here are some suggested ways to test book ideas:

- Read *Publishers Weekly* to learn what kinds of books are currently being published. Other sources of information are the *New York Times Book Review* and book sections of newspapers and magazines.
- Use the Subject Guide to *Books in Print,* available in the reference section of the library, to find the titles of similar books on the topic. Become familiar with these books. Then decide how this book will be different from books already written about the topic.
- Browse through bookstores to get a feel for publishing trends. If there are 20 books about cats, perhaps that market is already saturated. On the other hand, books about cats are obviously popular. A book that

deals with cats from a fresh perspective may have great potential.

- Consider how much research will be required to write the book. How long will it take to do the research? How much will it cost? Are sources readily available?
- Consider the people who are likely to be interested in the book. How many of these people are likely to buy the book?

Once an author has chosen and tested an idea, the next step usually is to query editors.

Query Editors.   Professional writers of nonfiction books almost always have contracts from publishers to write these books. How do authors get book contracts?

Some authors have agents who market their book ideas to editors. In general, agents work only with authors who have proven writing skills—those who have had at least one book published or those whose work has appeared in major magazines.

Agents usually charge a fee of 10 percent of the author's earnings from contracts they negotiate. Most reputable agents do not charge a fee for marketing authors' book ideas. They get paid only when they actually negotiate a contract for an author to write a book.

Beginning authors usually must market their own book ideas. They do so by sending book proposals to editors at various publishing houses. References such as *Writer's Market* and *Literary Market Place* list book publishers, types of books published, and editors' names and job titles. Many authors consult these references to choose publishers likely to be interested in a particular idea for a book and then send book proposals to the appropriate editors.

A book proposal is similar to a query letter (*see* page 316). The letter explains how a book will be different from other books on the same topic. It must clearly explain the book's *slant*—the point of view from which it will approach the topic. The proposal, in addition, should explain to the editor that a market already exists for the book, that the book will sell.

A book proposal must convince the editor that the author is qualified to write the book. Authors who are not experts on a subject need to do considerable research before writing on that subject; this research should be described in the book proposal. A list of articles and books already published should also be included as further evidence of the author's qualifications. Unless the author is well known, the book proposal usually must be accompanied by an outline of the book's contents and at least one sample chapter.

Some authors send book proposals to more than one editor at the same time, tailoring each proposal to the needs of the individual publishers. Authors should always inform editors when they are making multiple queries regarding the same book idea. Some editors will be less enthusiastic about a book proposal that has been submitted to other publishers. Other editors will be motivated to make a decision more quickly, knowing that other editors are considering the same proposal.

Editors generally take from several weeks to several months to reply to a book proposal. Even if an editor likes an idea, it must, in most cases, be approved by other people as well. These people include other editors as well as personnel from the sales and marketing, publicity, and production departments.

The procedure for finding a publisher for a fiction book is basically the same as finding one for a nonfiction book. However, beginning fiction writers must usually submit a complete manuscript rather than just an outline and a sample chapter or two.

The best way for a beginner to market a fiction manuscript is to write a letter that will interest an editor in the manuscript. The editor will then ask to see it and will probably give it careful consideration.

Unsolicited manuscripts—those that an editor has not asked to see—often end up in what is called a "slush pile." Junior editors or assistants are usually given the task of reading these manuscripts, many of which are poorly written. Most of these manuscripts are quickly read and rejected.

Established fiction writers sometimes get book contracts by writing query letters or by submitting an outline and sample chapters. Others hire agents to market their ideas or completed manuscripts.

Once an editor indicates that the publisher would like to buy the book, the next step is to negotiate the contract.

Negotiate the Contract. A book contract spells out, often in great detail, both the publisher's and the author's obligations and rights. The contract covers, among other things, agreement on advances and royalties; the time of manuscript delivery; who will register and hold the copyright; what the publisher will pay for; who is legally responsible in case anything in the book should be proved libelous; and conditions under which the contract might be terminated. Book contracts also cover subsidiary rights, including television and movie rights, book-club rights, and paperback reprint rights.

Some authors, especially beginning ones, are so thrilled that someone has decided to buy their book that they sign the publisher's contract without negotiating any of its terms. This is usually a mistake, since contracts are written with the publisher's, not the author's, interests in mind.

Most established authors have their agents negotiate book contracts. Even authors who market their own book proposals may engage an agent to negotiate the contract. Agents are listed in such sources as *Writer's Market* and *Literary Market Place.*

Publishers sometimes buy all rights to a book by paying the author a flat fee. But in most cases, the book contract includes a royalty agreement. Royalties consist of small payments the author gets for every copy of the book that is sold. For hardcover books, royalties are typically 10 percent of the book's retail price for the first 5,000 copies sold; 12½ percent for the next 5,000 copies; and 15 percent for any additional copies sold.

Authors usually receive royalty statements and payments (if any) twice a year. Royalty checks generally dwindle in number and amount after a relatively short time, as few books sell well for a long time. However, a book that sells steadily over a number of years can provide regular income for an author.

Publishers commonly give authors an advance against royalties. Such monies are not bonuses; advances must be paid back from the royalties a book earns. The publisher does not send any royalty checks to an author until the entire advance has been paid back.

The size of advances varies widely. First-time authors working for small publishers may get an advance of only a few hundred dollars; well-known authors working for large publishing houses may get as much as half a million dollars. Royalties and advances, like everything else concerning the author-publisher agreement, are spelled out in the book contract.

Once the contract has been negotiated and signed, the author still has a great deal of work to do: he or she must write and deliver an acceptable manuscript to the publisher.

Write the Book.   The book contract may specify that the manuscript is to be submitted by chapters or sections. Or it may simply indicate the date when the entire manuscript must be delivered to the editor. In the case of a fiction manuscript, the author may have had to submit a complete manuscript to the editor before the contract was issued.

For both fiction and nonfiction books, the editor's job is to read the manuscript and suggest ways to improve it. Minor changes may be suggested, such as rewarding several sentences or paragraphs, or adding or deleting small amounts of copy. In some cases, the editor may suggest that entire chapters be added or dropped or that the book be organized differently.

Some authors resist making any changes to a manuscript. This is usually unwise, since few manuscripts are perfect. On the other hand, authors should not allow editors to pressure them into making changes they do not want to make. After all, it is the author's name, not the editor's, that appears on the cover of the book.

Once the editing process is complete, the book will be typeset and the author will receive copies of the galley proofs. *Galley proofs* are long, narrow sheets of typeset copy with wide margins for showing corrections. Although the publisher will have a proofreader check the galley proofs, the author should proofread them as well. In addition to finding typographical errors, the author may find that words, lines, or even entire paragraphs have been misplaced or dropped.

Authors may make minor changes or even do some rewriting as they read the galley proofs. These changes, called *author's alterations,* require type to be reset at additional cost. Most book contracts stipulate that authors may make such alterations at the publisher's expense, as long as these changes do not exceed 10 percent of the original typesetting costs.

Promote the Book.   Once the book is published, the author should get involved in promoting it. The publisher's promotion department may arrange a book tour in which the author appears on radio and television interview or talk shows, gives interviews to newspaper reporters, and autographs copies of the book at local bookstores. The promotion department will also send copies of the book to book reviewers. In addition, the book may be advertised on radio and television and in newspapers and magazines.

Few books are heavily promoted, however. Promotion budgets are usually limited, especially for books by first-time or unknown authors. Nevertheless, authors can and should work to promote their books themselves. They can volunteer to autograph copies at bookstores; send press releases to newspaper, radio stations, and television stations; and try to arrange interviews on local radio and television shows.

After an author has done everything possible to promote the book, the only thing left to do is wait for the royalty checks to arrive.

Textbooks

Textbook publishing is the largest branch of the book industry. Each year, buyers spend more than $2 billion to purchase about 350 million copies of textbooks and workbooks. The textbook industry is generally divided into two categories: elementary and secondary textbooks; and college textbooks.

Elementary and Secondary Textbooks.   Publisher of elementary and secondary textbooks generally originate the concept for a textbook and then develop it using both in-house and outside personnel. A textbook or series of textbooks may take years to develop, since most are produced as a team effort. Team members include editors, authors, free-lance writers, educational consultants, designers, and illustrators.

Textbooks at the elementary and secondary levels must meet exacting standards. They must be written at an appropriate reading level and interest level. They must contain information that is accurate and up-to-date. In general, they must avoid issues that are overly controversial or that are likely to offend certain groups of people.

Whenever possible, textbooks should include an equal number of males and females and should depict a variety of racial and ethnic groups. In addition, textbooks should include people of all ages and those with physical disabilities. Finally, elementary and secondary textbooks must be able to compete with similar books or series produced by other publishers.

The high standards these textbooks must meet and the competition from other publishers result in a high degree of editorial input. Editors often do a substantial amount of editing and rewriting to ensure that materials conform to both the publisher's and the industry's standards.

In addition, educational publishers rely on outside consultants and advisers to review textbooks and other materials. These advisers evaluate whether material is presented clearly, accurately, and in agreement with accepted educational practices.

Who writes elementary and secondary textbooks? Some authors are practicing classroom teachers or former classroom teachers. Others are writers or consultants who are also experts in a particular subject area, such as reading, mathematics, history, or biology. Some authors are college or university professors who write about a particular academic discipline. Most textbook authors have some teaching experience in the particular field, academic training in the subject area, or both.

Some textbooks are written by teams of authors under the direction of an editor. This may be done to allow the publisher to meet a production schedule or because each author is a specialist in one particular area. In other cases, a free-lance writer may write parts of a textbook based on an author's or editor's detailed outline.

Most elementary and secondary publishers also produce materials to accompany textbooks. These *ancillary materials* include workbooks, tests, practice manuals, and duplicating worksheets. Free-lance writers are often hired to write ancillary materials.

Book contracts for authors of elementary and secondary textbooks may include royalty agreements, or authors may sell all rights to the book in a work-for-hire agreement.

Once the writing and editing processes are complete, the manuscript is sent to a typesetter, who returns galley proofs to the publisher. These may or may not be sent to the author, depending on the contract provisions or the policy of the individual publisher. Authors of textbooks are generally not involved in the illustration program or in the design, layout, and production processes.

Textbooks are sold mainly by traveling salespeople who visit schools, school systems, and state agencies. In some states, adoption committees decide which textbooks will be used by students in public schools throughout the state.

College Textbooks.　College textbooks are usually written by scholars. Such scholars are often college or university professors; many are well-known in their respective fields of study.

Authors may propose textbook ideas to publishers based on research they have done or courses they have taught. Publishers sometimes commission authors to write particular textbooks for which there is a market need. Some publishers have a field staff that seeks out and encourages potential authors or looks for authors with manuscripts in progress.

Book proposals or complete manuscripts are chosen based on the recommendation of an editor or an editorial committee. The editorial department may also seek advice from consultants and experts in appropriate academic disciplines. Book contracts for college textbooks usually include a royalty agreement, although some publishers may purchase all rights in a work-for-hire agreement.

Once the author submits the complete manuscript, the editor reads it to evaluate its content, format, and organization. He or she usually does a readability test to make sure the manuscript is written at a level that is suitable for college students.

Next, a copy editor edits the manuscript, correcting errors in spelling, grammar, and punctuation. The copy editor may reword sentences or paragraphs that are unclear. He or she also checks that the manuscript reads smoothly and follows a consistent style.

After the manuscript is typeset, the author is sent galley proofs to read and correct. The author may do some minor rewriting at this stage, which will result in additional typesetting costs. In most cases, the publisher will pay for these changes as long as they do not exceed 10 percent of the original cost for typesetting.

College textbooks are usually marketed by salespeople who call on faculty members at colleges and universities. Although the books are usually sold through campus bookstores, it is the faculty members who determine which books will be used in the courses they teach.

Other Kinds of Books

In addition to trade books and textbooks, free-lance writers write other kinds of books as well. These include business, law, technical, scientific, and medical books. Buyers purchase more than 52 million copies of such books each year, at a total cost of about $1 billion.

Other Markets

Some successful free-lance writers have never had a magazine article or a book published. Yet many of these writers earn a comfortable or even handsome living from their writing. They work for clients in an almost unlimited number of markets outside the publishing industry. Many free-lancers find that these markets pay better and offer them more security than book and magazine publishers.

Where can free-lance writers use their skills outside the publishing world? The answer to this question is limited only by the imagination and ambition of the individual free lancer. Almost any for-profit or not-for-profit organization may need the services of a free-lance writer. Examples of organizations that employ free-lance writers include businesses, trade and professional associations, school districts, colleges and universities, religious and charitable organizations, government agencies, and hospitals.

How can free-lance writers use their skills in various organizations? It depends on the organization's needs and the free-lancer's ability to discover and meet those needs. Here are some ways in which free-lance writers are currently using their writing skills in various organizations. Resourceful free-lancers will undoubtedly be able to think of other possibilities.

Ghostwriting

Many people in a variety of organizations are required to write as they carry out their job responsibilities. Others choose to write to enhance their professional reputations or to share special knowledge they have gained. However, many of these people are not skilled writers or do not have time to devote to writing. Such people may hire ghostwriters—professional writers—who do the actual writing.

Ghostwriting can be a profitable venture for good writers who are willing to let others take credit for their work. Ghostwriting assignments may range from short magazine and journal articles to complete books or series of books.

Speechwriting

Free-lancers may write speeches for a variety of individuals, including business managers and executives, politicians, government officials, and community leaders. Such people may be too busy to write their own speeches. Also, some good speakers are not good writers. So they hire professional writers to write speeches that may inform, entertain, or persuade the audience. Speeches that are well written may help enhance the speaker's professional reputation or standing in the community.

Speechwriting is actually a form of ghostwriting in which the writer allows another person to take credit for what he or she has written. However, many or most of the ideas presented are the speaker's.

Writers usually begin by meeting with the speaker to discuss the subject of the speech as well as its tone and emphasis. The next step may be to do some research to find facts that support the speaker's ideas or statements. In addition, the writer may include stories or jokes to vary the pace of the speech and keep the audience's attention.

If the audience does not respond well to the speech, the speaker may blame the free-lancer and find a new speechwriter. On the other hand, an enthusiastic audience response will probably result in more speechwriting assignments. Like ghostwriting, speechwriting can be quite a profitable venture for good writers who do not mind letting others take credit for their work.

Organization Publications

Organizations may publish newsletters, newspapers, or magazines for their employees, customers, or the general public. Free-lance writers may contribute to these publications in various ways. If the organization has a publications department, free-lancers may be hired to assist staff members in writing or editing articles. If no publications department exists, the organization may hire a free-lancer to write, edit, and produce the entire publication. Some free-lancers specialize in this kind of work and have contracts with one or more clients to handle organization publications on a continuing basis.

Reports and Brochures

Organizations may hire free-lancers to write a variety of reports, including the organization's annual report and various reports for internal and external use. Free-lancers may also be involved in writing and producing brochures. They may work under the supervision of staff members or may handle entire projects themselves.

Advertising and Public Relations

Some organizations have separate advertising and public relations departments. These departments may hire free-lance writers to do special projects or to assist staff members during peak periods. Organizations without such departments may engage free-lancers to write advertising copy or press releases for newspapers, radio, and television. In addition, advertising and public relations agencies sometimes hire free-lance writers to help out during busy periods or to handle special assignments.

Catalogs

Free-lance writers are sometimes hired to write copy for retail catalogs and for catalogs issued by schools, colleges and universities, and other nonprofit organizations. Free-lancers may work under the direction of staff members or may contract to write and produce an entire catalog on their own.

Fund-Raising

Charitable organizations may engage free-lancers to write materials used in fund-raising campaigns. Such materials include campaign proposals, press releases, fund-raising letters, and reports for internal and external use.

Training and Development

Many organizations have training and development departments. Such departments may hire free-lancers to help develop and write training programs. Organizations without such departments may engage free-lancers to develop, write, and sometimes even present training programs to employees.

Stringing

Local and national newspapers, magazines, and other publications often employ stringers, who are part-time reporters for these publications. Stringers may be given an assignment by an editor, or they may develop their own stories and submit them for publication. Networks of stringers allow publications to get stories quickly from a variety of sources and locations.

Careers

This section contains information on free-lance careers, including nature of the work, education and preparation, and employment opportunities.

Nature of the Work

Free-lance writers are entrepreneurs—people who organize and manage a business. They need good business skills and business judgment as well as writing talent to operate their businesses successfully. They must constantly market their skills, gain the confidence of publishers and clients, and keep that confidence by producing high-quality work. They must always be on the alert for new ways to serve clients or for ideas they can use to write articles and books. They must also take care of business matters such as billing clients, keeping track of earnings and expenses, and filing quarterly income tax statements.

Free-lance writers must be able to write well. They usually have a love for language and are willing to spend considerable time revising and rewriting their work. They must understand the importance of accuracy and thus be willing to do thorough and sometimes tedious research. In addition, free-lancers must be able to work under pressure and meet deadlines. This may sometimes involve putting in long hours.

Free-lance writers may be generalists or specialists. For example, some may write about a variety of topics for various general-circulation magazines. Others may specialize in writing language arts materials for elementary textbook publishers. Still others may make a career out of writing materials for training and development programs in various organizations. Some fiction authors specialize in one kind of fiction, such as romance novels, science fiction, or teen-age adventure stories. Others write several kinds of fiction.

Working conditions for free-lance writers are generally good. Many free-lancers work at home in a separate room or a space set aside for writing. When working at home, free-lancers set their own hours. Many establish and maintain regular office hours. Because they work without supervision, they must be self-disciplined and highly motivated.

Free-lancers sometimes work at clients' offices, especially if the work involves a great deal of interaction between the client and the writer. Free-lance writers may also do research at libraries, newspaper offices, public buildings, and museums. In addition, they may conduct interviews in person or on the teephone. They may cover events such as plays, political rallies, and musical concerts for magazines or newspapers.

Education and Preparation

There are no set requirements for becoming a free-lance writer. Anyone can submit material to book and magazine publishers. However, unless the material is well written and suits the publisher's needs, the publisher will not buy it. Also, the publisher may not even read it unless it is properly submitted.

Although free-lance writers are not required to have college degrees, many do. Some have liberal arts backgrounds, while others have bachelor's or advanced degrees in various specialized areas.

Some colleges and universities offer courses in writing for publication. These courses may deal with magazine articles, novels, short stories, plays, children's literature, and various kinds of nonfiction books. Other courses teach business writing and may be helpful to those interested in free lancing for various organizations. Free-lance writers sometimes attend conferences and seminars conducted by accomplished writers and authors. Others learn more about writing by reading books and magazine articles about the topic. Some free-lance writers get writing experience by working at newspapers, magazines, book publishers, and radio and television stations.

Most free-lancers would probably say that they learned to write by writing and that they improve their writing by continuous practice. Thus, persons considering a career in free-lance writing should write as often as possible. They should set aside a time to write each day.

Students should take advantage of the many writing opportunities at school. These include class assignments, essay contests, and research and term papers. The school newspaper and yearbook also provide excellent opportunities for young writers to learn their craft.

Employment Opportunities

Free-lance writers may work for book and magazine publishers. They may also work for a wide variety of organizations outside the publishing world. (For more information on opportunities for free-lance writers, *see* the sections on Magazines, Books, and Other Markets on pages 312–329.)

Persons considering a career in free-lance writing should remember that free-lancers have no fringe benefits. Because they are self-employed, they must buy their own health insurance and provide their own pension plans. In addition, they have no paid vacations or sick days.

Earnings for free-lancers vary widely depending on a number of factors. These include the writer's talent, ambition, and sometimes, luck. As noted earlier, the writer's choice of markets also greatly influences earnings.

Radio and Television Writers

Radio and television, like newspapers and magazines, are important communications media. The United States has about 8,700 radio stations and about 1,000 television stations. Americans own about 456 million radios; the average American household includes six radios. At least one television set can be found in 98 percent of American homes. Americans own a total of about 156 million television sets.

The majority of commercial radio and television programs are designed to entertain the audience. A relatively small number of such programs are intended to inform or teach. In contrast, public radio and television stations focus mainly on cultural and educational programming rather than entertainment. Both commercial and public stations broadcast the news and may air various news programs.

In addition to watching commercial and public television, millions of Americans view programs offered on cable television and pay-television systems. These subscription program services are offered to viewers for a fee.

This section deals with writing for radio and television. Let's begin by discussing newswriting.

Newswriting

Most radio stations broadcast news every hour or half-hour. All commercial television stations air newscasts every day, as do most public television stations.

Many stations hire reporters who gather the news in much the same way newspaper reporters do. These reporters may gather the facts and then give them to staff newswriters, who prepare scripts for the newscasters to read. Or the reporter may actually write the story as well as gather the facts.

At some stations, newscasters write all or part of the scripts that they read on the air. Reporters who do live, filmed, or taped reports for broadcast may write their own scripts or may be assisted by the station's newswriters.

News broadcast over the radio is usually gathered and written by professional reporter/writers who prepare a typescript that is styled to be read by a newscaster or disc jockey.

Radio and television stations get news stories from wire services as well as from their own reporters. Newswriters or newscasters may rewrite these wire service stories to conform with the station's or the individual newscaster's style. Wire service stories may also need to be shortened because of limited air time.

Writers who work with wire service copy must be able to do their jobs quickly. They may have only a few minutes to prepare broadcast copy about late-breaking stories. In television, they may not only write copy, but also coordinate it with the visual material.

In addition to news stories, radio and television reporters and newswriters may also write feature stories, news analyses, special reports, sports news, and weather forecasts. Other kinds of writing include commentaries, which express the opinion of the individual reporter and editorials, which express the views of the management of the news department.

Radio and television reporters may also do investigative reporting to expose corruption and other types of wrongdoing. The station then airs the results of these investigations.

Radio and television stations may provide live coverage of important news events, such as Presidential speeches, political conventions, and Congressional hearings. The commentators who cover these events generally do not read from a script. However, they may read prepared copy as they open and conclude the broadcast. In addition, they may refer to notes that they or other writers have prepared about the event.

Radio and television news reporting differs from newspaper reporting in several important ways. In general,

Television newscasters often write their own copy or edit another writer's stories to fit their particular style. Nationally known newscasters, such as Walter Cronkite who began his career as a reporter, may be involved in deciding what stories will be reported as well as what kind of emphasis should be given to various aspects of a day's news.

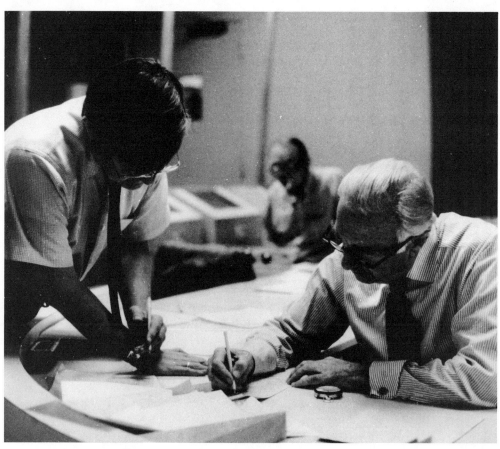

newspapers cover stories in much greater depth than the broadcast media. This is because local newspapers usually have larger reporting staffs than local radio and television stations. Also, newspapers generally devote more space to news than stations allot air time for newscasts. Stories average less than 30 seconds each in a typical five-minute radio newscast. The script for a half-hour television newscast would not even fill the front page of a standard-sized newspaper.

Radio and television newscasts also cover fewer stories than do newspapers. This is due not only to their limitations, but also to the need to appeal to a wide audience. While newspaper readers can skip stories that do not appeal to them, radio and television listeners cannot.

Radio and television stations can, however, report the news more quickly than newspapers. Stations can interrupt programs to give the latest news from their own reporters or from the wire services. Newspapers, on the other hand, must be printed and distributed before the public can get the news.   Television also allows the viewer to be an eyewitness to news events. The visual elements of live, taped, or filmed television news reports often helps viewers better understand the news.

Radio and television news stories, like newspaper news stories, focus on the 5W's: *who, what, when, where,* and *why.* The opening sentence of a broadcast news story should summarize the important facts of the story. The rest of the story should give more information about these facts.

Radio and television newswriters must write clearly and simply, keeping in mind that listeners will hear the story only once. Unlike newspaper readers, they cannot go back to the story if they did not understand a particular part of it.

Broadcast newswriters must also keep in mind that the words they write are to be spoken rather than printed. In general, broadcast news is less formal than print news; its tone and style are more conversational.

Whenever possible newswriters must avoid using tongue twisters and words that are difficult to pronounce. They should give the pronunciation of difficult words or names in parentheses. In addition, newswriters must write copy that conforms to the station's style and to the broadcast style of the newscaster who will read the material.

Scriptwriting

The following sections discuss the work of radio and television scriptwriters.

Radio

Relatively few opportunities exist for radio scriptwriters today. This was not always the case, however. During the "golden age" of broadcasting, which lasted from about 1925–1950, scriptwriters created material for a wide variety of radio programs. These programs included situation comedies, dramas, variety shows, soap operas, and adventure shows for children.

Popular dramas included "The Lone Ranger," "Superman," and "Buck Rogers in the 25th Century." Situation comedies such as "Amos 'n' Andy" and "Fibber McGee and Molly" were also popular. In addition to writing scripts for radio actors and actresses, writers also wrote the material announcers used to introduce and conclude each program.

As television's popularity grew during the 1950's, most of these radio shows went off the air. Recorded music became the chief type of radio programming. Today, few radio stations broadcast original comedies, dramas, or other programs like those that were so popular during the golden age. Television is the major medium for airing such programs.

Some radio stations broadcast talk shows in which the host leads a discussion or interviews guests. Writer may supply the host with a list of questions to ask or an outline of topics to cover on such shows. Or a writer may do research on the discussion topic or the person being interviewed in order to provide the host with background material.

Radio scriptwriters may also write short scripts for disc jockeys to use when they are not playing music. Such scripts may include information about the music being played, interesting or amusing stories, or gags and jokes.

Some radio stations produce programs for children. Such programs provide another opportunity for radio scriptwriters.

Television

Although the field of television scriptwriting is extremely competitive, it offers many opportunities for talented writers. These include writing scripts for weekly programs such as dramas, situation comedies, and variety shows;

Writers of such radio shows as "Amos 'n' Andy" developed formulas that provided the basis for television's hit programs. A team of scriptwriters create strong, vivid personalities, around which they weave everyday situations. Characters, such as Archie and Edith Bunker, become so well established in the public's mind that their creators, who "burn out," or run out of new ideas, can be replaced without the public perceiving a change in the show.

Writing a creative, entertaining script under the gun of a weekly deadline may be the hardest single aspect of a career as a scriptwriter.

and creating material for soap operas and children's shows.

Programs such as these may be written by individual writers or teams of writers. In some cases, the story editor may give the writer a script idea to develop. In other cases, the writer may have to come up with the story idea and also develop it.

Staff writers on regularly scheduled programs may work under a great deal of pressure. The material they produce must fit the time allotted for the program. It must also appeal to the intended audience. Writers must try to be creative—they must either come up with original ideas for scripts or new ways of presenting old ideas. In addition, scriptwriters must often give detailed instructions about the visual aspects of the program. All these things must be accomplished within a short period of time.

Scriptwriters may also write *documentaries.* These programs present factual information in a dramatic way. Documentaries may cover social issues such as poverty, crime, or drug abuse. Or they may deal with such topics as animals, foreign cultures, or the lives of famous people. Documentaries sometimes focus on an important topic in the news, such as United States foreign policy in a particular region of the world. Writing a documentary often involves a great deal of research, observation, and interviewing.

Talk shows and interview shows offer another opportunity for television scriptwriters. Such writers may create material for the host's opening statements or comedy monologue. Or they may write questions for the host to ask guests or outline possible topics to cover. Writers may also gather background information on guests or topics and summarize this information for the host.

Other kinds of scriptwriting include creating material for miniseries, made-for-television movies, teleplays, comedy or variety specials, and special dramatic presentations.

Careers

This section focuses on careers for radio and television writers. It discusses the nature of the work, education and preparation, and employment opportunities.

Nature of the Work

Careers in radio and television news reporting offer many of the same rewards and drawbacks as careers in newspaper reporting. Rewards may include the opportunity to influence people, help protect the public interest, travel, and meet a variety of interesting people. Drawbacks may include working under pressure to meet deadlines, long or irregular hours, and dangerous assignments.

Like newspaper reporters, broadcast journalists should be curious about people and events. They should have a "nose for the news" and sound news judgment. They must have good research skills and be persistent about getting all the facts for a story. They should also be good writers. This is particularly important for newswriters who must write stories quickly based on facts supplied by reporters or wire service stories.

Scriptwriters, like reporters and newswriters, must also be able to work under pressure to meet deadlines. They must be good writers who can create their own material or follow someone else's outline or format for a script. They must be able to cooperate with a variety of people, including other writers, directors, producers, actors, and program hosts.

Scriptwriting often requires a high degree of creativity. In addition, scriptwriters should have good research skills, since they often must do research before writing.

College courses in radio and television broadcasting usually include training in technology as well as writing and speaking techniques.

Education and Preparation

Preparing for a career in radio or television news reporting is in many ways similar to preparing for a career in newspaper reporting. (*See* pages 300–307 for more information on this topic.)

It should be noted that about 260 colleges and universities in the United States offer a major course of study in radio and television broadcasting. Aspiring broadcast journalists may wish to enroll in such programs. In addition, high school and college students should try to get experience at school or local radio and television stations.

Radio and television scriptwriters do not necessarily need a college degree, although a degree may prove useful. College courses in radio and television writing may be particularly helpful. Such courses may help writers learn how to create interesting plots, write dialogue, and make characters seem believable. Courses may also deal with such topics as writing documentaries and children's programs.

Employment Opportunities

Competition is keen for jobs in broadcast news reporting and writing, especially at the national networks and at stations in larger cities. Opportunities are usually better at smaller local stations. Many broadcast journalists begin at small stations and then move on to larger markets.

Small stations are often good places to learn. News department employees may be involved in a variety of tasks, including reporting, newswriting, announcing, and writing special reports.

Some broadcast journalists begin their careers as newspaper reporters. Experience in print journalism is usually considered good preparation for a career in radio or television news.

The growth of cable television and increased emphasis on news at many local radio and television stations may result in more job openings for broadcast journalists. Radio stations with an all-news format offer opportunities for reporters who wish to do thorough or in-depth coverage of news stories.

In general, salaries for broadcast journalists are higher than salaries for print journalists. Salaries vary depending on the size of the station, its location, and the individual journalist's experience and merit.

As discussed earlier, relatively few opportunities exist for radio scriptwriters. (*See* pages 336–337 for more information on these opportunities.)

Television and radio scriptwriters may work as staff writers on a particular program or may write and submit scripts on a free-lance basis. Although the field is highly competitive, there are opportunities for talented and persistent writers. The growth of cable and public television may result in even greater opportunities.

Scriptwriters generally need an agent to help them get jobs in television. To get an agent, a beginning scriptwriter might write a sample script for a series that is already on the air. He or she then sends the script to an agent, who reads it and decides whether or not to represent the writer. Once an agent accepts a scriptwriter as a client, the agent works to help the writer get writing jobs on television shows.

Another way to get started in scriptwriting is to write scripts for locally produced television shows. In addition, scriptwriters may work for independent production companies that produce programs for television.

Pay for scriptwriters is generally quite good. Minimum fees for television scriptwriting are set by the Writer's Guild of America. However, there may not be much job security, since television programs are frequently dropped or canceled.

Many scriptwriters live in or near New York City or Hollywood, as most television shows are produced in these cities. Writers hoping to work on these shows may need to relocate.

Advertising and Public Relations Writing

Who will buy designer X's new line of swimwear? What do the citizens of Pleasantville think about their local police department? Will a magazine ad convince readers that Brand Y is a better laundry detergent than Brand Z? How does the public feel about the economy, its public library, or its local sports teams?

These are all questions of concern to advertising and public relations writers. Advertising is critical in attracting buyers to a product or service. Without interested consumers, companies or agencies with a product or service to sell would fail. Therefore, it is the job of the advertising writer to create that necessary interest in a specific product.

Similarly, public relations writers are often responsible for what the public thinks about a variety of issues or concerns. They are responsible for maintaining a superior public image for the company or agency they represent. Indeed, it is the advertising or public relations writer who, with the right or wrong choice of words, can make or break the future of a company, an agency, a product, a candidate, or a public official.

The Advertising Copywriter

Advertising is an intense, fast-paced, and extremely competitive field. To be successful in this industry, a writer must be top-notch, hard-working, and above all, creative. His or her job is to write ad copy that will appear in print in newspapers, magazines, brochures, or posters, or in commercials on radio or TV. In this section we will discuss some of the inherent traits and developed qualities of an advertising copywriter and where and for whom copywriters work.

Traits

Most copywriters share certain traits. Obviously, they must love to write. They must have an interest in words and an appreciation for language. Beyond this, though, a copywriter must possess an aptitude for expression. This aptitude can be influenced a great deal by a rich background of experiences from which a writer can draw for information, vocabulary, and reference. In the process of developing this demanding craft, you will find that everything you have ever done, read, seen, or thought will be valuable to you. Not one human experience is ever wasted.

Other qualities that are characteristic of a good advertising copywriter include intelligence, imagination, objectivity, patience, curiosity, an interest in human nature, self-confidence (tempered, of course, with humility), integrity, verbal skills, and empathy, that important human characteristic that allows you to see things from another person's point of view. Mental and physical stamina are also job prerequisites. Copywriters generally must develop ideas and work under the pressure of deadlines. They must be able to integrate their efforts smoothly with the overall objectives of the job at hand.

Advertising copywriters work closely with artists in the development of successful campaigns. Ads that attract the public's attention combine the right words with the right illustration.

Where Do Copywriters Work?

As a copywriter you might work at any one of a variety of business organizations, such as:

- Ad agencies
- Large or small retail stores
- Mail order firms
- Manufacturing companies
- Newspapers
- TV or radio stations

Ad agencies are privately-owned businesses staffed by advertising specialists and hired by companies with goods or services to sell. They offer their clients all the necessary advertising functions from research to the production of final ad copy. Beyond your duties of writing ad copy for the media, you might, as an employee of an ad agency, additionally be asked to write anything from a product instruction tag to a company president's speech. Always, however, the client is the final judge of all ad copy.

Many manufacturing companies, while they may hire ad agencies for some of their advertising, still maintain an "in-house" advertising department. These departments are responsible for preparing copy for local newspaper fliers, catalogs, merchandising brochures, display pieces, sales training booklets, and the like. Often, manufacturers of highly specialized goods like to hire writers with training or experience in the technology involved.

All retail operations employ advertising writers, from famous department stores to small corner grocery stores. In fact, there is more retail advertising done in this country than any other kind. Your job as a retail copywriter would be to spread the word in the marketplace via newspapers, TV and radio, and direct mail. The job is often a grueling one of meeting day-to-day deadlines and using your creative efforts to the maximum.

Mail order writers are responsible for preparing catalogs and periodical fliers for major merchandising firms. These writers very quickly learn the importance of effective writing. The bottom line is sales and that is the scale by which their effectiveness is measured.

Newspapers and TV and radio stations often hire full-time advertising writers as a service to their advertisers. These writers write ad copy for local merchants who wish to use that particular medium to sell their goods or services. These writers also write advertising copy or promotional commercials for the newspaper or station itself.

Writing an Advertisement

Advertising writing is a unique and demanding form of communication. An advertisement, whether directed toward a reader, a listener, or a viewer, must attract attention. It must be informative. And, above all, it must persuade the reader, the listener, or the viewer to action. In this section we will discuss planning and writing an advertisement, various types of ad copy, and some aspects of good copywriting.

Planning the Ad

Before copywriters begin to write ad copy, they must acquire a vast amount of background knowledge. They must become extremely familiar with the product. They must also know the market well. They must know their potential consumers and what makes them buy. They must be aware of their competition as well. To do all this, copywriters will talk extensively with the client to learn the aims and objectives of the client and to study the way the product is made. Copywriters should talk to designers, engineers, salespeople, and account executives. Former customers are an excellent source of information as well. The inquisitive writer will also check company history and sales records. And, of course, the ad writer must communicate with research directors.

Research is critical to the writing of advertising. Information gathered in research is used to determine such factors as the kinds of people advertisements will be aimed at, which media to place ads in, and what kinds of appeals to use in the ad.

An appeal is a statement that will motivate or persuade a consumer to action. An ad's appeal must relate to a person's interests, desires, or specific problems. Consumers buy products for the benefit they will obtain from them. That benefit, thus, becomes the appeal of the advertisement. For example, one person might buy a specific car because it is economical. Another person might be interested in the same car because of its sporty looks. And a third person might want to buy that car because of its size and alleged ease in handling. Research, therefore, helps determine which appeal would be most advantagious for the advertiser to use in attempting to sell the product.

Ad appeals can take a factual approach or an emotional approach. Factual appeals present facts about the product—what it is, how it is made, or how it works. They are

Distinctive slogans and an emphasis on youth and enjoyment have long characterized Coke® ads. Soft drink companies have, through research, long understood that their primary customers fall within certain age ranges and gear their ads accordingly. Girls and young women identify with attractive women pictured in ads and, therefore, identify with the product; young men are attracted to the women pictured in the ads and, therefore, notice the product.

aimed at the practical side of the consumer. Emotional appeals, on the other hand, are aimed at satisfying a specific need such as love, security, or prestige. Perhaps the consumer who is interested in the sporty-looking car has a need to feel attractive to members of the opposite sex, or a need to feel prestigious, a need which a fancy car could fill.

Sometimes copywriters use both emotional and factual appeals in their ads. They might even use more than one appeal. Or they might limit the ad's appeal to a small group of consumers such as single men under thirty years old, senior citizens, or young married couples. Obviously, young people would not be good prospects for hearing aids. Senior citizens would probably not be interested in roller skates. And teen-agers would not be likely candidates for a Caribbean cruise. Similarly, Florida or southern California would not be a good marketplace for snow blowers. And air conditioners will have a greater year-round demand in Phoenix than in northern Minnesota. Clearly, copywriters must be familiar with their audience and keep it firmly in mind at all times. Research helps attain this familiarity.

As a point of reference, let's take a moment to very briefly discuss some types of research. There are three basic kinds of research:

- market research
- motivation research
- media research

Market Research.   Market research gathers information about the buying habits of consumers. This information is obtained from a sampling of consumers by using questionnaires, surveys, or interviews, and it helps determine the best method for presenting the product or service.

Motivation Research.   The purpose of motivation research is to try to determine why consumers buy certain products. This is often done on a personal interview basis with consumers who are or could be buyers of the product in question. However, due to the costly nature of a one-to-one interview, this type of research is sometimes done in a group called a *focus group*. The researcher's hope is to find the most effective appeal to use in the advertisement. What makes this method difficult, however, is the very complex nature of consumers' motivations.

Media Research.   Media research gathers information about radio and TV audiences—their size and makeup at various times of the day. The hope is to select the most effective medium in which to place an ad.

When the advertising copywriter has talked to all the necessary people and feels confident that he or she has the product, the audience, the market, and the competition clearly and thoroughly in focus, the writing can begin.

The Structure of the Print Ad

Advertising copy, whether directed toward the reader of a magazine or newspaper, a TV viewer, or a radio listener, must deal with one person at a time. A consumer must feel that an ad is speaking directly to him or her; otherwise, he or she will not pay attention. Although we will discuss print ads specifically, you will find that many factors hold true in writing for other media as well.

Most advertisements take a four-step form.

- The promise of product benefit
- The amplification or body copy
- The proof of claim
- The action to take

First, let's consider the promise of the product benefit.

Advertising copywriters produce more than copy for newspaper, radio, and television ads. The same creativity may be employed on billboards, grocery store displays, and even on the sides of fruit trucks.

This generally takes the form of a headline. Sometimes the promise can be the entire ad. Most experts believe that the headline coupled with the illustration (art or photography) is the most important part of the advertisement. As an ad writer, you will not be expected to be an artist, but you will be expected to be aware of and concerned about the total effect of the ad. Copywriters generally work on both a headline idea and an art idea at the same time. An attention-getting headline in tandem with a spectacular drawing or photo can create a superior advertisement.

A good headline includes the following points:

- It must get immediate attention.
- It must appeal to an interested audience.
- It must persuade.

■ It must offer a reward for reading it.

A headline can be as long or short as necessary—from one pertinent word to several sentences. One effective advertisement for house slippers displayed only the headline "Tranquilizers." As a copywriter you must be ready to write many, many different headlines for one ad—sometimes as many as hundreds—before you arrive at just the right one. In fact, most employers probably would not look too favorably upon a copywriter who submitted just one headline with an ad. Keep in mind, however, that leftover headlines often make excellent copy for the main body of the ad.

There are generally considered to be four major types of headlines.

■ Those that present a new product benefit
■ Those that promise or remind the reader of an existing product benefit
■ Curiosity or provocative headlines
■ Selective headlines, which are often combined with one of the above

High interest in a product occurs when it first offers a new benefit. Here are some examples of headlines that present new product benefits.

For those who haven't heard.
New ways to listen.

A Whole New Walk of Life.

A good thing. . . .
just got better.

The long-distance service that gives you more
now costs you less.

Obviously, products do not offer new benefits all the time. Therefore headlines sometimes simply remind buyers of existing benefits of the product. Here are some examples of that kind of headline.

Come to Where the Flavor Is.

South America. It's not foreign to us.

The headlights wink.
The engine growls.
The styling flirts.

The Magazine for the Successful Man

The curiosity headline offers a change of pace. It generally prods the reader to read further for the key message. Some examples follow.

Eyeglasses to sunglasses
in less than 60 seconds.

How many stamps can you lick
before you come unglued?

He had plenty of life insurance.
Unfortunately, his wife died.

Selective headlines appeal to people belonging to a particular group, such as teachers, people watching their diet, people who work in an office, or mothers with young children. Here are some examples of selective headlines.

Born Salt-Free.

Who can help your sesquipedalian freshman?

At last, a pager for people
who don't like to carry pagers.

Sometimes a headline needs further explanation. A subheadline, often called a *subcaption* or *subcap,* does this.

The copywriter uses the subcap to spell out more specifically the promise in the headline. It often provides a transition from the headline to the opening lines of the body copy.

Headline

**Losing your headache
just got easier.**

Subcap

Discover _____ in new capsule form.

Following the headline and subcap would come the second step in writing the ad—the amplification or body of the ad. The body of the ad should be written to explain the promise and how it will be fulfilled. More expensive products, such as major appliances or automobiles will require more explanation than low-cost items such as soft drinks or cologne. When writing the body of the ad, it is important to maintain a simple, friendly, conversational tone. The body must flow from the headline using the same writing style and focusing on the same points. For example, a headline that reads, "Half price sale today!" would not, or should not, be followed by text that explains the history of the store where the sale is taking place. It would, of course, give details of the sale—where it is, when it is, exactly what is on sale.

The prospective consumer might ask, "Can I really count on what this ad claims?" This is the third factor a writer must deal with when writing an ad—the proof of the claim. Some types of proof writers might use in their ads include:

- Warranties
  Slogans such as "We put that in writing" are often used by car and tire companies.
- Trial offers
  These are usually used for low-cost or nonconsumable products.
- Money-back guaranties
  We have all seen in ads such lines as, "Satisfaction guaranteed or your money back."

- Seals of approval
  These are generally from well-known magazines or organizations, such as the American Medical Association or Underwriters Laboratories.
- Testimonials
  These are usually by persons associated with a particular field, such as an athlete for running shoes or a doctor for a headache remedy.

Before writers begin writing an ad, they must keep in mind exactly what it is they want the reader to do. This is the action portion of the ad. A writer might end the ad with an "urge line."

Enjoy _____ coffee with your dinner tonight!

For more costly products, the writer might suggest:

See your local dealer for a demonstration

A cents-off coupon might be included in the ad as an incentive to buy the product on the very next trip to the grocery store.

Whatever the product, whatever the tack taken by the advertising copywriter, there are some basic criteria for evaluating advertising writing. As an ad writer, you should etch these somewhere in your brain and keep them clearly in mind while writing. If your advertising copy meets these criteria, you have probably done your job well.

- The ad should offer a reward for reading it.
- It must elicit immediate and complete understanding from the group addressed.
- It must be truthful and believable.
- It must be informative and persuasive.
- The ad must be memorable.
- It must be fitting to the product or service.
- It must reflect well on the overall image of the advertiser.
- The ad must be successful in its planned objective.

Other Kinds of Ads

Advertising writers often create ads for other media besides print, namely commercials for radio and television. Writing for radio and television follows many of the same guidelines as writing for print. There are, however, some distinctive features of radio and TV writing, which we will discuss now.

Writing Radio Ads. In writing a radio advertisement, it is important to visualize not only who the listener might be, but also what the listener might be doing. People who listen to the radio usually do so while engaging in some other activity—cooking, reading, eating, driving a car, or perhaps studying.

Radio ads, obviously, contain no visual illustrations—no colorful photographs or drawings. The copywriter, in effect, must write for the ear not the eye. But the radio copywriter does have the advantage of being able to use a warm, persuasive voice. With the aid of sound, the writer can conjure up any scene or set any stage. A colorful imagination is all that is necessary. Words, music, and sound effects are the only needs of a radio copywriter in communicating an ad's message.

Of course, time is of the essence. The writer has only a matter of seconds, usually 30 to 60 seconds, in which to deliver the message. In this short time span, the radio ad must, like all other ads, attract attention. It must quickly pull the listener in and then state the promise or benefit of the product. This can be done using some form of entertainment—humor, music, drama—whatever fits the product or service.

There are, however, some definite points to remember and keep in mind when writing a radio advertisement.

- Keep it simple. Use familiar words and short phrases and sentences.
- Keep it clear. Maintain a single train of thought and delete any unnecessary words. Keep rewriting until your script is as clear and concise as possible.
- Maintain a logical sequence.
- Develop rapport with your listener. Use a warm, personal tone. Use the word "you" often.
- Be pleasant, as if talking to a friend.
- Be believable. Tell the truth.
- Keep the ad interesting and informative.
- Be distinctive. Use music or phrases that set your ad apart from other commercials.
- Maintain a sense of urgency, especially in the first seconds of the commercial. Register the product name and repeat the promise of product benefits. Then urge the listener to act immediately.

Writing Television Ads. TV commercials offer the viewer all that print and radio ads offer—pictures, color, voices, sound, music. In addition, however, the TV commercial offers motion and people. TV is a picture medium. Therefore, it is not wise to have an announcer read radio copy into a television camera. Although strong copy is vital to a successful commercial, the television commercial depends on pictures, or *visuals.*

A good TV copywriter, though, need not be skilled in the mechanics of film. The writer is, however, responsible for the idea that generates the advertisement.

A TV commercial consists of two parts: the audio or the words and music; and the video or the visual presentation. In writing a script for a TV commercial, you should first divide your paper into two columns. In the left column you will write the promise of the product benefit and the supporting evidence in the form of the audio copy. In the right column, next to the corresponding audio copy, you will write a verbal description of the video portion of the commercial. After a rough script is completed, you will work with an art director who develops a *storyboard.* A storyboard is a master chart of the commercial. It consists of a series of blank TV screens on which the video portions of the ad are drawn using stick figures or some other form of rough sketches. Details are not necessary at this point. Under each TV screen, the corresponding audio portions of the commercial are typed, scene by scene. The copywriter and art director work together to develop a cohesive, meaningful commercial, which then goes to the client for approval.

The visual technique used by the TV copywriter is important. These techniques include:

- Spokesperson—an individual acts as an announcer
- Testimonial—uses a famous personality
- Demonstration—demonstrates a product benefit such as the absorbancy of a brand of paper towels or a cleanser's ability to remove stains
- Customer interview
- Animation
- Close-ups
- A combination of the above techniques

In writing the audio portion of a TV commercial, there are some important guidelines which should be followed.

- Maintain one basic idea throughout the commercial.
- The copy should stress the promise of the product benefit. State it, give supporting evidence, demon-

strate it if possible, and repeat it at the end of the commercial.

- Remember to use simple, everyday words.
- Read the copy out loud in order to catch any possible tongue twisters.
- The audio must relate to the video.
- Do not bother describing what is obvious in the pictures.

Public Relations

Public relations is a highly specialized field of communication. It can be defined as a planned effort concerned with winning favorable public opinion or gaining understanding for an organization or individual. Corporations, educational institutions, religious groups, labor unions, and even individuals in politics or entertainment all use public relations. Their wish is to gain the good will of the public.

Most public relations writing follows the same guidelines as advertising writing. Many of the same insights are necessary. After all, public relations is very similar to selling a product or service. Its job is to promote an idea, a feeling, or a public image.

Hodding Carter served as President Carter's news secretary and public relations expert.

Research, again, plays a vital role in determining public opinion. What do people think about a particular idea? How do they feel about a certain action? What do they think should be changed? These are the types of questions research sets out to answer. Information is obtained from the public by means of surveys. Then communication with the public can begin.

Like product advertising, public relations communication is usually aimed at a particular group, such as bankers, farmers, senior citizens, students, or homeowners. This is where the public relations writer comes in. There are four basic methods of communication in the public relations field.

- advertising—paid communications in the media, that is, radio, TV, newspapers, magazines, mail, or billboards
- lobbying—influencing the voting of legislators to support the interests of an organization
- publicity—favorable media coverage
- press agentry—promotes favorable media coverage

Writing Assignments

As a public relations writer, you will probably have an array of diverse writing assignments. Some of your assignments will include writing news releases, publicity stories, articles, speeches, brochures, print advertisements, letters to customers, or house organs. Let's take time to discuss just a few of these types of assignments.

Most public relations writers spend the majority of their time on *news releases.* A news release must have a broad interest for the reader or viewer. It must contain all the necessary facts in a small amount of space. These are the kinds of things a newspaper or broadcast editor will look for when deciding which news releases to print or air on a TV or radio broadcast. When writing a news release, you should follow the guidelines for writing a news story. (For more information on writing news stories, *see* pages 300–303.)

Publicity stories are also an important part of public relations writing. Their aim is to make a person, organization, or product well known to the public. Publicity stories are often used in the entertainment business. An agent will write a story about his or her client in order to improve their public image. These are also written much like news stories, but there are three primary rules in writing a publicity story.

- Report the truth as closely as possible.
- State all the necessary facts as early in the story as possible.
- Write the story so that it can be cut at any point without seriously altering the key points.

Finally, let's discuss writing for a house organ. A house organ is a communication between management (usually of a large company, though not always) and employees. It often takes the form of a company newspaper or newsletter and is generally used in influencing employee attitudes. A house organ should be written with some basic rules in mind.

- The writing should be objective. All sides of a story should be explored.
- Interesting, newsworthy items should be explored editorially to avoid possible subjective bias.
- The interests of the employees and their families should be recognized and dealt with.
- Write your articles as if you were writing for a commercial publication. Poor writing and editing will not go unnoticed by the reader.

Anyone with an interest in words, ideas, and people can develop skill in public relations writing. Fortunately, integrity and a belief in truth have become important characteristics of this professional field, which began as a manipulative craft. The goal of influencing public opinion has become a credible profession.

Careers

The following section discusses careers in advertising and public relations writing, including nature of the work, education and preparation, and employment opportunities.

Nature of the Work

We have seen that advertising and public relations writing is done for nearly every area of our society. It is a demanding craft performed for both private and public organizations. Its aim is to sell products or services, promote ideas, and support social, educational, or religious agencies.

Copywriters in advertising and public relations do much more than simply spew words and phrases out of a typewriter all day long. They are business people with obligations within an organization. Writers attend meetings of all sorts—training seminars, briefing sessions, and planning meetings. They often communicate with administrators, sales managers, and buyers. They deal with suppliers who mechanically produce the creative material of an advertisement. Writers frequently explain or sell ideas to clients, boards of directors, or management groups. They often work closely with art directors in discussing the arrangement of illustrations, type faces and type sizes, and the overall design of an ad. They have to do research and correct grammar, spelling, and punctuation.

Copywriters do have the satisfaction of seeing their work in print or on TV or radio. They have the advantage of a fairly decent paycheck. But they often work long hours and frequently under the pressure of meeting deadlines. Disagreements or friction among workers occasionally occur. Clients can, as well, be critical or unfair. Like any intense, creative work, advertising and public relations writing, though usually very exciting, can be exhausting.

Education and Preparation

To get a job as an advertising or public relations copywriter, you will need at least a bachelor's degree. A degree in public relations or in communications, with an emphasis on public relations would be ideal. A liberal arts degree with a specialization in journalism or communications would also be a good choice. A business degree with an emphasis in advertising is also excellent. Often journalism graduates transfer to a public relations job at a later date. Publishing, broadcasting, or writing experience is also ideal for public relations work.

Studying areas of broad general knowledge such as English literature, sociology, history, psychology, political science, economics, and foreign languages would certainly be helpful in understanding people. Courses in marketing or business practices would be useful. As a future writer, it would be to your advantage to take as many writing courses as possible.

Writing for the school newspaper or yearbook and taking part in student government or debating clubs would certainly have its advantages. Summer or part-time jobs in writing or communications would be helpful. Future copywriters should prepare a portfolio containing some of the best samples of their work to show prospective employers at interviews.

Employment Opportunities

The tough competition among manufacturers and sellers of products requires top-notch, effective advertising. Thus, the number of trainee jobs in advertising will go down, while fewer, though better qualified workers will be hired by ad agencies. Competition for these jobs will be keen. Advertising writers might find jobs with retail stores, chain stores, mail-order firms, or manufacturing companies.

Billions of dollars, on the other hand, will be spent on public relations by business, government, and industry. Public relations among smaller firms is expected to grow in the near future. A demand has been created for specialists in this area. But the number of graduates in the fields of journalism and communications is on the rise and competition for these positions will be sharp. Most available jobs will be found in large corporations, foundations, consulting firms, and colleges.

Many public relations writers find work in large cities where corporation headquarters are located and where press services are nearby. Exploring jobs in TV or radio broadcasting, publishing, or fund-raising often proves fruitful.

Salaries for advertising and public relations writers vary widely depending on the size of the agency, corporation, or organization and the skills of the writer. Occasionally writers will be paid overtime for any extra hours they might work to meet deadlines. Many agency or corporation writers receive such fringe benefits as sick pay, paid vacations, medical insurance, and stock or pension plans.

Appendix A

Spelling

You can learn to spell any word in the English language. Begin by looking up the word in the dictionary.

Using the Dictionary

Almost everyone is unsure of how to spell some words, especially words that are pronounced one way and spelled another. The dictionary gives you the correct spelling. But how do you look up a word you cannot spell?

Before you give up in despair, try to decide exactly what you need to know. If you want to spell the word *separate*, but cannot remember whether an *a* or an *e* follows the *p*, all you need do is check *sepa-*. If you want to spell the word *wagon*, but cannot remember whether to use one *g* or two, look up *wagg-* and see what you find. Your greatest problems will be in words that have a combination of letters that do not look like the sounds they represent—the *a* sounds of *plaid*, *half*, and *laugh* for example, or the silent letters that begin *gnaw*, *knife*, and *pneumonia*.

Multiple Spellings

Some words have more than one acceptable spelling. When one spelling is used almost as often as another, the two spellings appear together in a single entry joined by "or."

cal|o|rie or **cal|o|ry**

Alternate spellings may be combined in a single entry when: an entry can be written with or without a hyphen, such as *orangutan* or *orang-utan;* an entry can be written with a capital or a lower case letter, such as *burley* or *Burley;* an entry can be written with or without a possessive ending, as in *bachelor's* or *bachelor hall;* an entry can be written in the singular or the plural, such as *Canterbury bell* or *bells;* an abbreviation can be written with or without periods, as in *GI* (no periods) or *G.I.*

In cases where the two forms of the word are not equally used or belong in different alphabetical places, the alternate spelling appears at the end of the entry for the preferred spellings, introduced by the word *also,* as in *catabolism . . . .* Also, *katabolism.* Such alternate spellings appear in their own alphabetical places in the dictionary, but only as cross references to the preferred spelling, such as *katabolism = catabolism.*

When the pronunciation of an alternate form differs from the pronunciation of the preferred spelling, the alternate form has a separate cross-reference entry.

> **i|o|dide** (ī'ə dīd, -did), *n.* a compound of
> iodine with another element or radical;
> a salt of hydriodic acid. [<*iod-* + *-ide*]
>
> **i|o|did** (ī'ə did), *n.* = iodide.

When more than one spelling is given for an entry, which should you choose? Where several forms are combined in a single entry joined by "or," the first spelling is considered the more commonly used.

> **co|deine** or **co|dein** (kō'dēn), *n.* a white, crys-
> talline drug obtained from opium and used to
> lieve pain and coughs, and to cause sleep:
>
> **quan|dong** or **quan|dang** (kwon'dong'), *n.* **1** an
> Australian tree related to the sandalwood, that
> has an edible fruit and a nutlike seed with an
> edible kernel. **2** the fruit of this tree. **3** the
> seed or kernel. [<the native Australian
> name]

You will be among the majority if you choose *codeine* and *quandong.*

When different spellings of the same word are listed as separate entries, the spelling of the defined entry is preferred to the entry that is cross referred.

> **co|coa|nut** (kō'kə nut', -nət), *n., adj.* = coconut.
>
> **co|co|nut** (kō'kə nut', -nət), *n., adj.—n.* **1** the
> large, round, brown, hard-shelled nut of the
> coconut palm. Coconuts have a white lining
> that is good to eat and a whitish or clear liq-
> uid called coconut milk, used as a drink. The
> white lining is cut up into shreds and used for
> cakes, puddings, and pies. **2** the fruit of the
> coconut palm, containing the nut within a
> thick, ovoid, fibrous husk: *The coconut yields*
> *six commercial products: copra, coconut oil,*
> *coconuts, shredded coconut, oil cake, and*
> *coir fiber* (Colby and Foster). **3.** = coconut
> palm.
> **—*adj.*** of or made from the fruit of the coco-
> nut. Also, **cocoanut.**

You should choose *coconut.*

Inflections

Inflections or inflected forms are the forms of a word that show grammatical differences such as the plurals of nouns, the past tense and present participle of verbs, and the comparative forms of adjectives and adverbs. Most inflections are regular. That is, they follow simple rules, such as the rule to add *s* to the end of a singular noun to form the plural.

> **bab|ble** (bab′əl), *v.,* **-bled, -bling,** *n.—v.i.* **1** to make sounds like a baby: *My baby brother babbles and coos in his crib.* **2** to talk foolishly; prattle: *She babbled on and on about her new dress.*
>
> **e|mul|si|fy** (i mul′sə fī), *v.t.,* **-fied, -fy|ing.** to make or turn (an oil, fat, resin, or other substance) into an emulsion: *Juice from the pancreas emulsifies fat in the digestion of food.*

Only the syllable or syllables that differ from the spelling of the main entry are given:

> **ad|vance** (ad vans′, -väns′), *v.,* **-vanced, -vancing,** *n., adj.—v.t.* **1** to put or move forward; push forward: *The general advanced the troops.* **2** to help forward; further: *The President's speech ad-*
>
> **ka|tab|a|sis** (kə tab′ə sis), *n., pl.* **-ses** (-sēz). **1** a military retreat, especially that of Cyrus the Younger and the Greeks who fought against Artaxerxes. **2** the act or process of going down. [<Greek *katábasis* descent<*katabainein* to go down]

Common irregular inflections have main entries themselves:

> **da|ta** (dā′tə, dat′ə, dä′tə), *n.pl. of* **da|tum.** things known or granted; information; facts: *Names,*
>
> **me|di|a**[1] (mē′dē ə), *n.* **1** a plural of **medium**: *Newspapers, magazines, and billboards are important media for advertising.* **2** = medium (def. 2). **3** = mass media.
> ►See **medium** for usage note.

When two or more spellings are listed for inflected forms, the one listed first is the most acceptable.

> **a|quar|i|um** (ə kwãr′ē əm), *n., pl.* **i|ums, -i|a** (-ē ə). **1** a pond, tank, or glass bowl in which living fish and other water animals and water plants are kept. **2** a building used for showing collections of living fish, water animals, and water plants: *The aquarium had large tanks with glass fronts for different kinds of fish.*

ge|nus (jē′nəs), *n., pl.* **gen|e|ra** or **ge|nus|es.**
1 any group of similar things; kind; sort;
class: *Assuming, however, that there still ex-*
ists the genus serious reader (Hayden Car-
ruth). **2.** a

Some inflected forms are spelled one way in American English
and another way in British English. These spellings are labeled:

bev|el (bev′əl), *n., v.,* **-eled, -el|ing** or (*espe-*
cially British) **-elled, -el|ling.** *adj.—n.* 1 a
sloping edge or surface. There is often a
bevel on the frame

Once you have looked a word up in the dictionary, make the
word yours by following these steps:
- Write the word neatly and clearly
- Close your eyes and visualize the word in your mind
- Spell the word out loud
- Study the syllables if it has more than one
- Pronounce the word out loud
- Study its meaning; it may have more than one
- Make up a sentence with the word
- Use the word at every opportunity in writing and talking

Once you learn how to spell a word, most spelling problems
arise when the word is changed to show number, person, tense,
or comparison.

To help you with these problems, a list of spelling rules and a
table of common spellings of English sounds is included in this
appendix. When you have a spelling problem look it up here, and
learn the rules and exceptions by using them.

Which is correct?	Correct spelling	This rule explains why	Some exceptions
beleive or believe relieve or releive sliegh or sleigh	believe relieve sleigh	Use *i* before *e* except after *c* or when sounded as *a* as in neighbor and weigh.	*counterfeit, either, foreign, forfeit, height, leisure, seize, weird*
handkerchieves, handkerchiefs, or handkerchiefes	handkerchiefs	Most singular words are made plural by adding *s*.	Some nouns ending in *f* or *fe* form the plural by changing the *f* or *fe* to *ve* and adding *s: knives, elves, halves, calves, leaves, loaves, sheaves, shelves, wives.*

Which is correct?	Correct spelling	This rule explains why	Some exceptions
armys or armies	**armies**	Nouns ending in *y* preceded by a consonant, form the plural by changing *y* to *i* and adding *es*.	Proper names ending in *y* form the plural by adding *s*: "There are four *Marys* in this class."
monkeys or monkies	**monkeys**	Nouns ending in *y* preceded by a vowel, form the plural by adding *s*.	*soliloquies*
churchs or churches topazs or topazes	**churches** **topazes**	Words ending in *ch, j, s, ss, sh, x,* or *z* are made plural by adding *es*.	
cameos or cameoes radioes or radios	**cameos** **radios**	Nouns ending in *o* preceded by a vowel, form the plural by adding *s*.	
tomatos or tomatoes volcanoes or volcanos	**tomatoes** (both)	Nouns ending in *o* preceded by a consonant, form the plural by adding *es*.	Some words add *s* only: *silos, dittos, dynamos*. In other cases, either *s* or *es* is correct: *buffalos* or *buffaloes*. Check the dictionary if you are not sure.
brother-in-laws or brothers-in-law cupsful or cupfuls	**brothers-in-law** **cupfuls**	Compound nouns add *s* to the main word to form a plural. Add *s* to words ending in *ful*.	
1920s or 1920's four 7's or four 7s	**1920's** **7's**	Form the plural of numbers, dates, letters, and signs by adding *'s*.	
desireable or desirable caring or careing	**desirable** **caring**	Words ending in *e*, drop the final *e* before adding a suffix beginning with a *vowel*.	*mileage, saleable*
humaneness or humanness arrangement or arrangment	**humaneness** **arrangement**	Words ending in *e*, keep the final *e* before adding a suffix beginning with a *consonant*.	*argument, duly, ninth, wholly*
changeable or changable advantagous or advantageous	**changeable** **advantageous**	Words ending in soft-sounding *ce* or *ge*, retain the final *e* when adding suffixes.	
canoing or canoeing lovly or lovely	**canoeing** **lovely**	Words ending in *e* preceded by a vowel, keep the *e* before adding a suffix, except a suffix beginning with *e*.	*truly*
dying or dieing	**dying**	Words ending in *ie*, change the *ie* to *y* before adding a suffix.	
prefered or preferred begining or beginning	**preferred** **beginning**	Words ending in a consonant preceded by a single vowel, double the consonant before adding a vowel suffix.	*crocheting, ricocheted, filleted*
benefiting or benefitting revealling or revealing boilling or boiling	**benefiting** **revealing** **boiling**	Words ending in a consonant preceded by more than one vowel, or not accented on the last syllable, do not double the final consonant.	

Which is correct?	Correct spelling	This rule explains why	Some exceptions
accidentaly or accidentally	**accidentally**	Words ending in one *l*, keep the final *l* before a suffix beginning with *l*.	Words ending in *ll* drop one *l* before an *ly* suffix: *hilly, fully*.
allready or already mouthfull or mouthful	**already** **mouthful**	Omit one *l* in adding prefixes or suffixes ending in *ll*.	
supplyed or supplied occupys or occupies	**supplied** **occupies**	Words ending in *y* preceded by a consonant, change *y* to *i* before a suffix, unless suffix begins with *i*.	Words of one syllable ending in *y*, keep the *y* before a suffix: *shy, shyly; dry, dryly*.
stayed or staied	**stayed**	Words ending in *y* preceded by a vowel, retain the *y* before a suffix.	*daily, laid, paid, said, slain*
dissatisfy or disatisfy imortal or immortal	**dissatisfy** **immortal**	Prefixes *dis-, il-, im-, mis-, over-, re-*, and *un-* do not change the spelling of the root word.	

Common spellings of English sounds

This table shows the various sounds of English and the most common spellings for those sounds. It will help you find words in this dictionary when you are unsure of how to spell them. Many words are pronounced differently from the way they are written. For example, *laugh* is pronounced (*laf*) and *phrase* is pronounced (*frāz*). If you are unsure of how a word begins or ends or of some of the letters in between, this table will give you the clues you need to look it up in the dictionary.

Symbol	Spelling
a	hat, plaid, half, laugh
ā	age, aid, gaol, gauge, say, break, vein, weigh, they
ã	care, air, prayer, where, pear, their
ä	father, half, laugh, sergeant, heart
b	bad, rabbit
ch	child, watch, righteous, question, future
d	did, add, filled
e	many, aesthetic, said, says, let, bread, heifer, leopard, friend, bury
ē	Caesar, quay, equal, team, bee, receive, people, key, machine, believe, phoenix
ėr	pearl, stern, first, word, journey, turn, myrtle
ər	liar, mother, elixir, honor, honour, augur, zephyr
f	fat, effort, laugh, phrase

Symbol	Spelling
g	**g**o, e**gg**, **gh**ost, **g**uest, catalo**gue**
h	**h**e, **wh**o
hw	**wh**eat
i	**E**nglish, b**ee**n, b**i**t, s**ie**ve, w**o**men, b**u**sy, b**ui**ld, h**y**mn
ī	a**i**sle, **ay**e, h**ei**ght, **ey**e, **i**ce, l**ie**, h**igh**, b**uy**, sk**y**, r**ye**
j	bri**dg**e, ver**d**ure, sol**di**er, tra**g**ic, exa**gg**erate, **j**am
k	**c**oat, a**cc**ount, **ch**emistry, ba**ck**, a**c**quire, sa**cque**, **k**ind, fol**k**, li**qu**or
l	**l**and, te**ll**
m	dra**chm**, paradi**gm**, ca**lm**, **m**e, cli**mb**, co**mm**on, sole**mn**
n	**gn**aw, **kn**ife, **mn**emonic, **n**o, ma**nn**er, **pn**eumonia
ng	i**nk**, lo**ng**, to**ngue**
o	w**a**tch, h**o**t
ō	b**eau**, **yeo**man, s**ew**, **o**pen, b**oa**t, t**oe**, **oh**, br**oo**ch, s**ou**l, th**ough**, l**ow**
ô	**a**ll, **U**t**ah**, w**a**lk, t**augh**t, l**aw**, **o**rder, br**oa**d, b**ough**t
oi	b**oi**l, b**oy**
ou	h**ou**se, b**ough**, n**ow**
p	cu**p**, ha**pp**y
r	**r**un, **rh**ythm, ca**rr**y, **wr**ong
s	**c**ent, ni**ce**, **ps**ychology, **s**ay, **sc**ent, **sch**ism, mi**ss**
sh	o**ce**an, ma**ch**ine, spe**ci**al, **psh**aw, **s**ure, **sch**ist, con**sci**ence, nau**se**ous, **sh**e, ten**si**on, i**ss**ue, mi**ssi**on, na**ti**on
t	stopp**ed**, bou**ght**, **pt**omaine, **t**ell, **Th**omas, butto**n**
th	**th**in
ŦH	**th**en, brea**the**
u	c**o**me, d**oe**s, fl**oo**d, tr**ou**ble, c**u**p
u̇	w**o**lf, g**oo**d, sh**ou**ld, f**u**ll
ü	man**eu**ver, thr**ew**, ad**ieu**, m**o**ve, sh**oe**, f**oo**d, cr**ou**p, thr**ough**, r**u**le, bl**ue**, fr**ui**t
v	o**f**, Ste**ph**en, **v**ery, fli**vv**er
w	ch**oi**r, q**u**ick, **w**ill
y	opin**i**on, hallelu**j**ah, **y**es
yü	b**eau**ty, f**eu**d, q**ueue**, f**ew**, ad**ieu**, v**iew**, **u**se, c**ue**, **y**ou, **y**ule
z	ha**s**, di**s**cern, **sc**i**ss**ors, **x**ylophone, **z**ero, bu**zz**
zh	gara**g**e, mea**s**ure, divi**si**on, a**z**ure, bra**z**ier
ə	**a**lone, fount**ai**n, mom**e**nt, penc**i**l, c**o**mplete, cauti**ou**s, circ**u**s

Parts of Speech

Every word in an English dictionary belongs to one of eight parts of speech: nouns, pronouns, adjectives, verbs, adverbs, prepositions, conjunctions, and interjections.

Many words belong, in fact, to more than one part of speech, depending on how they are used. A noun is a word used as the name of a person, place, thing, event, or quality. *Cream* is a noun when you speak of cream for coffee. An adjective describes or modifies a noun, so that *cream* becomes an adjective when you speak of banana cream pie. A verb is a word that expresses action. *Cream* becomes a verb when you cream butter and sugar together to make a cake.

You need to know how a word is used in a sentence to label it properly. But that is not as difficult as it may sound.

Nouns

Nouns are the easiest to recognize. You are a noun. So is every person, every place, and every thing: *Susan, man, Mrs. Smith, England, Michigan, ocean, truck, car, Golden Gate Bridge.*

There are two kinds of nouns: common and proper. Proper nouns name particular persons, places, or things: *Susan, England*, and *Golden Gate Bridge* are proper nouns. Common nouns do not tell us the particular person, place, or thing, and they are not capitalized. *Man, ocean,* and *truck* are common nouns.

Common nouns are divided into three groups: abstract, concrete, and collective.

Abstract nouns name qualities, actions, and ideas: *courage, helpfulness, loyalty.* Most of the time, you use *the* before abstract nouns, but not *a.* Ordinarily, you would not say *a* helpfulness.

Concrete nouns name things that you can see or touch: *door, pencil, car.* Most of the time, you use either *a* or *the* before a concrete noun, depending on the meaning you want to convey. Also, concrete nouns can be plural—*doors, pencils, cars*—whereas you would not ordinarily say *courages* or *helpfulnesses*.

Collective nouns are singular, but they refer to a group of persons or things: *team, class, herd, set.* Collective nouns are usually followed by singular verbs: "Our *team was* defeated." But they can be followed by a plural verb, especially where they emphasize the individuals more than the group: "The *people were* discontented."

Pronouns

Pronouns take the place of nouns. Our language would be cumbersome without them. You could say, "Mrs. Smith asked John to be careful with Mrs. Smith's car when John borrowed the car to take John's date home." But it is easier to say, "Mrs. Smith asked John to be careful with her car when he borrowed it to take his date home."

The noun that is replaced or referred to by the pronoun is called the antecedent. Every pronoun must have an antecedent, either stated or understood. In our example, *Mrs. Smith, John,* and *car* are antecedents, and the pronouns *her, he, his,* and *it* relieve you of the necessity of repeating the nouns.

There are five kinds of pronouns: personal, relative, interrogative, demonstrative (definite), and indefinite.

Personal pronouns stand for the name of a person, a place, or a thing. English has seven personal pronouns: *I, you, he, she, it, we,* and *they.* All seven are subject form. They "do" the action. Any one will take the place of a noun in the sentence: ". . . saw Mary."

Each of the seven personal pronouns has an object form. The object forms are: *me, you, him, her, it, us,* and *them.* They receive some kind of action. Some action happens "to" them. Any one will take the place of a noun in the sentence: "Mary saw . . . ."

In speaking and writing, people often misuse personal pronouns in sentences with verbs such as *is, are, am, was, were,* and *to be.* After such verbs, the subject form of the personal pronoun is always used: "It is *I.*"

Choosing the right pronoun to follow a preposition—such as *to, for, at, between*—can be troublesome, too. Prepositions call for the object form of the pronoun. "She talked to Mary and *me.*" (Not Mary and *I.*)

If we add *self* or *selves* to a personal pronoun, it becomes a compound form: *myself, yourself, herself, itself, ourselves, themselves.* This form may be intensive (giving emphasis) or reflexive (expressing action turned back on the subject). Do not use the compound form when you should use a simple personal pronoun. It is wrong to say "My brother and *myself* are going." You may say "I *myself* am going" (intensive), and you may also say "He shaves *himself*" (reflexive).

Relative pronouns serve a double purpose. First, they connect two clauses (groups of words containing a subject and a verb): "She did not buy the same book *that* he did." Second, they relate back to a noun or a pronoun in a preceding clause. "She went with the boy *who* lives on Oak Street." Words frequently used as relative pronouns are *that, what, which, who, whom, whose.* Compound relative pronouns in common use are *whatever, whichever,* and *whoever.*

Interrogative pronouns—*what, which,* and *who*—are used to ask questions. They ask the identity, the nature, or the possessor of whatever is in question. "*Who* was there?" "*Which* of the books is yours?"

Demonstrative pronouns. *That, these, this,* and *those* answer the question "Which?" by pointing out a particular person or thing. They are sometimes called definite pronouns. *"That* is all wrong." *"This* is the one I want." *"Those* are too expensive." *"These* are just perfect."

Indefinite pronouns also answer the question "Which?" But in so doing, they do not refer to definite persons or things. *"Somebody* took my pencil." *"Neither* will do the job." Other indefinite pronouns include *both, each, many, one, other.* Like demonstrative pronouns, many indefinite pronouns are adjectives. *"Both* boys were absent." *"Neither* book is mine."

Adjectives

An *old* man; a *black* cat; a *long* bill. *Old, black,* and *long* are adjectives. Each is used to modify, or to give a more exact meaning to, a noun. It is not just any man, it is an *old* man; it is not just any cat, it is a *black* cat; it is not just any bill, it is a *long* bill.

Descriptive adjectives describe a quality or condition of a noun: a *short* stick, a *sad* girl, a *grassy* slope. Limiting adjectives single out the object talked about or indicate quantity: *this* book, *that* ring, *two* words. Notice that some limiting adjectives are regularly used as pronouns (*that, these, this, those*). *A, an,* and *the,* also limiting adjectives, are sometimes called articles.

Phrases and clauses may also serve as adjectives. "The man *with the green hat* saw me." In addition to modifying nouns, adjectives modify a word or group of words that is acting as a noun: *"Going to school* (noun) is *necessary* (adjective)."

Verbs

The most important word in a sentence is the verb. A verb expresses action or a state of being. In "John the ball," we have a subject, *John,* and we have an object, *ball.* But only after adding a verb, such as *threw,* do we have action, and a sentence. "John threw the ball." Sometimes the action is mental rather than physical. "She *believed* the story."

Not all verbs express action. Those that do not may be either linking verbs or auxiliary verbs. Linking verbs join the subject of the sentence to another word, in order to make a statement. "Sara *felt* ill." The verb *felt* links the subject *Sara,* with the word *ill,* to make a statement about Sara's health. Some linking verbs regularly used are *appear, be, grow, look, remain, seem, smell, stay, taste.*

Auxiliary verbs are used with other verbs to form a verb tense, voice, or mood. "I studied" becomes "I *have* studied," with the addition of the helping, or auxiliary verb, *have.* Other common auxiliary verbs are *be, do, may, will.*

Verbs may be either transitive or intransitive. A transitive verb takes an object. "He *lifted* the hammer." An intransitive verb does not take an object. "They *ran* fast." Many verbs are transitive in some sentences and intransitive in others. "She *sang* the song." (Transitive) "She could not *sing.*" (Intransitive)

Adverbs

Adverbs, like adjectives, give a more exact meaning to other words. But adjectives modify only nouns and words acting as nouns. Adverbs modify verbs, adjectives, other adverbs, entire sentences, or clauses. "The boat was *absolutely* waterproof." (Adverb modifying adjective) "The radio worked *unusually* well." (Adverb modifying adverb) "I went to school *yesterday.*" (Adverb modifying sentence)

An adverb *usually* answers the questions: *How? When? Where?* or *To what extent?* "He ran *quickly* down the road." (How) "She went to school *today.*" (When) "She dropped the ball *there.*" (Where) "John sang *loudly.*" (To what extent)

Interrogative adverbs ask questions. "*Where* did she go?" "*Why* did she go?" Other common interrogative adverbs are *when* and *how.*

Conjunctive adverbs appear between clauses and serve the double function of connecting the two clauses and modifying one. "You signed a contract; *therefore,* we demand payment." Other conjunctive adverbs are *however, moreover, nevertheless, otherwise, still.*

Words commonly used as adverbs are *almost, fast, very,* and most words ending in *-ly: badly, sorely.*

Prepositions

Prepositions may be short words (*in, for, on, to*), long words (*alongside, concerning*), or groups of words (*in spite of, as far as*). But they all do the same thing. They show the relation of one word (usually a noun or a pronoun) to some other word in the sentence. Some of the relations are:

Position—"The book is *on* the table."
Direction—"He walked *toward* the door."
Time—"She left *before* him."

Words frequently used as prepositions are *at, between, by, down, for, in, of, on, over, toward, up, with.*

Conjunctions

Conjunctions join together words or word groups. There are coordinating, correlative, and subordinating conjunctions.

Coordinating conjunctions are the simplest, linking two words or word groups that are grammatically the same. "She bought meat *and* potatoes." Other coordinating conjunctions are *but* and *yet.*

When two coordinating conjunctions are used together, they are called correlative conjunctions. "*Both* Henry *and* Bill are gone." Other correlative conjunctions are *either . . . or, though . . . yet.*

Subordinating conjunctions connect a subordinate clause to the main clause of a sentence. In the following instance, the subordinating conjunction *because* introduces the subordinate clause. "Mary was happy *because* she found her mother at home." Other subordinating conjunctions include *as, before, if, since, unless.*

Interjections

Ah! Alas! Oh! Ouch! These are interjections. A unique characteristic of interjections is that they bear no grammatical relation to other words in a sentence. They neither affect other words—as do adjectives—nor are they affected by other words—as are nouns. A second property held in common by interjections is that they all express emotion. *Ouch!* It hurts. *Alas!* It is a shame. *Ah!* Here comes Mary.

Capitalization

Capital letters are used in writing to make reading easier. They distinguish specific or proper names from general or common names. They signal the beginning of new sentences, quotes, and thoughts. English has many rules for using capitals. The main ones follow:

What to capitalize	Examples
Proper nouns	John Jones Chicago Bill of Rights
Proper adjectives	Paris fashions Kennedy administration Persian rugs
Personified nouns	All Nature sang. Let not Evil triumph.
The first word of a sentence, a phrase, or a word that has the force of a sentence	What are you doing? Nothing. Stop!
The first word of a direct quotation	Bob called, "Hurry up."
The first word of a complete statement following a colon (:)	This is our conclusion: The trial was fair.
The first words and all important words in titles of books, magazines, newspapers, songs, and other writings. (Capitalize *a; an; and; the;* prepositions, and conjunctions only when they come at the beginning or end of a title or when they consist of five or more letters.)	Ivanhoe *Business Week* *Evening News* "Roll Out the Barrel"

What to capitalize	**Examples**
The pronoun *I* and the interjection *O*	I was right. Rejoice, O ye people
The days of the week, months, and holidays	Tuesday February Easter Christmas
Words used instead of, or as part, of a family member's name	I asked Father for a dollar. He called Uncle Bob.
Nicknames, titles, and their abbreviations	Old Hickory Senator Brown Dr. Ph.D.
Specific political and geographical subdivisions	Chicago Queens County Italian Sioux Indians
Specific rivers, mountains, and other geographical features	Amazon River Rocky Mountains Atlantic Ocean
Specific streets, highways, buildings, and other locations	Michigan Avenue Fifth Ave. Empire State Bldg.
Political parties, religious denominations, and their members	Democratic Party Baptist Church Republicans
Organizations, business firms, and institutions	Camp Fire Girls General Motors Columbia University
Sacred writings and words that refer to a Supreme Being	Bible Holy Writ God Trust in Him Vishnu
Specific historical events, wars, treaties, documents, etc.	Louisiana Purchase World War II Treaty of Ghent
Branches, departments, and other divisions of government	Congress Parliament Department of State
Specific trains, planes, ships, satellites, submarines, and other vehicles	*Golden State Limited Concorde Titanic* *Sputnik Nautilus*
Stars, planets, constellations, and other heavenly bodies	Sirius Mars Big Dipper Milky Way
Creeds and confessions of faith	Nicene Creed Augsburg Confession
Specific historical periods	Age of Reason Renaissance
Military decorations	Purple Heart Navy Cross Victoria Cross
Preface, contents, chapter, index, and other parts of a book when referred to specifically	

Appendix B

Preparing Manuscripts

If you contribute or submit an article to a newspaper, magazine, or other publication, it should be prepared in a professional way. Once you have done this, and mailed or delivered the manuscript, your responsibility ends. But you might want to know what happens to the manuscript, sometimes called copy, after it reaches an editor and the printer.

The Author's Manuscript

Your manuscript should be neatly typed, double-spaced, using only one side of the paper. If possible, begin each page with a paragraph. Avoid hyphenating words at the end of lines, and never divide a word from one page to another.

Pages. Number the pages consecutively at the top. Type the word *more* at the bottom of each page except the last. On the last page, type an end mark, such as ###, below the last line of your manuscript.

Corrections. Write or type the correction above the line. Be neat and be sure that your writing is clear.

Spelling. Consult your dictionary for preferred spelling, and stick to that spelling throughout the manuscript. Be consistent.

Capitalization and Punctuation. Be consistent with an accepted style, such as the one suggested in Appendix A of this book. Keep in mind, however, that every publication has its own style and that your copy may be changed to conform to "house" rules.

Copy Editing

When your manuscript reaches the publisher, an editor is assigned to copy edit your work. It is the editor's responsibility to see that what the author has said is clear, accurate, and orderly; to see that capitalization and punctuation are correct; and to mark the manuscript in such a way that the typesetter will have no difficulty setting it in type.

Both editor and typesetter need to know and use the same set of marks. These marks, called proofreaders' marks, are used in marking the manuscript for the typesetter and in correcting proofs. In the manuscript, the proof marks are indicated either on a line or between lines; on a galley or page proof, the proof-readers' marks are put in the margin left or right, next to the line in which the correction is to be made. Marks in the line indicate where the correction should be made. All corrections should be neatly and clearly indicated.

Proofreading

After your manuscript has been set into type, the typesetter prints a proof, which is compared with the original copy by a proofreader, the editor, and sometimes the author. There is more than one way to indicate errors in proofs, but the style shown in this appendix is one commonly used by many editors and proof-readers. All directions to the printer that are not to be set in type should be circled.

Marking Manuscripts

In text	Explanation
Introduction	Set in boldface type
mckinley high school	Use capital letters
foot ball team	Close up space
spring spring semester	Delete letter or word and close up
"Fourscore and seven years ago our fathers	Indent
The new laboratory should	Insert letter or word
Read Paradise Lost	Set in italic type
Mr. Smith, the Janitor	Use lower-case letter
⑤	Spell out
The senior prom	Begin new paragraph
held Saturday, June 1 (stet)	Let it stand
after final examinations. (This is the first time	Run in—no paragraph
examinations willbe	Separate words
the Booster	Set in small capitals
began Jan. 1	Spell out or abbreviate
421 First Street	
gymnasium (decorated is)	Transpose
Jim Browne ——— (follow copy)	Unusual spelling

Marking proofs

In margin	In test	Explanation
e	The rule is, nver	Insert
◡ ⌒	tomorroow, and	Delete
(tr)	yesterday—never but	Transpose
	Chap 5	Spell out
(ital)	jam today	Use italic type
(Rom)	It must	Use roman type
(b.f.)	Introduction	Use boldface type
(l.c.)	THE WALRUS AND	Use lower case
(caps)	the carpenter	Use capital letters
(w.f.)	Come sometimes	Wrong font (used when a character is the wrong size or style)
x	to jam today	Broken letter
ↄ	Ʌlice objected	Inverted letter
◡	No, it c an't	Close up
#	said theQueen	More space
(stet)	It's jam	Let it stand

In margin	In text	Explanation
(?)	every other night	Is this correct?
(see copy)	today any	Something left out
⊏	other day	Move left
⊐	you know	Move right
(¶)	you know. When	New paragraph
(no ¶)	you know. When it	No paragraph
=	I use a word	Straighten line
(X)	said the Queen. Now	Insert period
⌃	Now, here you see	Insert comma
⌄	Everythings	Insert apostrophe
?	are you asking me. No,	Insert question mark
⌄⌄	it means just what	Insert quotation marks
/=/	*Looking Glass*	Insert hyphen
(:)	other day. today isn't	Insert colon
□	And whether pigs	Indent one em
//	Queen the running	Align type

Index